Ethics in a Multicultural Context

Sherlon P. Pack-Brown
Bowling Green State University

Carmen Braun Williams
University of Colorado at Denver

Multicultural Aspects of Counseling Series 19

SAGE Publications
International Educational and Professional Publisher
Thousand Oaks ▪ London ▪ New Delhi

For information:

Sage Publications, Inc.
2455 Teller Road
Thousand Oaks, California 91320
E-mail: order@sagepub.com

Sage Publications Ltd.
6 Bonhill Street
London EC2A 4PU
United Kingdom

Sage Publications India Pvt. Ltd.
B-42 Panchsheel Enclave
Post Box 4109
New Delhi 110 017 India

Printed in the United States of America

Library of Congress Cataloging-in-Publication Data

Pack-Brown, Sherlon P.
Ethics in a multicultural context / Sherlon P. Pack-Brown, Carmen Braun Williams.
    p. cm.—(Multicultural aspects of counseling series ; v. 19)
Includes bibliographical references and index.
ISBN 0-7619-2426-4—ISBN 0-7619-2427-2 (pbk.)
   1. Cross-cultural counseling-Moral and ethical aspects-United States.
I. Williams, Carmen Braun. II. Title. III. Series.
BF637.C6 P235 2003
174.'9362—dc21

2002153687

03   04   05   06   10 9 8 7 6 5 4 3 2 1

Acquisitions Editor:	Art Pomponio
Editorial Assistant:	Heather Scafidi
Production Editor:	Melanie Birdsall
Copy Editor:	Carla Freeman
Typesetter:	C&M Digitals (P) Ltd.
Proofreader:	Kristin Bergstad
Indexer:	Teri Greenberg
Cover Designer:	Janet Foulger
Production Artist:	Sandra Ng Sauvajot

Ethics in a
Multicultural
Context

MULTICULTURAL ASPECTS OF COUNSELING SERIES

SERIES EDITOR

Paul Pedersen, Ph.D., *University of Alabama at Birmingham*

EDITORIAL BOARD

VOLUMES IN THIS SERIES

Contents

Foreword

Multicultural counselors are often faced with a moral dilemma of whether to *either* follow the ethical guidelines of their professional counseling organization and act in a way they consider inappropriate *or* take the appropriate action while bending or violating the ethical guidelines. This book addresses that dilemma and provides guidance to multicultural counselors thinking through the ethical implications and consequences of competent multicultural counseling. Because all behaviors are displayed and learned in a cultural context, it should not be a surprise that ethical guidelines developed in one cultural context might not exactly fit when applied to a quite different cultural context.

The purpose of this book is first of all to identify culturally troublesome issues that need to be examined. It is often easier to overlook these cultural issues than to struggle with them, which is perhaps why cultural diversity has so often been minimized in psychological research, training, teaching, and administration. The second purpose of this book is to promote culturally appropriate interpretation of the ethical guidelines already in place. This book does not disregard the extremely hard work that has already been done to develop culturally sensitive ethical guidelines over the years, but it also documents why the task of culturally appropriate interpretation is not yet complete. The third purpose of this book is to promote ethical behavior within multicultural contexts. This is the most difficult task of all. For a variety of reasons, even those who "know the good and right thing to do" will not always do it. The professional ethical standards do a fairly good job of outlining a counselor's responsibility but they are either (a) so abstract that they are subject to interpretation by culturally encapsulated counselors or (b) taught as a simplistic list of rules for staying out of trouble rather than as guidelines for "ethical thinking."

Many concerns raised in this book focus on two questions. The first question is this: "Are counselors ethical?" We would like to say yes, of course, and yet we know that while we aspire to be ethical in all situations, we do not always achieve that standard of behavior. The second question is this: "Are the professional ethical codes appropriate?" Each set of professional ethical guidelines *inevitably* reflects the cultural perspective and values of its designers. As the guidelines for professional counseling are applied to diverse cultural groups around the United States and increasingly across the other cultures of the world, it is apparent that those professional guidelines need constant modification. There is no shortcut or simplistic solution to defining ethical behavior in multicultural counselors in these professional guidelines or in any other culturally encapsulated perspective. This text does a good job of helping readers evaluate both their own behavior and the guidelines they use in their behavior.

The book is divided into three parts. The first part describes the purpose of the text and why it is important for training multicultural counselors. The purpose of this book is not to develop a new "multicultural" perspective about counseling, but to achieve accurate, meaningful, and appropriate competencies among multicultural counselors. The second part is divided according to the three-stage developmental sequence of multicultural awareness, knowledge, and skill. This framework of multicultural competence is now widely recognized and accepted in the field of counseling. The third part of this book is focused on specific ethical dilemmas and problem areas to provoke classroom discussion. The book is both practical and comprehensive. It is comprehensive in reflecting the ethical guidelines of the American Counseling Association, the American Psychological Association, and the National Association of Social Workers. It is practical in raising numerous critical incident examples of the multicultural dilemma in practice.

The hot topics for discussion in the last part of the book are particularly useful for classroom discussion. Are dual relationships ethical or not? In many multicultural contexts, ethical counseling behavior demands that the counselor accept dual relationships despite the ethical mandate to the contrary. How do you manage unintentional cultural bias? If you are making the wrong culturally learned assumptions, it will not matter how well intentioned or competent you are, you will be unethical in your behaviors. How do we manage the client's welfare? Often the guidelines seem more interested in protecting the provider against the client than protecting the client. Can you barter for counseling services? The assumptions of a cash economy do not apply to many cultural groups in which bartering is more sensitive to the cultural context. Does counseling foster dependence? The individualistic dominant culture sees dependence as wrong even though many, and perhaps most, world cultures emphasize the importance of dependency to maintain the social fabric. What are the boundaries of competence? How can the same person become competent in a variety of different cultural contexts in which the rules and assumptions are so completely different? This is not an easy task.

Do not expect this book to answer all your questions. Rather, expect that, after reading this book, you will have many more questions than you had in the beginning! Do not think of complexity as your enemy, but rather as your friend in managing the reality of an inevitably complex multicultural world. Do not minimize the difficulty of doing the right thing, but rather recognize inadequacies and aspire toward higher standards of ethical behavior in your practice of counseling multicultural clients.

—Paul B. Pedersen
Professor Emeritus
Syracuse University,
Visiting Professor,
University of Hawaii,
Department of Psychology

Preface

The purpose of *Ethics in a Multicultural Context* is threefold. First, we seek to point out culturally troublesome issues and aspects of current ethical codes for the American Counseling Association (ACA), the American Psychological Association (APA), and the National Association of Social Workers (NASW). Next, we seek to promote culturally appropriate interpretations of existing ethical codes for mental health professions. Our goal is to encourage ethical thinking rather than rule following. Finally, we seek to promote ethical behavior, within a multicultural context, among professionals and within the profession. Here, we address professional and ethical issues that affect ethical thinking within a multicultural context. We provide a practical text and reference materials to assist practitioners and practitioners-in-training to make culturally appropriate and sensitive interpretations of mental health codes of ethics and to make ethical decisions within a cultural context.

Introduction

The preamble to *The American Counseling Association Code of Ethics and Standards of Practice* (ACA, 1995) initiates with the following statement,

> The American Counseling Association is an educational, scientific and professional organization whose members are dedicated to the enhancement of human development throughout the life span. Association members recognize diversity in our society and embrace a cross-cultural approach in support of the worth, dignity, potential, and uniqueness of each individual. (p. 1)

Following the preamble, Section A, "The Counseling Relationship," emphasizes two ethical codes addressing difference under Section A.2, "Respecting Diversity":

> A.2.a. Nondiscrimination: Counselors do not condone or engage in discrimination based on age, color, culture, disability, ethnic group, gender, race, religion, sexual orientation, marital status, or socioeconomic status. (p. 2)

> A.2.b. Respecting Differences: Counselors will actively attempt to understand the diverse cultural backgrounds of the clients with whom they work. This includes, but is not limited to, learning how the counselor's own cultural/ethnic/racial identity impacts her/his values and beliefs about the counseling process. (p. 2)

The ACA (1995) *Code of Ethics and Standards of Practice* gives guidelines on ways to (a) address the diversity and multiculturalism of ACA clientele, (b) promote ethical behavior, and (c) process ethical complaints.

Similarly, the 2002 version of the preamble of the APA *Ethical Principles of Psychologists and Code of Conduct* contains a statement implying consideration for diversity. The preamble advises that, "Psychologists respect and protect civil and human rights and the central importance of freedom of inquiry and expression in research, teaching, and publication." This value is reflected in several of APA's ethical standards. For example, Standard 2.01.b, "Boundaries of Competence," states,

> Where scientific or professional knowledge in the discipline of psychology establishes that an understanding of age, gender, race, ethnicity, culture, national origin, religion, sexual orientation, disability, language, or socioeconomic status is essential for effective implementation of services or research, psychologists have or obtain the training, experience, consultation, or supervision necessary to ensure the competence of their services, or they make appropriate referrals, except as provided in Standard 2.20, Providing Services in Extraordinary Circumstances. (p. 5)

And Standard 3.01, "Unfair Discrimination," states,

> In their work related activities, psychologists do not engage in unfair discrimination based on age, gender, race, ethnicity, culture, national origin, religion, sexual orientation, disability, socioeconomic status, or any basis proscribed by law. (p. 10)

The 1996 National Association of Social Workers (NASW) *Code of Ethics* also includes a statement concerning diversity and multiculturalism in its preamble. A portion of this statement reads as follows: "Social workers are sensitive to cultural and ethnic diversity and strive to end discrimination, oppression, poverty, and other forms of injustice" (p. 1). Again, the value for multiculturalism and diversity is spelled out in several NASW standards. For example, Standard 1.05, "Cultural Competence and Social Diversity," states,

> (a) Social workers should understand culture and its function in human behavior and society, recognizing the strengths that exist in all cultures.

> (b) Social workers should have a knowledge base of their clients' cultures and be able to demonstrate competence in the provision of services that are sensitive to clients' cultures and to difference among people and cultural groups.

> (c) Social workers should obtain education about and seek to understand the nature of social diversity and oppression with respect to race, ethnicity, national origin, color, sex, sexual orientation, age, marital status, political belief, religion, and mental or physical disability. (p. 6)

Collectively, the authors have taught for more than 24 years as counselor educators and are committed to enhancing the development of ethical and culturally competent counseling and helping professionals. Over the years, numerous students at various levels of their graduate studies have voiced their awareness that ethical counselors act in the "best interests of their clients." However, few understood the relationship between diversity, multiculturalism, and ethical behavior. In fact, few students without the benefit of culturally purposive teaching considered the impact of culture on a client's "best interest." Often, students attribute their lack of understanding and consideration of the impact of culture on clients to the fact that many, if not all, of their counseling graduate programs imparted helping philosophies reflecting education and training built on Eurocentric organizational, theoretical, clinical, supervisory, and research models (Ivey, Ivey, & Simek-Morgan, 1997; Pack-Brown, Whittington-Clark, & Parker, 1998; Pedersen, 1997a; Sue & Sue, 1999).

Two critical concerns for the counseling profession are (a) whether professionals are engaging in culturally appropriate interpretations of mental health ethics codes and subsequently competently practicing within a cultural context and (b) whether the codes themselves are ethical outside of a Eurocentric model. A review of the literature reveals that diverse cultural groups are underrepresented in school and community programs. One reason for this underrepresentation is that many diverse and multicultural populations believe that White counselors (currently the majority of practitioners) do not share similar values, life experiences, worldviews, and expectations (Brown, Parham, & Yonker, 1996; Ivey et al., 1997; Pack-Brown, 1999; Pack-Brown et al., 1998; Sue, 1991; Sue & Zane, 1987).

Research also reveals difficulties many White clients experience with mental health practitioners due to perceived dissimilarities in regard to experiences related to gender, sexual orientation, and class (Sue & Sue, 1999). If these populations are correct in their beliefs or their perceptions of counselors, it is important for counseling professionals to become more sensitive to their personal assumptions, worldviews, and biases and the subsequent helping implications. Ethical professionals must provide competent helping services that are more in-line with the life experiences and worldviews of those they serve. Pedersen (1995) and many other scholars in the field of multiculturalism and diversity promote a broad definition of culture; that is, a definition that includes demographics, status, affiliation, and ethnographic variables. However, a controversy exists among professionals as to whether the terms *multiculturalism* and *diversity* and what they mean are one and the same. Pedersen and many other cross-cultural authors contend that culture in its broadest sense implies that all behavior must be understood in its sociocultural context. If so, they contend that "the construct of 'multicultural' becomes generic to all counseling relationships" (Pedersen, 1995, p. 16).

The authors of this book agree with another group of cross-cultural scholars in the field of multiculturalism and diversity scholars (e.g., Arredondo et al., 1996; Pack-Brown et al., 1998; Parham, 1993; Sue & Sue, 1999) that the two constructs (multiculturalism and diversity) are different. Given the historical and continuing struggles around "isms" in the United States, the authors of this book believe acknowledging a difference in definition remains critical. Thus, in this book, we define multiculturalism as the racial and ethnic differences of a particular group of people. We define diversity as the many types of other differences that exist among people, including but not limited to gender, sexual orientation, socioeconomic status, and so on. Of significance is that within diversity, race and ethnicity offer guidelines for how differences are manifested. For example, if we look at gender, we notice that Black/African American women are aligned with White/European American women on the basis of gender. At the same time, their racial and ethnic values, life experiences, and worldviews generate thematic differences that transcend gender. To illustrate, Black/African American women in terms of communication styles tend to value direct and affective expressions of both thoughts and feelings. White/European American women tend to value indirect expression of thoughts and direct affective expressions of feelings.

For more than 26 years, counseling professionals have struggled with ways to translate the words specified in professional codes of ethics from personal awareness to professional action. Most recognize that ethical practice requires a multicultural orientation; however, few understand the cultural realities of the codes and how to interpret and implement the codes within a cultural context.

Part of the struggle encompasses being able to accurately and appropriately view the world through more than monocultural lenses without imposing "self" on interpretations of problems, life experiences, and problem-solving behaviors. As the profession contends with struggles specific to ethics and culture, questions and concerns emerge as to whether the mental health profession and its practitioners and practitioners-in-training are (a) straddling ethical boundaries, (b) crossing ethical boundaries, or (c) ethically meeting the needs of a pluralistic society. There are also struggles related to culturally biased assumptions inherent to the existing codes of ethics. Our objective is to help practitioners recognize culturally biased assumptions in professional codes of ethics and standards so that those codes and standards can be changed and applied appropriately in a variety of sociocultural contexts.

The purpose of *Ethics in a Multicultural Context* is threefold. First, we seek to point out culturally troublesome issues and aspects of current ethical codes for the ACA, the APA, and the NASW. Next, we seek to promote culturally appropriate interpretations of existing ethical codes for mental health professions. Our goal is to encourage ethical thinking rather than rule following. Finally, we seek to promote ethical behavior, within a multicultural context, among professionals and within the profession. Here, we address professional and ethical issues that have an impact on ethical thinking in a multicultural context. We provide a practical text and reference book to assist practitioners and practitioners-in-training to make culturally appropriate and sensitive interpretations of existing mental health codes of ethics and make ethical decisions within a cultural context. Furthermore, this text will facilitate the process of revising codes of ethics within a culturally intentional and competent manner.

The goals of *Ethics in a Multicultural Context* are as follows:

1. To promote accurate and appropriate discussion about culture and ethics

2. To enhance cognitive skills related to ethics from a multicultural and diverse context

3. To develop skills in recognizing culturally biased assumptions related to the existing mental health codes of ethics

4. To present critical incident scenarios that demonstrate culturally competent and ethical behavior by mental health professionals

5. To identify experiences that mental health experts (counselors, psychologists, and social workers) cite as critical in their development of cultural competence

6. To veer practitioners away from "either/or" to "both/and" (i.e., constructivist) thinking with regard to ethics.

Coverage

Ethics in a Multicultural Context is a practical text and resource book intended to help mental health practitioners and trainees to develop ethical decision-making skills that reflect cultural responsiveness. The main focus is ethical decision making in an applied counseling context. The text covers ethical dilemmas arising in face-to-face counseling interactions, the supervisory relationship, and the teaching of counseling.

This text is divided into three sections. Section I introduces readers to the purpose of the text, reviews the literature on ethics within a multicultural context, and discusses the importance of multicultural counseling competency. This latter area addresses the critical need for counselor awareness, knowledge, and skill regarding the difficult issues that often arise when counseling across cultures. Specific topics include the importance of counselors' exposure to and comfort with cultural differences early in their training, how the "experts" evolved personally and professionally, and the importance of forming and maintaining collaborative networks with racially and ethnically diverse individuals. Section II examines, in-depth, the three core components of multicultural counseling competencies: awareness, knowledge, and skills. Included in this section are discussions of the concept of difference, the pervasiveness of the influence of culture, and emotional knowledge, cultural bias, and development of an ethical multicultural framework. Section III introduces ethical dilemmas frequently encountered by practitioners working with a multicultural and diverse clientele.

Each chapter presents a different ethical problem under headings, including dual relationships, unintentional cultural bias, client welfare, bartering for services, fostering dependency, and practicing beyond one's competence. Each of these chapters is divided into four sections: (a) presentation of the case, or "critical incident," (b) identification of the relevant professional codes and moral principles, (c) multicultural experts' discussion of critical questions and concerns, and (d) the experts' stance on the appropriate action to take.

A topic that others in the mental health profession might expect this text to cover is an examination of existing professional codes for cultural biases. Although this topic is addressed indirectly throughout the chapters in the second section, it is not a main focus of the book. The authors are choosing to focus instead on strategies to promote critical thinking in regard to ethical multicultural practice.

Approach

This text constitutes the most comprehensive and practical treatment to date on ethical decision making within a multicultural context. The cases presented include clients of color and clients from other stigmatized groups, as well as White clients. This coverage is designed to "shake up" the current thinking that cultural issues are relevant only to those who have been historically stigmatized. The authors' approach is one that asserts that culture and its impact on all clients is important to examine and that ethical counseling practice takes this into account.

This text also is unique in that the counseling literature covering ethical concerns rarely offers in-depth analyses of multicultural issues. More often, multicultural concerns are covered in a separate chapter in casebooks, and then often superficially. Furthermore, the literature on multicultural counseling does not cover ethics in-depth. This text therefore fills an important gap in the scholarship on ethics and multicultural counseling.

Specifications

Each chapter of *Ethics in a Multicultural Context* includes cases, or critical incidents. These cases are followed with suggested exercises that can be used in counselor education settings. This book also includes an ethical decision-making chart, a glossary, and references.

Acknowledgments

The authors of *Ethics in a Multicultural* context are indebted to a number of persons for their contributions to and assistance with the development of this book. We thank Dr. Nick Ruiz for his initial involvement in the development of this book. We appreciate Nick's commitment to cultural competence and ethical thinking and commend him for knowing when it is necessary to "take care of self" and having the sense to do so. We are particularly grateful to Ms. Nancy Hale, Ms. Heather Scafidi, Ms. Carla Freeman, and Dr. Paul Pedersen for their comments. We thank Mrs. Judy Maxey and Mrs. Sherry Haskins for their word processing work and expertise, patience, and editorial advice. We thank Mrs. Antoinette Banks, Ms. Amelia Fleming, and Miss Jill Oswald, who at the time of writing this book were master's students in the Guidance and Counseling Program at Bowling Green State University, for their assistance in locating references and information pertinent to the development of our work.

We are particularly grateful to the following persons, who offered their multicultural expertise, comments, and suggestions in the critical incident sections: Dr. Michael Garrett, Dr. Colleen Logan, and Dr. Sandra Lopez-Baez.

We give praises to our families (immediate and extended) who endured some neglect during our work on this book. Thank you for your love, support, understanding, sensitivity, and cultural heritage. We hold in high esteem the foundations you helped build for us and the cultural values, beliefs, attitudes, and life experiences you passed down to us.

Grateful praises, acknowledgment, and love from Sherlon Pack-Brown to my family. To my lovely daughter, Allison Sherlon Brown-Smith, thanks for your love and commitment to nurture our relationship. I cherish

WE ARE BECAUSE YOU ARE, YOU ARE THEREFORE WE ARE,

the fact that we are both mother and daughter and we are sister friends. To the four precious men in my life, I thank you. To my eldest and handsome son Scott Allen Brown, praise God for who you ARE and how we (as mother and son) have grown together in the Lord. To my handsome "baby," Tony Olson Brown, thanks for your commitment and your love. We are one in spirit and one in the Lord. To my beloved husband, Al Brown, thank you for your mild manner and the gift that no matter what, ours is a love that will last forever. To my son-in-law, Dwayne Smith, "Mama Brown" welcomes you to the family. A very special thank you to my two granddaughters (Taylor Sheral and Courtney Breanna) and my grandson (Camryn Charles) from "Granny Mom," for your love and your innocence, which has helped me learn to enjoy the basic and important things that life has to offer. To my beautiful Mama, Mildred Guy, without you, I would not be the woman I am today: thanks for your love, vision, discipline, wisdom, and our relationship. Rest assured that even as an elder myself, "I still know who the Mama is and who the daughter is!" Heartfelt thanks to my coauthor, Carmen Williams, and colleagues, such as Paul Pedersen, Mike Espina, Nick Ruiz, Rick Gressard, Linda Keel, Jo-Ann Lipford Sanders, and others from whom I learned a great deal about the power of culture, differences, and similarities in the operationalization of ethics within a cultural context.

I, Carmen Braun Williams, wish to express appreciation to the gifted teachers early in my life whose interest and belief in me helped me to achieve in ways that I dared only to dream. Mr. Henry, you will never know the impact you had on my life! I thank the professors who mentored me during my graduate training. Without their guidance, I surely would have fallen short of my goal. I thank the graduate students in the Counseling Psychology and Counselor Education program at the University of Colorado at Denver for the energy, humor, and intellectual stimulation they bring to my professional life. It is because of them that I strive to be the best teacher I can be. I am thankful to Dr. Judy Lewis for the opportunity to be part of the American Counseling Association Ethics Committee. My service on the Ethics Committee allowed me to work with exceptionally talented and principled people, such as my coauthor Sherlon Brown, Paul Pedersen, Mike Espina, Nick Ruiz, Rick Gressard, Linda Keel, and others from whom I learned a great deal about fairness and justice. A special thanks to my furry companion, Mallorca, whose gentle reminders that it was time to take a walk saved me from becoming too singularly focused on work. And last, very special thanks to my life partner, Jim, who took up golf so that I could commit myself fully and guiltlessly to this project! His support, encouragement, and interest in everything I write made the completion of this project possible.

This book is dedicated to the multicultural and diverse individuals and groups that make our society a kaleidoscope of beauty, gifts, and perspectives. May our multiple cultures, worldviews, and heritages continue to be passed from one generation to another generation. May the passage of cultural and individual differences and similarities unite us personally and professionally.

We are because of each other; each of us is, therefore we are.

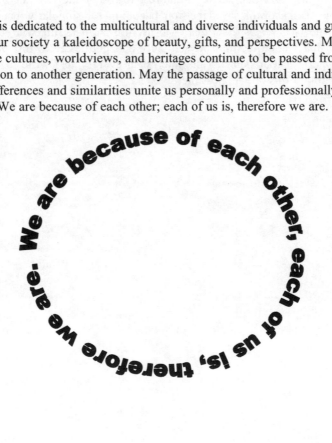

Section I

Overview

Few counseling and mental health professionals understand the relationship between diversity, multiculturalism, and ethical behavior. Many struggle with recognizing the impact of culture on a client's "best interest." One reason is that formal training imparts helping philosophies reflecting education and training built on Eurocentric organizational, theoretical, clinical, research, and supervisory models (Ivey, & Ivey, & Simek-Morgan, 1997; Pack-Brown, Whittington-Clark, & Parker, 1998; Sue & Sue, 1999). Another reason is possession of a tenuous ability to accurately view the world through more than monocultural lenses without imposing "self" on interpretations of problems, life experiences, and problem-solving behaviors. A third reason for the struggle is related to culturally biased assumptions inherent in existing codes of ethics. A fourth reason is the existence of culturally biased assumptions that those interpreting the codes bring with them while making interpretations. As the profession contends with struggles specific to ethics and culture, questions and concerns emerge as to whether the mental health profession and its practitioners are (a) straddling ethical boundaries, (b) crossing ethical boundaries, or (c) ethically meeting the needs of a pluralistic society.

Section I of this book introduces readers to (a) the purpose of the text, (b) a preliminary review of the literature on ethics in a multicultural context, and (c) the fundamental importance of multicultural counseling competency. This latter area will address the need for counselor awareness, knowledge, and skill regarding difficult issues that arise when counseling across cultures. Specific topics will include the importance of counselors' exposure to and comfort with cultural differences early in their training, how "experts" evolved personally and professionally, and the importance of forming and maintaining collaborative networks with racially and ethnically diverse individuals. Section I is divided into three chapters. Chapter 1 provides a review of underlying principles and goals of the ethical codes of three professional associations, the American Counseling Association (ACA), the American Psychological Association (APA), and the National Association of Social Workers (NASW). Chapter 2 offers a review of the literature on ethics in a multicultural context. Chapter 3 identifies important areas that have not been fully explored regarding multicultural context and implications.

1

Brief Review of Principles and Goals of Three Ethical Codes

Herlihy and Corey (1996) describe the most basic functions of an ethics code as educating members about sound ethical conduct, providing a mechanism for professional accountability, and providing a catalyst for improving practice.

—Pedersen (1997a, p. 23)

Perhaps one of the most important messages emerging from the Herlihy and Corey statement is that in order for mental health practitioners and practitioners-in-training to obtain an accurate understanding of, assume accountability for, and improve practice, they need to fully comprehend the underlying principles and goals of ethical codes specific to their professional associations. Of significance, however, is that many practitioners and practitioners-in-training experience feelings of ambiguity and concern over the multiple ways the codes may be perceived and interpreted. This is in part due to the fact that some have not looked beyond the "face value" of the codes, while others have trouble putting the codes into real-life situations and engaging in ethical thinking rather than rule following.

This chapter reviews the underlying principles and goals of ethical codes for three professional associations: the American Counseling Association (ACA), the American Psychological Association (APA), and the National Association of Social Workers (NASW). Each association will be presented separately. This review will serve as a precursor to an in-depth examination of existing ethical codes and as a catalyst for practitioners and practitioners-in-training to question the need to consider codes of ethics in a multicultural context. Each review begins with the preamble, to serve as a precursor to principles defining ethical behavior and standards of practice for association members. The review of the preamble will set the stage for ethical thinking as it relates to sections of the code. Two questions guide the overview: What are guidelines for ethical behavior? How are professionals and professionals-in-training expected to process ethical complaints? Each question will be presented separately. Basic assumptions and thematic values and their impact on ethical conduct, professional accountability, improved practice, and ethical thinking will follow. The chapter concludes with a "critical incident." The reader is asked to share his or her opinions about the incident to foster the development of ethical thinking by responding to the questions at the end of the chapter.

Ethics are rules of conduct or moral principles that guide professional practices. Ethical codes empower professional associations to clarify ethical responsibilities for their members and identify methodology for processing complaints and correcting unethical behavior. The codes promote professional empowerment by assisting professionals and professionals-in-training to (a) keep good practice, (b) protect their clients, (c) safeguard their autonomy, and (d) enhance the profession.

The American Counseling Association

The 1995 ACA *Code of Ethics and Standards of Practice* preamble reads,

> The American Counseling Association is an educational, scientific and professional organization whose members are dedicated to the enhancement of human development throughout the life span. Association members recognize diversity in our society and embrace a cross-cultural approach in support of the worth, dignity, potential, and uniqueness of each individual.
>
> The specification of a code of ethics enables the association to clarify to current and future members, and to those served by members, the nature of the ethical responsibilities held in common by its members. As the code of ethics of the association, this document establishes principles that define the ethical behavior of association members. All members of the American Counseling Association are required to adhere to the ACA *Code of Ethics & Standards of Practice*. The *ACA Code of Ethics & Standards of Practice* will serve as the basis for processing ethical complaints initiated against members of the association. (p. 1)

As students and practitioners review their professional codes of ethics and (a) define ethical behavior, (b) strive to adhere to ethics, and (c) process ethical complaints, they must have an accurate understanding of the foundation upon which the codes are built. The following questions serve to assist in understanding that foundation. First, what are specific guidelines for ethical behavior prescribed to counselors? Second, how are counselors expected to process ethical complaints? The way a person responds to these questions governs the accuracy of understanding the underlying principles and goals of the code. For it is in these responses that definitions of criteria for ethical behavior and methodology for processing ethical complaints originate. Keys to accuracy include basic and requisite awareness, knowledge, and skill to identify assumptions and thematic values and their subsequent impact on interpretation of reality, ethical thinking, and ethical decision making.

Guidelines for Ethical Behavior

What are the specific guidelines for ethical behavior prescribed to counselors? How do these guidelines serve as pillars for accurate understanding of the foundation upon which the ACA code of ethics is built? This section is not meant to be a comprehensive effort, but to simply initiate a process for ethical thinking based on randomly selected sections of the code and answers to the questions above. The ACA (1995) *Code of Ethics and Standards of Practice*, more commonly referred to as "the foundation to ethical practice for counselors," provides guidelines for promoting ethical thinking and maintaining ethical behavior. Beginning with the preamble, the stage is set for ethical thinking as it informs members that the ACA is able to clarify common ethical responsibilities for its members as well as for persons served by its members. Yet to fully understand and interpret what constitutes ethical behavior, those reading the code must at the very least know the underlying assumptions, principles, and goals inherent to the code.

Eight sections follow the preamble. Each section makes specific assumptions and presumptions about what is considered ethical behavior. Each provides principles that outline rules for personal conduct while engaging in ethical behavior. Each specifies goals toward which movement is expected as members behave ethically. Finally, each offers a statement that demonstrates what someone with a mistaken view might say about (a) ethical behavior, (b) rules for personal conduct while engaging in ethical behavior, or (c) goals toward which movement is expected as one behaves ethically.

Section A: The Counseling Relationship

An assumption in this section of the ACA code relates to the welfare of clients. An underlying principle is that counselors will act in the "best interests" of those they serve. Those reading the code are provided with 12 subheadings offering specific guidelines and goals related to personal conduct needed to exhibit character as defined by the ACA, particularly in developing and maintaining a counseling relationship. The section begins with issues such as primary responsibility of counselors, positive growth and development of clients, developing counseling plans, and family involvement in the counseling process. Furthermore, this section offers a mandate for respecting diversity and provides goals for members to strive toward, such as nondiscrimination and respecting differences. Guidelines are provided for client rights and include disclosure to clients and freedom of choice. A statement reflecting a potential mistaken view of the counseling relationship is, "If I respect my client, my client will respect me," as if respect were a universal concept and had no cultural implications or demanded no cultural considerations.

Additional sections of the ACA code address personal needs and values of the counselor and their potential impact on areas such as the counseling relationship, dual relationships between client and counselor, and sexual intimacies between counselor and client. This section offers the value of independence rather than dependence. Section A.1.b, "The Counseling Relationship—Positive Growth and Development," states that "Counselors encourage client growth and development in ways that foster the clients' interest and welfare; counselors avoid fostering dependent counseling relationships" (p. 2). There is an expressed value for nondiscrimination. Section A.2.a, "Respecting Diversity-Nondiscrimination," states that, "Counselors do not condone or engage in discrimination based on age, color, culture, disability, ethnic group, gender, race, religion, sexual orientation, marital status, or socioeconomic status" (p. 2). An assumption is that those who engage in nondiscrimination are believed to be respectful of diversity and acting in the best interests of clients.

Section B: Confidentiality

An assumption specific to this section of the ACA code relates to the client's right to privacy for information shared during sessions and of record. A critical value is confidentiality. Personal boundaries are placed on counselors around information considered private property or confidential, as if personal space and time were valued as property to be privately owned. An underlying principle is that counselors will adhere to the client's right to privacy and confidentiality. A mandate for confidentiality is offered, and goals for members to work toward are shared. For example, Section B.1.a, "Respect for Privacy," states, "Counselors respect their clients' right to privacy and avoid illegal and unwarranted disclosures of confidential information" (p. 3). Guidelines are offered for clarification to include client waiver, exceptions, court-ordered disclosure, and explanation of limitations. Section B.4.b, "Confidentiality of Records," states that, "Counselors are responsible for securing the safety and confidentiality of any counseling records they create, maintain, transfer, or destroy whether the records are written, taped, computerized, or stored in any other medium" (p. 4). An assumption about privacy may be "I believe in privacy, so my client(s) must believe in privacy too." This assumption reflects a potential mistaken view of confidentiality and serves as the impetus for ethical thinking. Of significance is the impact of worldview perspective on definitions of terms such as *privacy*. For example, a counselor believes in privacy, and this belief (consciously or unconsciously) is interpreted from the counselor's worldview perspective. That is, privacy is information perceived as property, and a critical question becomes this: What impact does my worldview perspective have on my ethical thinking within a cultural context?

Section C: Professional Responsibility

Assumptions about competence are presented in this section of the ACA code. Immediately, counselors are charged with the responsibility not to only read but also to understand and follow the ACA code of ethics. From this point on, assumptions, values, and guidelines are offered to facilitate the process of behaving in a competent manner. For example, there is an assumption that competence is related to formalized education and training. Section C.2.a, "Boundaries of Competence," states that, "Counselors practice only within the boundaries of their competence, based on their education, training, supervised experience, state and national professional credentials, and appropriate professional experience" (p. 4). This section continues by directing members as to what behaviors they must engage in to exhibit their commitment to working with diverse populations.

Section D: Relationships With Other Professionals

This section of the ACA code highlights the importance of respecting professionals in related mental health professions. One value inherent to this section is that of collaborative relationships. Section D.1.b, "Agreements," states,

> Counselors establish working agreements with supervisors, colleagues, and subordinates regarding counseling or clinical relationships, confidentiality, adherence to professional standards, distinction between public and private material, maintenance and dissemination of recorded information, workload, and accountability. Working agreements in each instance are specified and made known to those concerned. (p. 5)

An assumption is that sharing working agreements with "concerned" entities is a viable way to display ethical behavior. A statement reflecting a potential mistaken view of professional responsibility is, "I think any ethical and competent counselor engages in culturally appropriate helping behavior." Another guideline is Section D.1.i, "Discrimination." The directive here is as follows:

> Counselors, as either employers or employees, do not engage in or condone practices that are inhumane, illegal, or unjustifiable (such as considerations based on age, color, culture, disability, ethnic group, gender, race, religion, sexual orientation, or socioeconomic status) in hiring, promotion, or training. (p. 5)

There is a value placed on not using difference as a viable factor in decision making about hiring, promoting, or training, so an assumption is that difference is not something to be valued; rather it is to be ignored.

Section E: Evaluation, Assessment, and Interpretation

Section E of the ACA code contains standards that govern the use of tests in counseling. Section E.1.a, "Appraisal Techniques," states,

> The primary purpose of educational and psychological assessment is to provide measures that are objective and interpretable in either comparative or absolute terms. Counselors recognize the need to interpret the statements in this section as applying to the whole range of appraisal techniques including test and non-test data. (p. 6)

This section presents an assumption that educational and psychological assessment is done to provide measures that are objective and interpretable in either comparative or absolute terms. That is, there appears to be a value placed on the use of empirical and linear assumptions used to substantiate quantitative, rather than qualitative, methodologies as criteria for accuracy when evaluating, assessing, and making interpretations.

Section F: Teaching, Training, and Supervision

This section of the ACA code emphasizes ethical guidelines for counselor educators and trainers, for counselor preparation programs, and for students and supervisors. Immediately, for example, in Section F.1.a, "Educators as Teachers and Practitioners," guidelines for responsible and ethical behavior are offered. This section states,

> Counselors who are responsible for developing, implementing, and supervising educational programs are skilled as teachers and practitioners. They are knowledgeable regarding the ethical, legal, and regulatory aspects of the profession, are skilled in applying that knowledge, and

make students and supervisees aware of their responsibilities. Counselors conduct counselor education and training programs in an ethical manner and serve as role models for professional behavior. Counselor educators should make every effort to infuse material related to human diversity into all courses and/or workshops that are designed to promote the development of professional counselors. (p. 7)

Values include the possession of teaching and clinical skills; knowledge of and ability to apply ethical, legal, and regulatory aspects of the counseling profession; and serving as role models for professional behavior. A statement reflecting a potential mistaken view of evaluation, assessment, and interpretation is, "I appreciate testing as a viable helping tool, so it seems appropriate to expect that others appreciate testing as a viable helping tool." "I believe counselor educators, supervisors, and clinicians possess educational and clinical skills and infuse material related to human diversity into their work" exemplifies a statement reflecting a potential mistaken view of teaching, training, and supervision.

Section G: Research and Publication

This section of the ACA code addresses a range of issues that includes protection of human subjects, informed consent for research participants, honesty and accuracy in reporting research results, and ethical problems in seeking publication. Values include a protection of human dignity, diminishing harm or injury to subjects, and informed consent. Attention is given to the impact of cultural factors, such as language, on understanding what and how work is to be done. For example, Section G.2.a, "Topics Disclosed," offers guidelines specific to informed consent and states,

In obtaining informed consent for research, counselors use language that is understandable to research participants and that (1) accurately explains the purpose and procedures to be followed; (2) identifies any procedures that are experimental or relatively untried; (3) describes the attendant discomforts and risks; (4) describes the benefits or changes in individuals or organizations that might be reasonably expected; (5) discloses appropriate alternative procedures that would be advantageous for subjects; (6) offers to answer any inquiries concerning the procedures; (7) describes any limitations on confidentiality; and (8) instructs that subjects are free to withdraw their consent and to discontinue participation in the project at any time. (p. 9)

However, there is an implied value for counselors interpreting the guidelines from an unspecified reference, which might be the self-reference of the person actually reading this section. A statement reflecting a potential mistaken view of research and publication is, "I value self-reference, so you must value it too."

Section H: Resolving Ethical Issues

Section H of the ACA code emphasizes the responsibility of counselors to know the ethical standards of practice and explain procedures for resolving and reporting suspected ethical violations. Section H.1, "Knowledge of Standards," states,

> Counselors are familiar with the Code of Ethics and Standards of Practice and other applicable ethics codes from other professional organizations of which they are member[s] or from certification and licensure bodies. Lack of knowledge or misunderstanding of an ethical responsibility is not a defense against a charge of unethical conduct. (p. 10)

Values inherent to this section include familiarity with existing guidelines, expectation for all counselors to adhere to the code of ethics, and consultation for clarification when uncertain about the code. Several assumptions are inherent to this section. One assumption is that counselors can informally work with each other to ensure that ethical behaviors are upheld. Another assumption is that counselors value working with each other to ensure professional and ethical behavior. "I am familiar with the code of ethics, and my colleagues are familiar as well" demonstrates a statement reflecting a potential mistaken view of resolving ethical issues.

Processing Ethical Complaints

How are counselors expected to process ethical complaints? This question serves as another pillar for accurate understanding of the foundation upon which the ACA code of ethics is built. This section is not meant to be a comprehensive effort, but to simply initiate a process of ethical thinking based on randomly selected sections of the code and answers to this question. How one responds to this question governs the accuracy of understanding the underlying principles and goals of the code that define criteria for ethical behavior and methodology for processing ethical complaints. Appropriate awareness, knowledge, and skills remain critical to identifying requisite assumptions, thematic values, and their subsequent impact on interpretation of reality, ethical thinking, ethical decision making, and action taken when ethical codes are broken. Violations of the ethics code and subsequent sanctions as determined by the ACA Ethics Committee include (a) remedial requirements imposed for completion within a specified time, (b) probation for a specified time subject to review of compliance by the committee, (c) suspension from ACA membership for a specified time, and (d) permanent expulsion from ACA membership. Penalties exist: First, failure to satisfactorily meet remedial requirements as a result of a probation sanction automatically brings forth suspension until the requirement is met. However, the committee may also determine that the remedial requirement needs modification based on *good cause* (i.e., efforts made by the charged member to meet the specifications of the committee) as shown prior to the end of probation. The second relates to a penalty for failing to satisfactorily fulfill remedial requirements specific to the committee's decision for suspension. If the member fails to respond, he or she may be automatically and permanently expelled unless the committee determines the remedial requirement should be modified, based on good cause, to the end of the suspension period. It should be noted that actions violating the ACA ethics code may lead to the imposition of sanctions by other bodies that include other professional groups, professional boards, state or federal agencies, and payers for health services.

Section H.2.a of the ACA code, "Suspected Violations: Ethical Behavior Expected," reads that, "Counselors expect professional associates to adhere to the Code of Ethics. When counselors possess reasonable cause that raises doubts as to whether a counselor is acting in an ethical manner, they take appropriate action" (p. 10). Values inherent in this statement include going to someone who has participated in "inappropriate" behavior and directly sharing with that person what was ethically wrong, then collaboratively working to correct the behavior. If that direct attempt fails, the next step is to report inappropriate behavior to others outside the immediate community (e.g., the ACA Ethics Committee). ACA members are to strive toward the goal of assisting the association in monitoring the profession and its professionals by serving as watchdogs over each other. An assumption is that all members wish to promote professionalism among members and for the association via the goals specified. That is, when one member believes that another member is in violation of an ethical code, the complainant culturally values personally and directly attempting to correct the behavior, and if that direct attempt fails, then he or she culturally values taking the problem to a higher authority. For example, Section J.2, "Filing Complaints," reads,

> Individuals eligible to file complaints will send a letter outlining the nature of the complaint to the Committee at the ACA Headquarters. The complaint should include, if possible, (a) the name and address of the complainant, (b) the name and address of the charged member, (c) the names and addresses of any other persons who have knowledge of the facts involved, and (d) a brief description of the reason why the complaint is being filed. (p. 14)

Of significance is that interpretations of the underlying principles and goals that guide directives for determining ethical misconduct and processing ethical complaints are motivated in part by personal and/or professional assumptions, presumptions, and thematic values originating within a cultural context. Note that the cultural context could be that of the ACA, the person filing the complaint, or the person in violation. It becomes critically important for persons to engage in accurate ethical thinking and decision making when reviewing the ACA code, making determinations about misconduct according to the code, and making decisions on when to process ethical complaints to engage in accurate ethical thinking and decision making. At the very least, persons electing to file complaints need to be cognizant of the basic ACA assumptions (beliefs that are considered factual), presumptions (beliefs that originate from the formation of a judgment based on probable grounds and remain open for further evidence to substantiate accuracy), and thematic values (values that emerge over and over again) that undergird the ACA (1995) *Code of Ethics and Standards of Practice*. Exercise 1.1 presents a model for identifying basic assumptions, presumptions, and thematic values inherent to sections of the ACA code, thus facilitating a better understanding of the culture upon which the code was built.

This information will serve as one of the pillars needed to enhance ethical thinking within a multicultural context. The reader is advised that this model is useful with codes of ethics across mental health professions.

Further clarification of the cultural context of the ACA code of ethics mandates knowledge and understanding of thematic cultural values, assumptions, and presumptions inherent to a code. To facilitate the process, further discussion of the ACA code of ethics follows.

Basic Assumptions, Presumptions, and Thematic Values

Immediately, the preamble of the ACA code reads, "Association members recognize diversity in our society and embrace a cross-cultural approach in support of the worth, dignity, potential and uniqueness of each individual" (p. 1). Of significance is the potential impact of subconscious cultural programming about terms such as *unique* and *individual*. If, for example, unique and individual are culturally defined as the importance of the individual taking priority, the terms may mean self-actualization, or self-worth, ultimately placing an emphasis on the individual. On the other hand, if unique and individual are culturally defined as the importance of self in relation to others, the terms may mean, "I am because we are; we are, therefore I am." In this case, self is perceived in relation to others. In reviewing the literature, individualism is suggested as the predominant definition specific to the ACA code of ethics. Given this reality, many reading the preamble are consciously or unconsciously prone to believe that the ACA code is based on a preference for individualism.

A further review of the ACA (1995) *Code of Ethics and Standards of Practice* as well as the literature specific to the code reveals a number of underlying principles and goals. Many authors (Pedersen, 1997a;

Exercise 1.1   Basic Assumptions, Presumptions, and Values Inherent to
                    the Culture of the ACA Code of Ethics

Section(s) of the Code	*Basic Assumption(s)*	*Basic Presumption(s)*	*Thematic Value(s)*
Section A.1.c. ***Counseling Plans.*** Counselors and their clients work jointly in devising integrated individual counseling plans that offer reasonable promise of success and are consistent with abilities and circumstances of the clients. Counselors and clients regularly review counseling plans to ensure their continued viability and effectiveness respecting clients' freedom of choice.	The individual is the building block of counseling	An individualistic perspective.	Individualism
Section			
Section			

Note: The reader is encouraged to take each section of the ACA code of ethics that is applicable to the issues at hand and complete the chart using Section A.1.c as an example. An outcome of this effort will be a clearer picture of the thematic cultural assumptions, presumptions, and values inherent to the existing ACA code of ethics.

Pack-Brown & Williams, 2000) suggest that the code defines ethics from a predominantly European American cultural perspective, such that numerous rules, checklists, principles, and guidelines for ACA members are presented within a Eurocentric worldview and value system. Kitchner (1984) discovered four universal moral principles woven throughout the ACA code. Those principles are found under specific subheadings that provide a foundation for the code and include (a) autonomy, which is a clients' freedom for self-definition; (b) beneficence, which encompasses the actions that promote the growth and development of clients; (c) nonmaleficence, which is the act of refraining from hurting clients; and (d) fairness, which mandates equal treatment of all people.

The American Psychological Association

The 2002 version of the APA's *Ethical Principles of Psychologists and Code of Conduct* (more commonly referred to as the "Ethics Code") is divided into four sections: (a) an introduction, (b) a preamble, (c) five general principles, and (d) ethical standards. The preamble and general principles are referred to as nonenforceable rules designed to help psychologists arrive at ethical actions and used to assist in interpreting the ethical standards. On the other hand, the ethical standards are considered enforceable rules for conduct. The Ethics Code applies to psychologists' work-related activities, which are activities considered part of the psychologist's scientific and professional functions, or clinical or counseling functions that are believed to be psychological in nature.

The preamble to the APA (2002) *Ethical Principles of Psychologists and Code of Conduct* reads,

> Psychologists are committed to increasing scientific and professional knowledge of behavior and people's understanding of themselves and others and to the use of such knowledge to improve the condition of individuals, organizations, and society. Psychologists respect and protect civil and human rights and the central importance of freedom of inquiry and expression in research, teaching, and publication. They also strive to help the public in developing informed judgments and choices concerning human behavior. In doing so, they perform many roles, such as researcher, educator, diagnostician, therapist, supervisor, consultant, administrator, social interventionist, and expert witness. This Ethics Code provides a common set of principles and standards upon which psychologists build their professional and scientific work.
>
> This Ethics Code is intended to provide specific standards to cover most situations encountered by psychologists. It has as its goals the welfare and protection of the individuals and groups with whom psychologists work and the education of members, students, and the public regarding ethical standards of the discipline.
>
> The development of a dynamic set of ethical standards for a psychologist's work-related conduct requires a personal commitment and a lifelong effort to act ethically; to encourage ethical behavior by students,

supervisees, employees, and colleagues; and to consult with others concerning ethical problems. (p. 3)

Guidelines for Ethical Behavior

What are specific guidelines for ethical behavior prescribed for psychologists? This question serves as a pillar for accurate understanding of the foundation upon which the APA code of ethics is built. This review is not meant to be comprehensive, but to simply initiate a process for ethical thinking.

The APA (2002) *Ethical Principles of Psychologists and Code of Conduct* provides guidelines on promoting ethical thinking and maintaining ethical behavior. Beginning with the preamble, the stage is set for thinking as it informs members that the APA provides a set of values upon which psychologists build their work. The code provides general principles and decision rules to cover situations encountered by psychologists. The primary goal of the code is the welfare and protection of individuals and groups served by psychologists. However, as with the ACA code of ethics, to fully understand and interpret what constitutes ethical behavior, those reading the APA code must at the very least know APA's underlying assumptions, principles, and goals.

Five general principles follow the preamble. Each principle offers specific assumptions and presumptions about what is considered ethical behavior. Each outlines rules for personal conduct while engaging in ethical behavior. Finally, each specifies goals toward which movement is expected as members behave ethically. Though these principles are considered unenforceable, they do guide thinking. To give a flavor of the unenforceable guides to thinking, the first three will be reviewed.

Principle A: Beneficence and Nonmaleficence

Principle A of the APA code emphasizes the responsibility of psychologists for maintaining a positive effect on persons with whom they work while simultaneously ensuring that no harm comes to those served. A portion of this principle reads, "Because psychologists' scientific and professional judgments and actions may affect the lives of others, they are alert to and guard against personal, financial, social, organizational, or political factors that might lead to misuse of their influence" (p. 3).

There are numerous values, such as understanding others in order to have a positive effect, so that competence and its variance depend on distinct characteristics of populations served. Two specified goals are that psychologists aspire to (a) maximize the benefits of their work and (b) prevent or minimize harm to populations served. Another value is scientific professional information.

Principle B: Fidelity and Responsibility

Fidelity and responsibility are the areas of emphasis in Prinicple B of the APA code. To illustrate, a portion of this principle states,

> Psychologists establish relationships of trust with those with whom they work. They are aware of their professional and scientific responsibilities to society and to the specific communities in which they work. Psychologists uphold professional standards of conduct, clarify their professional roles and obligations, accept appropriate responsibility for their behavior, and seek to manage conflicts of interest that could lead to exploitation or harm. (p. 3)

Several goals are evident in this principle and include consulting with, referring to, and cooperating with other professionals in order to better serve the interests of students, research participants, patients, and clients. Values include loyalty and trust. A guideline for psychologists is to be aware of professional and scientific responsibilities to society and to communities served.

Principle C: Integrity

Integrity is the emphasis in Prinicple C of the APA code. To illustrate, a portion of this principle states, "Psychologists seek to promote accuracy, honesty, and truthfulness in the science, teaching, and practice of psychology. In these activities psychologists do not steal, cheat, or engage in fraud, subterfuge, or intentional misrepresentation of fact" (p. 3).

Several goals are evident in the "Integrity" principle and include seeking to promote integrity in the science, teaching, and practice of psychology. Psychology is assumed to be a science. Values reflected include candid and forthright behavior to promote trust in relationships. A guideline for psychologists is to keep promises and avoid bad-faith excuses, unwise or unclear commitments, and conflicts of interest.

Ethical Standards

Section 1: Resolving Ethical Issues

An assumption in Section 1 of the APA code relates to acceptable methodology for addressing and resolving ethical issues. A presumption of competence exists as psychologists identify acceptable methodology specific to ethical issues. An underlying principle is that psychologists help other psychologists to abide by ethical standards and appropriately address ethical issues. Eight subheadings are offered to provide guidelines and goals for resolving ethical issues:

Section 1.01   Misuse of Psychologists' Work

Section 1.02   Conflicts Between Ethics and Law, Regulations, or Other Governing Legal Authority

Section 1.03   Conflicts Between Ethics and Organizational Demands

Section 1.04   Informal Resolution of Ethical Violations

Section 1.05   Reporting Ethical Violations

Section 1.06   Cooperating With Ethics Committee

Section 1.07   Improper Complaints

Section 1.08   Unfair Discrimination Against Complainants and Respondents

Thematic values evident in this standard include direct communication of information and behavior and cooperation specific to ethics investigations and proceedings. "I believe in directly confronting my colleagues to help them engage in acceptable behavior, and my colleagues believe in directly confronting too" may reflect a mistaken view of resolving helping issues. The reader is reminded that values such as direct communication have a cultural frame of reference. These values affect assumptions and influence definitions of normal and appropriate behavior as well as decision making. For example, a counselor operating from a cultural perspective that views direct communication as an effective life approach may professionally embrace direct confrontation as normal, appropriate, and effective as a helping strategy. A counselor operating from a cultural perspective that embraces indirect communication as an effective life approach may personally and professionally emphasize the merits of indirect communication and view direct communication as abnormal and inappropriate behavior. A critical question for ethical counselors seeking to operate within a cultural context is this: What impact do my cultural and individual worldview perspectives and value systems have on my ethical thinking?

Section 2: Competence

An *assumption* in this section of the APA code is that scientific or professional knowledge obtained by psychologists via methodologies such as education, training, and supervision is culturally accurate, sensitive, and/or appropriate and has the potential to promote effective implementation of services or research. A *presumption* of desire and motivation to seek education and training to enhance competence exists, particularly as it relates to serving populations different from the psychologist. An underlying *principle* is that psychologists operate only within the boundaries of their competence. Six subheadings are offered to provide guidelines and goals for operating as a competent psychologist:

Section 2.01   Boundaries of Competence

Section 2.02   Providing Services in Emergency Circumstances

Section 2.03   Maintaining Competence

Section 2.04   Bases for Scientific and Professional Judgments

Section 2.05   Delegation of Work to Others

Section 2.06   Personal Problems and Conflicts

Values thematic of this standard include awareness of the importance of knowledge and understanding of diversity and multiculturalism to the quality of services offered and protection of persons from harm. A statement reflecting a potential mistaken view of competence is, "Scientific knowledge is culturally accurate, sensitive and/or appropriate."

Section 3: Human Relations

This section of the APA code offers an *assumption* that psychologists understand and appreciate human relations in their work-related activities. A *presumption* of competence and professionalism exists when psychologists understand and honor the multiple facets of human relations. A guiding principle is that psychologists do no harm to persons around issues such as age, gender, race, ethnicity, national origin, religion, sexual orientation, disability, socioeconomic status, or any basis prescribed by law. Values include engaging in professional behaviors that empower persons receiving services, regardless of their differences, and promoting the objectivity, competence, and effectiveness of psychologists in their work-related activities. "I appreciate the individualism in human relations, so other psychologists must too" reflects a potential mistaken view of human relations. Twelve subheadings offer assumptions, presumptions, guiding principles, and values for ethically addressing human relations:

Section 3.01   Unfair Discrimination

Section 3.02   Sexual Harassment

Section 3.03   Other Harassment

Section 3.04   Avoiding Harm

Section 3.05   Multiple Relationships

Section 3.06   Conflict of Interest

Section 3.07   Third-Party Requests for Services

Section 3.08   Exploitative Relationships

Section 3.09   Cooperation With Other Professionals

Section 3.10   Informed Consent

Section 3.11   Psychological Services Delivered to or Through Organizations

Section 3.12   Interruption of Psychological Services

Section 4: Privacy and Confidentiality

Section 4 of the APA code offers an assumption that psychologists have a similar value of and understanding of privacy and confidentiality. A presumption is that discussion of confidential information with others is not only appropriate and ethical but also minimizes intrusions on privacy. "Privacy is a universal value" is an example of a potential mistaken view of privacy and confidentiality. Seven subheadings present presumptions and guidelines for ethical behavior specific to privacy and confidentiality:

Section 4.01   Maintaining Confidentiality

Section 4.02   Discussing the Limits of Confidentiality

Section 4.03   Recording

Section 4.04   Minimizing Intrusions on Privacy

Section 4.05   Disclosures

Section 4.06   Consultations

Section 4.07   Use of Confidential Information for Didactic or Other Purposes

Each subheading of the APA code offers guiding principles for psychologists related to privacy and confidentiality. For example, a guiding principle for psychologist in Section 4.04.b, "Minimizing Intrusions on Privacy," is that, "Psychologists discuss confidential information obtained in their work only for appropriate scientific or professional purposes and only with persons clearly concerned with such matters" (p. 7).

Section 5: Advertising and Other Public Statements

Section 5 of the APA code addresses an assumption that psychologists will advertise and engage in other public representations. A presumption of false or deceptive representations exists in Section 5.01, "Avoidance of False or Deceptive Statements." A guiding principle is that psychologists do not consciously misrepresent themselves. Six subheadings present presumptions and guidelines for ethical behavior around advertising and engaging in other public representations:

Section 5.01   Avoidance of False or Deceptive Statements

Section 5.02   Statements by Others

Section 5.03   Descriptions of Workshops and Non–Degree Granting
                Educational Programs

Section 5.04   Media Presentations

Section 5.05   Testimonials

Section 5.06   In-Person Solicitation

For example, Section 5.04, discussing guidelines for media presentations,
states,

> When psychologists provide public advice or comment via print, internet,
> or other electronic transmission, they take precautions to ensure that
> tatements (1) are based on their professional knowledge, training, or
> experience in accord with appropriate psychological literature and
> practice; (2) are otherwise consistent with this Ethics Code; and (3) do not
> indicate that a professional relationship has been established with the
> recipient. (p. 8)

A thematic value inherent to this section is the presentation of accurate
information concerning professional behaviors (be they practice, products,
or activities), training, knowledge, or experience. A statement reflecting
a potential mistaken view of advertising and other public representations
is, "I value public advice as appropriate professional behavior, so others
will too."

Section 6: Record Keeping and Fees

An assumption in Section 6 of the APA code is that record keeping
serves multiple purposes, such as to (a) facilitate the provision of services,
(b) allow for replication of research design and analysis, (c) meet institutional requirements, (d) ensure accuracy of billing and payments, and
(e) ensure compliance with the law. Specific presumptions are evidenced in
the seven subheadings addressing record keeping and fees:

Section 6.01   Documentation of Professional and Scientific Work and
                Maintenance of Records

Section 6.02   Maintenance, Dissemination, and Disposal of Confidential
                Records of Professional and Scientific Work

Section 6.03   Withholding Records for Nonpayment

Section 6.04   Fees and Financial Arrangements

Section 6.05   Barter With Clients/Patients

Section 6.06   Accuracy in Reports to Payors and Funding Sources

Section 6.07   Referrals and Fees

Each subheading provides presumptions and guidelines for psychologists as they address ethical behavior around record keeping and fees. For example, a presumption of maintaining confidentiality of records and guidelines for psychologists is addressed and identified in Sections 6.02a and 6.02b:

> Psychologists maintain confidentiality in creating, storing, accessing, transferring, and disposing of records under their control, whether these are written, automated, or in any other medium. If confidential information concerning recipients of psychological services is entered into databases or systems of records available to persons whose access has not been consented to by the recipient, psychologists use coding or other techniques to avoid the inclusion of personal identifiers. (p. 9)

A value evident of record keeping and fees is confidentiality and the protection of confidential records. A statement reflecting a potential mistaken view of record keeping and fees is, "I like it, so you must like it too." Cultural merits related to accurate communication and documentation are inherent to this statement. The reader is reminded that communication and documentation have cultural foundations, so that the previous thought about communication and documentation when posed within a cultural context may be stated in at least two ways. One statement is, "In my culture, written documentation is appropriate record keeping." Another statement is, "In my culture, historical oral histories are appropriate record keeping."

Section 7: Education and Training

This standard of the APA code is built around the assumption that psychologists present appropriate information and experiences when teaching or training. Seven subheadings follow and present presumptions, guidelines, and values inherent to education and training:

Section 7.01   Design of Education and Training Programs

Section 7.02   Descriptions of Education and Training Programs

Section 7.03   Accuracy in Teaching

Section 7.04   Student Disclosure of Personal Information

Section 7.05   Mandatory Individual or Group Therapy

Section 7.06   Assessing Student and Supervisee Performance

Section 7.07   Sexual Relationships With Students and Supervisees

A presumption expressed in the first two subsections is that psychologists take "reasonable steps" in education and training. Guidelines are inherent in the statements. For example, Section 7.01 states,

Psychologists responsible for education and training programs take reasonable steps to ensure that the programs are designed to provide the appropriate knowledge and proper experiences, and to meet the requirements for licensure, certification, or other goals for which claims are made by the program. (p. 10)

Values include current and accurate descriptions of program content and readily available information to recipients of services. "There are universal guidelines for competence in education and training" reflects a potential mistaken view of education and training for psychologists.

Section 8: Research and Publication

Section 8 of the APA code highlights many assumptions, one of which is the assumption that psychologists engaging in research obtain prior approval from institutions or organizations in which they are employed. Fifteen subheadings clarify ethical behaviors expected in research and publication:

Section 8.01   Institutional Approval

Section 8.02   Informed Consent to Research

Section 8.03   Informed Consent for Recording Voice and Images in Research

Section 8.04   Client/Patient, Student, and Subordinate Research Participants

Section 8.05   Dispensing With Informed Consent for Research

Section 8.06   Offering Inducements for Research Participation

Section 8.07   Deception in Research

Section 8.08   Debriefing

Section 8.09   Humane Care and Use of Animals in Research

Section 8.10   Reporting Research Results

Section 8.11   Plagiarism

Section 8.12   Publication Credit

Section 8.13   Duplicate Publication of Data

Section 8.14   Sharing Research Data for Verification

Section 8.15   Reviewers

Each subheading offers presumptions, guidelines, and values related to ethical behavior. For example, there is a presumption of protection of students and subordinates in Section 8.04. A guideline for psychologists is, "When psychologists conduct research with clients/patients, students or subordinates as participants, psychologists take steps to protect the prospective participants from adverse consequences of declining or withdrawing from participation" (p. 11). There is a value of equitable alternative activities for prospective research participants. A possible mistaken view of research and publication is, "In my culture, the use of animals in research is appropriate, so it is appropriate universally."

Section 9: Assessment

Standard 9 of the APA code assumes assessment to be a critical piece of substantiating findings. Eleven subheadings outline presumptions, guidelines, and values to ensure that assessment and parallel behaviors are ethical in nature:

Section 9.01   Bases for Assessments

Section 9.02   Use of Assessments

Section 9.03   Informed Consent in Assessments

Section 9.04   Release of Test Data

Section 9.05   Test Construction

Section 9.06   Interpreting Assessment Results

Section 9.07   Assessment by Unqualified Persons

Section 9.08   Obsolete Tests and Outdated Test Results

Section 9.09   Test Scoring and Interpretation Services

Section 9.10   Explaining Assessment Results

Section 9.11   Maintaining Test Security

"I am aware of my worldviews and take this information into consideration during my assessments, recommendations, reports, opinions, and diagnostic or evaluative statements, and so do other psychologists" illustrates a possible mistaken view of assessment.

Section 10: Therapy

Standard 10 of the APA code assumes that psychologists engage in specific and universal behaviors (physical, intellectual, social, and emotional) when providing multiple types of therapy to clients/patients. Ten subheadings outline presumptions, guidelines, and values to ensure that therapy is ethical in nature:

Section 10.01   Informed Consent to Therapy

Section 10.02   Therapy Involving Couples or Families

Section 10.03   Group Therapy

Section 10.04   Providing Therapy to Those Served by Others

Section 10.05   Sexual Intimacies With Current Therapy Clients/Patients

Section 10.06   Sexual Intimacies With Relatives or Significant Others of Current Therapy Clients/Patients

Section 10.07   Therapy With Former Sexual Partners

Section 10.08   Sexual Intimacies With Former Therapy Clients/Patients

Section 10.09   Interruption of Therapy

Section 10.10   Terminating Therapy

Each subheading offers presumptions, guidelines, and values related to ethical behavior when providing therapy. For example, there is a presumption that psychologists are culturally "self-aware" in Section 10.03. "When psychologists provide services to several persons in a group setting, they describe at the outset the roles and responsibilities of parties and limits of confidentiality" (p. 15). A value inherent to this section is the "here and now" description of roles and responsibilities at the outset. "I value non-Western techniques and procedures, so other psychologists do the same" illustrates a potential mistaken view of therapy.

Processing Ethical Complaints

How are psychologists expected to process ethical complaints? This question is a pillar of accurate understanding of the foundation upon which the APA code of ethics is built. This section is not comprehensive, but is simply an attempt to help process ethical thinking on the basis of randomly selected sections of the code and answers to this question. How one responds to this question governs the accuracy of understanding the underlying principles and goals of the code defining specific criteria for ethical behavior and methodology for processing ethical complaints. Appropriate awareness, knowledge, and skills remain critical to identifying requisite assumptions and thematic values and their subsequent impact on interpretation of reality, ethical thinking, ethical decision making, and action taken when ethical codes are broken.

Standard 1 of the APA code is referred to as "Resolving Ethical Issues." Procedures for filing, investigating, and resolving unethical complaints are described in this section of the code. Violations of the Ethics Code may include actions such as (a) reprimand, (b) censure, (c) termination of APA membership, and (d) referral to other bodies. It should be noted that actions violating the APA ethics code may lead to the imposition of sanctions by other bodies, including state psychological associations, other professional groups, professional boards, state or federal agencies, and payers of health services.

The National Association of Social Workers

The NASW (1966) *Code of Ethics* identifies a set of values, principles, and standards that guide social workers' professional behavior. Within this code, there is a statement clarifying what the code does and does not do. Specifically, the code does not provide rules that prescribe how social workers are expected to act. Instead, it offers values, principles, and standards to facilitate decision making and conduct. NASW acknowledges that decision making must involve informed judgment of the individual (student or practitioner) and an understanding of how the issues would be judged in a peer review process.

The code of ethics of the NASW was approved by the 1996 NASW Delegate Assembly and revised by the 1999 NASW Delegate Assembly. The preamble reads:

> The primary mission of the social work profession is to enhance human well being and help meet the basic human needs of all people, with particular attention to the needs and empowerment of people who are vulnerable, oppressed, and living in poverty. A historic and defining feature of social work is the profession's focus on individual well-being in a social context and the well-being of society. Fundamental to social work is attention to the environmental forces that create, contribute to, and address problems in living.
>
> Social workers promote social justice and social change with and on behalf of clients. "Clients" is used inclusively to refer to individuals, families, groups, organizations, and communities. Social workers are sensitive to cultural and ethnic diversity and strive to end discrimination, oppression, poverty, and other forms of social injustice. These activities may be in the form of direct practice, community organizing, supervision, consultation, administration, advocacy, social and political action, policy development and implementation, education, and research and evaluation. Social workers seek to enhance the capacity of people to address their own needs. Social workers also seek to promote the responsiveness of organizations, communities, and other social institutions to individuals' needs and social problems. (p. 1)

In reviewing the NASW preamble, we seek to set the stage for accurately understanding the foundation upon which the ethical code is built. Two questions serve as pillars of understanding the foundation: (a) What specific guidelines for ethical behavior are provided for social workers?

and (b) How are social workers expected to process ethical complaints? Responses to these questions govern the accuracy of understanding the underlying principles and goals of the code and define the criteria for ethical behavior and methodology for processing ethical complaints.

Guidelines for Ethical Behavior

What specific guidelines for ethical behavior are provided for social workers? In response to this question, the NASW (1996) *Code of Ethics* identifies six principles for social workers: The primary goal is to (1) help people in need and address social problems, (2) challenge social injustice, (3) respect the inherent dignity and worth of the person, (4) recognize the central importance of human relationships, (5) behave in a trustworthy manner, and (6) practice within their areas of competence and develop and enhance their professional expertise (pp. 2–4). In addition, each ethical principle of the NASW code is prefaced with a core value and explanation of ideals. The following provides a sampling of the principles in terms of core values, assumptions, and principles.

Ethical Principles

Ethical Principle 1. In this principle of the NASW code, social workers are informed that they are to act as follows:

> Social workers elevate service to others above self-interests. Social work-
> ers draw on their knowledge, values, and skills to help people in need and
> to address social problems. Social workers are encouraged to volunteer
> some portion of their professional skills with no expectation of significant
> financial return (pro bono service). (p. 3)

A potential mistaken view of Principle 1 is, "I know what values and skills I possess and how they affect my services, so other social workers must know theirs as well." The primary goal specified for social workers is to help people in need and to address social problems. The core value identified is service. Principles include elevating service to others above self-interests and drawing on personal knowledge, values, and skills to help others address their social problems. An assumption is that social workers know their personal values and skills.

Ethical Principle 2. This principle of the NASW code presents information about what social workers will do by stating,

> Social workers pursue social change, particularly with and on behalf
> of vulnerable and oppressed individuals and groups of people. Social
> workers' social change efforts are focused primarily on issues of poverty,
> unemployment, discrimination, and other forms of social injustice. These

activities seek to promote sensitivity to and knowledge about oppression and cultural and ethnic diversity. Social workers strive to ensure access to needed information, services, and resources; equality of opportunity; and meaningful participation in decision making for all people. (p. 3)

The core value specified is social justice. A primary goal toward which social workers are to aspire is attending to issues of social injustice, such as poverty, unemployment, and discrimination. An assumption is that social workers desire to promote sensitivity to and knowledge about oppression and cultural as well as ethnic diversity. "I care about the dignity and worth of all populations that I serve, so my colleagues must care too" illustrates a potential mistaken view of this principle.

Ethical Principle 3. This principle of the NASW code states,

Social workers treat each person in a caring and respectful fashion, mindful of individual differences and cultural and ethnic diversity. Social workers promote clients' socially responsible self-determination. Social workers seek to enhance clients' capacity and opportunity to change and to address their needs. Social workers are cognizant of their dual responsibility to clients and to the broader society. They seek to resolve conflicts between clients' interests and the broader society's interests in a socially responsible manner consistent with the values, ethical principles, and ethical standards of the profession. (pp. 3–4)

The core value is the person's dignity and worth. One assumption evident in this principle is that social workers share a common definition of caring and respectful behavior. A goal toward which social workers are to aspire is possession of a personal awareness of their dual responsibility to clients and society at large.

Ethical Standards

Following the ethical principles in the NASW code are ethical standards that define professional guidelines and responsibilities in six areas: (1) to clients, (2) to colleagues, (3) in practice settings, (4) as professionals, (5) to the profession, and (6) to the broader society. Inherent in these guidelines and responsibilities are values and assumptions. Three of the five standards follow, along with thematic values, assumptions, and guidelines for ethical behaviors.

Social Workers' Ethical Responsibilities to Clients. The NASW standards offer 16 subheadings addressing ethical responsibilities to clients: (1) commitment to clients, (2) self-determination, (3) informed consent, (4) competence, (5) cultural competence and social diversity, (6) conflicts of interest, (7) privacy and confidentiality, (8) access to records, (9) sexual relationships, (10) physical contact, (11) sexual harassment, (12) derogatory language,

(13) payment for services, (14) clients who lack decision-making capacity, (15) interruption of services, and (16) termination of services. Given a limited amount of space, the first two responsibilities will be presented. Accompanying each responsibility will be assumptions, values, and guidelines for responsible behavior.

Ethical Standard 1.01 of the NASW code, "Commitment to Clients," states,

> Social workers' primary responsibility is to promote the well-being of clients. In general, clients' interests are primary. However, social workers' responsibility to the larger society or specific legal obligations may on limited occasions supersede the loyalty owed clients, and clients should be so advised. (Examples include when a social worker is required by law to report that a client has abused a child or has threatened to harm self or others.) (p. 5)

A core value is promoting clients' well-being. An assumption is that all who read the word *well-being* would define it in the same way. Guidelines are presented to help social workers understand situations in which the core value becomes secondary. An example is the mandate to report child abuse to legal authorities. A potential mistaken view of this ethical responsibility is, "I understand what is meant by the idea of well-being, and my colleagues have a similar understanding."

Ethical Standard 1.02 of the NASW code, "Self-Determination," states,

> Social workers respect and promote the right of clients to self-determination and assist clients in their efforts to identify and clarify their goals. Social workers may limit clients' right to self-determination when in the social workers' professional judgment, clients' actions or potential actions pose serious, foreseeable, and imminent risks to themselves or others. (p. 5)

A core value is individualism as represented in *self-determination.* An assumption is that all clients value self-determination rather than a more collectivistic approach to life, such as the self as a member of the group, which may then mean *group determination.* Guidelines are presented to assist social workers in determining when to limit a client's right to self-determination. One instance is that when a client's action is believed by the social worker to pose a risk to the client or others, the client's right to self-determination is limited and altered. A potential mistaken view of Section 1.02 is, "I value an individualistic perspective, and you must too."

Ethical Standard 1.05 of the NASW code, "Cultural Competence and Social Diversity," states,

> (a) Social Workers should understand culture and its function in human behavior and society, recognizing the strengths that exist in all cultures:

(b) Social Workers should have a knowledge base of their clients' cultures and be able to demonstrate competence in the provision of services that are sensitive to clients' cultures and to differences among people and cultural groups, and (c) Social Workers should obtain education about and seek to understand the nature of social diversity and oppression with respect to race, ethnicity, national origin, color, sex, sexual orientation, age, marital status, political belief, religion, and mental or physical disability. (p. 6)

A core *value* is cultural competence. An *assumption* is that social workers, currently and in the future, value culture and social diversity. Guidelines are presented to help social workers practice within a culturally competent framework. For example, there is a *guideline* that directs social workers to possess a strong knowledge base of culture. A potential mistaken view of Section 1.05 is, "I value and understand cultural competence and difference among people, and my colleagues share a similar value and understanding."

Social Workers' Ethical Responsibilities to Colleagues. This standard of the NASW code offers eleven subheadings addressing ethical responsibilities to colleagues: (1) respect, (2) confidentiality, (3) interdisciplinary collaboration, (4) disputes involving colleagues, (5) consultation, (6) referral for services, (7) sexual relationships, (8) sexual harassment, (9) impairment of colleagues, (10) incompetence of colleagues, and (11) unethical conduct of colleagues. Accompanying each responsibility are specific assumptions, values, and guidelines for responsible behavior related to colleagues.

Section 2.01.a of the NASW code, "Respect," reads, "Social workers should treat colleagues with respect and should represent accurately and fairly the qualifications, views, and obligations of colleagues" (pp. 10). There are clear values of fair treatment and respecting of one another. However, an assumption is that social workers share a common definition of respect and fair treatment. A possible mistaken view of respect and fair treatment is, "I respect my colleagues by looking them in the eye while we talk, and they respect me in the same way."

Section 2.02 of the NASW code, "Confidentiality," states that, "Social workers should respect confidential information shared by colleagues in the course of their professional relationships and transactions. Social workers should ensure that such colleagues understand social workers' obligation to respect confidentially and any exceptions related to it" (p. 11). Again, there seems to be a strong value of respect. An assumption continues to be that all social workers define respect in the same way and exhibit a common behavior related to showing respect.

Social Workers' Ethical Responsibilities in Practice Settings. This standard of the NASW code offers 10 subheadings: (1) supervision and consultation,

(2) education and training, (3) performance evaluation, (4) client records, (5) billing, (6) client transfer, (7) administration, (8) continuing education and staff development, (9) commitments to employers, and (10) labor management disputes.

Section 3.1.a of the NASW code, "Supervision and Consultation," states that, "Social workers who provide supervision or consultation should have the necessary knowledge and skill to supervise or consult appropriately and should do so only within their areas of knowledge and competence" (p. 13). There is a value of competent service. An assumption is that social workers collectively understand what is meant by necessary knowledge and skill to supervise or consult, particularly since no specific guidelines or criteria are specified in this section. However, guidelines immediately follow this section. For example, Section 3.1.b informs social workers that during supervision or consultation, they are expected to set clear, appropriate, and culturally sensitive boundaries. Section 3.1.c informs social workers that they are not to engage in dual or multiple relations with supervisees. "I know my cultural values and worldview, and so do my colleagues, and we use this information appropriately in supervision and consultation" illustrates a possible mistaken view of supervision and consultation for social workers.

Processing Ethical Complaints

How are social workers expected to process ethical complaints? Section 2.11.a of the NASW code, "Unethical Conduct of Colleagues," suggests that, "Social workers should take adequate measures to discourage, prevent, expose, and correct the unethical conduct of colleagues" (p. 12). There is an assumption that all social workers value correcting unethical conduct of colleagues. A primary value is exposing, correcting, or discouraging unethical conduct among colleagues. Guidelines specify that social workers take adequate measures to stop unethical behavior; however, the guidelines are not specific as to how to do so until farther into the standards. For example, Section 2.11.d states that, "When necessary, social workers who believe that a colleague has acted unethically should take action through appropriate formal channels (such as contacting a state licensing board or regulatory body, an NASW committee on inquiry, or other professional ethics committees)" (p. 13).

Impact of Assumptions
and Values on Ethical Thinking

Human beings see and understand the world through cultural guidelines (beliefs, values, life experiences). In fact, the literature reveals that people can better be reached by working within the context of their cultural foundations (Pack-Brown et al., 1998; Pedersen, 1987). Of significance is that counselors and counselors-in-training bring their cultural worldviews to the helping arena. That is, each brings a distinct outlook or philosophical system concerning the nature of reality that is strongly grounded in his or her cultural heritage. At the core of this worldview is a system of assumptions and beliefs held by the counselor or counselor-in-training about the meaning and reality of existence. This worldview affects his or her (a) approach to an organizational directive, such as a code of ethics, and (b) method of structuring reality while interpreting ethical codes and engaging in ethical thinking.

The ACA code of ethics has a worldview, or an outlook or philosophical system, concerning the nature of reality. As previously discussed, there are specific values, beliefs, assumptions, and presumptions that guide the code. The reader is reminded that a number of scholars report that the code reflects a predominantly Eurocentric worldview. Thus, it is critical that counselors and counselors-in-training possess knowledge about the impact of the underlying principles, assumptions, and values specified in the ACA code on what they read and how they make interpretations. Without an understanding of the similarities and differences in one's personal worldview and the worldview of the ACA code, the two cultures may clash. A consequence of this clash is that the person seeking to practice ethical behavior may misinterpret the code or become confused. This confusion affects ethical thinking and decision making. The following critical incident illustrates this point. Keep in mind that Section A.2.a of the ACA code, "Nondiscrimination," states that, "Counselors do not condone or engage in discrimination based on age, color, culture, disability, ethnic group, gender, race, religion, sexual orientation, marital status, or socioeconomic status" (p. 2).

Critical Incident

Billy Brown is a White European American master's level counselor who practices mental heath at a center located in a racially and ethnically diverse city in the Midwest. The counselors at the mental health center are predominantly White European Americans at the master's level, and some at the doctoral level. After a few months, Billy begins to notice that the population seeking services at the clinic is primarily White middle class. Lower socioeconomic status (SES) Whites, and people of other racial backgrounds are minimally represented at the mental health center. (See Exercise 1.2.)

Exercise 1.2   Critical Incident

Instructions: You are a consultant, and Billy has come to you for assistance with identifying ethical guidelines that will help him better serve the populations with whom he works. Your goal is to diminish the possible "clash of cultures" and help Billy gain knowledge about the impact of his worldview, his clients' worldviews, and the worldview of his professional association's code of ethics.

As Billy's consultant, respond to the following questions or statements:

1. Review the ACA code of ethics with Billy and identify two ethical principles that relate to his situation.

2. What values, assumptions, and presumptions are common to the worldview of ACA code of ethics?

3. What values, assumptions, and presumptions are common to Billy's worldview?

4. What values, assumptions, and presumptions are common to the majority of his clients when looking through cultural lenses (e.g., ethnicity, gender, SES)?

5. What are similarities and differences in the worldviews in #2, #3, and #4?

6. How do the similarities and differences affect interpretation of the code, ethical thinking, and ethical decision making?

Discuss insights gained relative to the possible clash of culture and appropriate ethical thinking.

Summary and Key Points

This chapter addresses three critical factors that affect the building of a foundation for ethical thinking within a multicultural context. First, the chapter provides a brief review of underlying principles and goals of three ethical codes: ACA, APA, and NASW. Second, the chapter serves as a precursor to an in-depth examination of each code of ethics. Finally, Chapter 1 serves as a catalyst for practitioners and practitioners-in-training to question the need to consider codes of ethics in a multicultural context. The following are key points of the codes relevant to cultural bias and the process of examining a code's cultural underpinnings.

- Ethical codes empower professional associations by (a) clarifying ethical responsibilities for members, (b) identifying common methods for processing ethical complaints, and (c) offering ways and resources to correct unethical behavior.
- Counselors, psychologists, and social workers are responsible for adhering to their professional association's code of ethics in order to (a) keep good practice, (b) protect clients, and (c) enhance the profession.
- Counselors, psychologists, and social workers are expected to follow specific guidelines for ethical behavior, that serve as pillars for accurate understanding of the foundation of the code, as well as a guide to ethical thinking.
- Counselors, psychologists, and social workers are expected to follow specific methodology for processing ethical complaints, which subsequently affects ethical thinking.
- Interpretations of ethical principles, directives for determining ethical misconduct, and processing ethical complaints are in part motivated by personal and/or professional assumptions, presumptions, and thematic values originating within a cultural context.
- Clarification of the cultural context of an association's code of ethics mandates knowledge and understanding of the thematic cultural values, assumptions, and presumptions inherent to the code.

2

Review of the Literature on Ethics in a Multicultural Context

We are all multicultural human beings; our very selfhood and identity are embedded in the language we speak, our gender, our ethnic/racial background, and our individual life path and experience.

—Ivey, Pedersen, and Ivey (2001, p. 1)

Culturally competent practitioners or practitioners-in-training understand and appreciate that cultural experiences and values undergird human behavior. Furthermore, they recognize and appreciate that human behavior (be it cognitive, affective, physical, or spiritual) is displayed within a cultural context. They understand that humans are multidimensional (e.g., age, gender, race, ethnicity, sexual orientation, etc.) and that these dimensions (more commonly referred to as *identities)* play an important role in the manifestation of behavior. For example, when reading and interpreting a professional code of ethics, a person's gender identity may play a larger role in the interpretation of the code than that person's ethnic identity. In part, these roles and how they are manifested are dependent on levels of identity development and life experiences.

A culturally competent counselor, psychologist, or social worker is skilled in placing an emphasis on the context in which the ethical decision is being made. For it is at this point that multiculturalism becomes critical to effective ethical thinking. However, the literature covering existing principles and goals of the American Counseling Association (ACA), the American Psychological Association (APA), and the National Association of Social Workers (NASW) ethical codes reveals that the ethical guidelines and standards of practice of these professional associations, more often than not, tend to promote the imposition of the dominant culture's value system on everyone. Of significance is that this imposition is couched "in the best interests of those served." This chapter looks more deeply into the ACA, APA, and NASW codes of ethics and reviews the existing literature addressing ethics within a multicultural context. We begin by acknowledging the discipline of philosophical ethics and highlight four major schools of ethics: absolutism, relativism, intentionalism, and consequentialism. Next, we offer an overview of how the helping professions have promoted ethics within a multicultural context. We follow with an investigation of the addition of multicultural helping, particularly within the counseling profession, as the "fourth force" among the previous forces that guide professional thinking and behavior. The chapter concludes with a brief review of the literature from 1980 to the present. This review sets the stage for a more in-depth discussion of explorations and implications related to ethical codes presented in Chapter 3.

Philosophical Ethics: Four Major Schools

Understanding and appreciating multicultural ethics mandates a solid knowledge base built on a historical context of the collective studies of philosophers and philosophical ethics over the years. Four major schools of ethics commonly found in the literature are absolutism, relativism, intentionalism, and consequentialism. Each school will be briefly addressed to initiate construction of a broader knowledge base that positions multicultural ethics in a historical context.

Absolutism

Absolutism is a school of ethics that upholds the fundamental belief that only one truth about human behavior exists. Differences in explaining, perceiving, and understanding behavior, particularly within a cultural context, are at best minimized, so that ethnocentrism (using one's own culture and worldview as the bases for judging other cultures and worldviews) and subsequent problems are neglected, omitted, or discounted when attending to human behavior. When and if the need to evaluate evidence of behavior emerges, those engaging in the evaluation process apply the same evaluative criteria across cultures in a fixed and unchanging manner. An outcome of the absolutist worldview is that behavior within a cultural context is minimized. When comparing groups is necessary, the comparison is to be done across groups. The same measures, strategies, theories, or ethical principles related to human behavior are to be used in the same way, across groups, and without respect for cultural differences.

Illustration: The concept of self and how to live more fully varies when looking at the world through Afrocentric (collectivistic) and Eurocentric (individualistic) lenses. The reader is encouraged to note that *Afrocentric* and *Eurocentric* are terms that reflect worldview perspectives, not racial perspectives. A counselor, social worker, or psychologist operating from the absolutist school of ethics and embracing an Afrocentric worldview would say that self is a member of the collective (i.e., the group) and anything an individual does has an impact on the group. So, if an individual were to live life more fully, that individual would engage in behaviors that would help both the group and the individual, thereby embracing a collectivistic (relationally oriented) approach to life. A counselor, social worker, or psychologist operating from the absolutist school of ethics and embracing a Eurocentric perspective would say that self is an individual and in order for the individual to live life more fully, that person would engage in behaviors that promote the development and maturation of the individual, thereby embracing an individualistic approach to life and modifying personal (individual) behaviors.

Relativism

Relativism is a school of ethics that embraces the idea that more than one truth exists in the determination of human behavior. The reality of different behavior is acknowledged. Those accepting this perspective avoid imposing value judgments. More important, they allow each cultural context and subsequent behavior to be addressed in its own right. Relativism is discussed in two terms: descriptive and normative. *Descriptive relativism* is based on the foundation that different people have different moral beliefs, which affects how they behave and define problems. Those operating from this philosophical position take no stand on whether beliefs about human behavior within a particular cultural context are valid or not. *Normative relativism* is based on the foundation that each culture's beliefs are right within that culture. Those operating from the normative relativism school believe it is impossible to validly judge another culture's values, beliefs, and attitudes from the outside.

Illustration: Taking the same example of an Afrocentric and an Eurocentric worldview, counselors, social workers, and psychologists adhering to the relativist school of ethics would say that regardless of the fundamental worldview, more than one truth exists in determining human behavior. Counselors, social workers, or psychologists advocating an Afrocentric approach to life recognize that a Eurocentric approach to life exists. Similarly, counselors, social workers, and psychologists advocating a Eurocentric approach to life recognize that an Afrocentric approach to life exists. Ultimately, worldview, cultural context, and subsequent behaviors are appreciated and recognized in their own right.

Intentionalism

Intentionalism is a school of ethics that espouses the idea that there is always a mindfulness of and realization that some aspect of reality exists. Some helping professionals link realism and intentionalism. Counselors, social workers, and psychologists adhering to the intentionalism school of ethics believe that the idea of morality is purposive and specific to a person's intent and/or motives.

Illustration: A White European American female attempts to communicate with her husband about their responsibilities as parents in raising their newborn child. Her husband says to her, "It's up to you dear, whatever you want to do is fine with me." She becomes angry at her husband because he will not talk with her and share his feelings about their moral responsibilities. She believes that her husband purposively ignored her request to talk with her and is intentionally placing the parental responsibilities for their child upon her.

Consequentialism

Consequentialism is a school of ethics that maintains a belief that the consequences of human behavior determine whether a behavior is considered by a group of people to be right or wrong. An assessment of the consequences of behavior is the major vehicle by which ideals of "correct" human conduct are determined. Sometimes consequentialism is linked with utilitarianism. *Utilitarianism* asserts that one type of human behavior is important morally and that behavior is whatever produces the greatest amount of utility for a group of people (e.g., pleasure, happiness, ideals, preferences).

Illustration: Asbestos is known to be carcinogenic (usually, the effects onset after 20 years of exposure). Removal is costly and time-consuming. Should it be required to be removed from elementary schools? Most would agree that it should, at any expense. Should the elderly (many of whom are on fixed incomes) be required to remove it from their private homes?

Promoting Ethics in a Multicultural Context

The idea of promoting ethics in a multicultural context generates a number of questions. For example, what venues promote ethical thinking? Are these venues generally promoting ethics from outside a monocultural perspective? What struggles have underscored the writing of ethical codes, particularly as they relate to cultural intentionality? Mental health professionals (counselors, psychologists, and social workers) are challenged to understand the literature on ethics and how multiculturalism has historically affected the creation and interpretation of ethical codes, standards, and guidelines. Such an understanding provides another pillar for developing a foundation for ethical thinking, particularly within a cultural context.

One highly visible and powerful medium for promoting ethics, ethical thinking, and ethical decision making is the formal educational system (academe). Second to the formal system is the professional development medium of training and workshops offered outside academe at local, state, and national levels. A third venue is that of leadership; that is, leaders in the profession sit on boards and committees and assume professional leadership roles, making decisions for the vision and future direction of the profession. A large part of the advancement of awareness, knowledge, and skills related to applying the basic behavior of perceiving ethics in a multicultural context is dependent on the cultural competence of educators, trainers, and leaders in positions to promote general interpretations and direct decision making for the profession.

Though many educators, trainers, and leaders in professional associations have supported the idea of culturally competent and intentional helping, efforts undertaken to ensure that professional associations and professionals, across the board, operate within a multicultural context and are held accountable for culturally appropriate behavior have not been received without criticism. Criticism, discussion, and efforts exhibiting struggles over operating within a multicultural context have been evident, for example, in articles published in professional journals. In 1987, *Counselor Education and Supervision* addressed the need for special multicultural training, highlighting questions and responses specific to the validity of including multicultural counseling in counselor education programs. Lloyd (1987) stated that, "An approach to multicultural counseling that emphasizes differences between groups and attempts to teach simplistic views of cultural traits, characteristics, and beliefs does not seem the type of instruction that should be part of teacher education or counselor education" (pp. 166–177). Many have rebutted: Ivey (1987), for example, responded to Lloyd's comments and revealed that his microtraining concepts evolved from recognizing that being culturally blind was insufficient to promote effective service delivery to all populations, such that his work lead to the recognition of cultural intentionality as the core of effective helping. His rebuttal to Lloyd was that, "Counselors' first step toward understanding the unique human being before them is awareness of multicultural content" (p. 170). Others, like Parker (1987), questioned Lloyd's awareness of developments in multicultural counselor training. Parker called for counselor flexibility in work with culturally different clients (i.e., clients who are culturally different from counselors) and emphasized the need to "affirm both likenesses and differences in our approaches to multicultural counseling" (p. 180).

Professional associations have also sought ways to resolve whether and how to operate within a multicultural context. An area of struggle is related to the idea of who can best address multicultural and diversity issues and implement research as the area of multicultural counseling develops. Many association leaders have discussed who would best be able to research multiculturalism and diversity. In 1990, Joseph Ponterotto organized a symposium, held during the APA convention, titled "The White American Researcher in Multicultural Counseling: Significance and Challenges." The purpose of the symposium was to examine the history of involvement by White researchers in cross-cultural research and to look at how researchers of color felt about the involvement of White researchers. Mio and Iwamasa offered highlights of and reactions to speakers at the 1990 APA symposium in the April 1993 edition of *The Counseling Psychologist*. Mio and Iwamasa discovered four lessons to be learned from the symposium for people of color and White persons attempting to promote the validity of counseling and helping within a multicultural context:

1. Resentment of White researchers exists among many researchers of color. An example is that some researchers of color believe that their research ideas and methodology are not considered by the general society to be important or empirically sound. Dr. Thomas Parham (1993), an eloquently spoken Black psychologist, suggested, however, that this resentment be taken as a given but not a stopping point.

2. White researchers attending the symposium used their personal discomfort experienced during the symposium to facilitate their personal understanding of oppression as experienced by many people of color.

3. People of color were called to recognize the good intentions of White researchers attempting to be part of the solution.

4. Both White researchers and researchers of color may have a moral imperative to try harder to find common groups to publish together.

Though the criticism was and continues to be evident, advocates of culturally intentional and ethical behavior continue to call for professionals and professionals-in-training to (a) recognize cultural differences (both in "self" and those served); (b) possess knowledge of the worldview, values, and life experiences of the diverse and multicultural populations served; and (c) exhibit skills in providing culturally appropriate services to all clients regardless of the difference(s) these clients bring to the helping arena (Arredondo et al., 1996; Herlihy & Corey, 1996; Pack-Brown & Williams, 2000; Pedersen, 1987). Cultural intentionality mandates helping behaviors that are fundamental to ethical mental health practice. The ways in which professional associations relay messages about ethics in a multicultural context are critical to understanding the rules of conduct and moral principles guiding the practices of the mental health profession and its professionals (current and future).

Many advocates of the application of ethics in a multicultural context suggest that ethical thinking that approaches the same ethical dilemma via critical incidents be done in four fundamental ways: (a) consequences, (b) intention, (c) relative terms, and (d) absolute terms. This way of thinking places value on classical ethical theories and puts more emphasis on the context in which the ethical decision is being made (i.e., multiculturalism and cultural intentionality) rather than on the imposition (consciously or unconsciously) of one culture's system (e.g., the White European American middle-class culture) on everyone.

Counselors, psychologists, and social workers are multicultural and diverse in nature. In fact, it is common knowledge that the meanings of *self, identity,* and *worldview* are products of our language, gender, and ethnic and racial backgrounds as well as our individual and collective life paths and experiences. Thus, the behaviors of helping professionals and professionals-in-training are learned and displayed within a cultural context. Consequently, these professionals bring their cultural experiences into their personal and professional lives as well as into their training and education environments.

Of significance is how diversity and multiculturalism are embedded in the ways in which educators and trainers of counselors, psychologists, and social workers think, perceive others, diagnose, determine appropriate helping methodology, and communicate with diverse and multicultural clienteles. If they are not careful, intentional, and properly trained, they will educate from within the worldviews and value systems of their cultures or the cultural previews of the education and training they received. For example, in professional meetings, we have heard some of our experienced colleagues question the need to consider ethics from within a cultural context. Comments are expressed such as, "People are people, so if we understand human nature, we will know how to best train others to behave ethically." Educators and trainers who profess the importance of multiculturalism and diversity in ethical training and thinking share that they believe ethical behavior is dependent on an individualistic life approach. For example, when discussing confidentiality, they express the importance of privacy and impose this value on all—when, in fact, some cultures hold a collectivistic life approach in high esteem and personal privacy is less valued, in some cases to the degree that those who engage in such behavior are considered selfish. Corey, Corey, and Callanan (1993) suggest the following:

> Ethics are moral principles adopted by an individual or group to provide rules for right conduct. Morality involves an evaluation of actions on the basis of some broader cultural context or religious standard. Thus, conduct that is evaluated as moral in one society might well be not exact and

uniform answers to moral dilemmas of counselors and clients in a culturally diversified society. (p. 3)

Ethical codes combine rules and principles in ways that require interpretation. Given the influence of multiculturalism and diversity on our lives, it is important for those training and educating counselors, psychologists, and social workers (current and future) to understand how multiculturalism and diversity affect interpretations of the standards and principles specific to their professional associations' ethical codes. However, understanding the basic language pertaining to culture, cultural competence, and diversity is critical to the task of understanding the concepts and their impact on training and educating.

Exercise 2.1 is recommended to assist educators, trainers, and leaders in assessing their personal competence in understanding the impact of multiculturalism and diversity on ethical thinking and education. Work through the list and think about how your characteristics influence who you are as an educator or trainer and their potential impact on your teaching and training.

Since 1980, many have questioned, studied, and scrutinized the importance of preparing mental health professionals for a multicultural and diverse society. Numerous courses have been developed to assist students preparing to become counselors, psychologists, and social workers in improving their training and facilitating the process of developing culturally sensitive thinking and behavior. In some cases, courses have been developed to promote culturally competent practice and thinking. Unfortunately, little has been done to assess the impact of this training and education on the development of students and, ultimately, practitioners.

Multicultural Counseling:
The Fourth Force in Counseling

Although North American society has historically been multicultural and diverse, it is currently undergoing a more visible transformation in terms of the multicultural and diverse composition of the American people. The literature suggests that most helping models specific to educating counselors, psychologists, and social workers, though designed to help people, are inherently deficient when it comes to providing help in addressing differences among people. However, these helping professions, in varying degrees, are taking a stance on emphasizing specific rules, values, and guidelines necessary to promote the quality of life for people they serve: people who bring their similarities and differences to the helping environment. The old rules, values, and guidelines for counseling, psychology, and social work are moving from a monocultural to a multicultural premise. The old rules, values, and

Exercise 2.1   Culturally Intentional and Competent Educators and
Trainers

Culturally competent educators and trainers possess specific skills
needed to promote culturally intentional education and training,
particularly around ethical thinking. Sue and Sue (1999) developed a
list of characteristics for culturally competent counselors. This list
has been modified to assist educators and trainers in determining
their effectiveness as promoters of cultural intentionality specific to
ethical thinking among their students and trainees. Notice that your
personal cultural background, life experiences, and values will
dictate your responses to this assessment. You may decide to use this
tool to assist your students in assessing themselves.

Instructions:

Rate yourself on the following. Use a rating scale of 1 = *Very
well,* 2 = *Well,* 3 = *Fairly well,* and 4 = *Not at all.* Place your rating
on the line in front of each number. Once you have completed this
form, circle areas that represent skills needing work and/or change.
Highlight areas that represent your strong and useful skills.

Skills:

As a culturally intentional and skilled educators or trainer, I do
the following:

_____ 1. Engage in a variety of verbal and nonverbal helping/
teaching behaviors to promote ethical thinking and understanding.

_____ 2. Apply various methods or approaches to helping/
teaching and recognize that my helping/teaching styles and
approaches may be *culture bound.*

_____ 3. Identify when my helping/teaching style(s) is/are
limited and potentially inappropriate to the impact of culture on
interpreting ethical codes.

_____ 4. Help those I help/teach to determine whether an
ethical code stems from an "ism" such as racism or bias in others.

_____ 5. Continuously develop sensitivity to issues of oppression, sexism, heterosexism, elitism, racism, and other "isms" when
those I help/teach are studying and interpreting ethical codes.

(Continued)

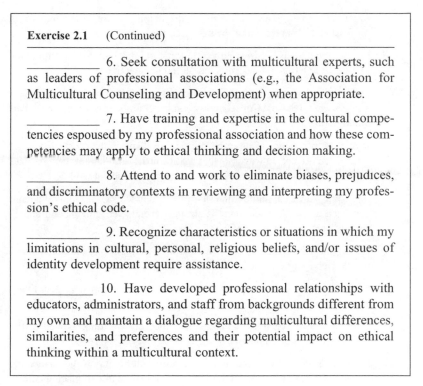

Exercise 2.1   (Continued)

_____ 6. Seek consultation with multicultural experts, such as leaders of professional associations (e.g., the Association for Multicultural Counseling and Development) when appropriate.

_____ 7. Have training and expertise in the cultural competencies espoused by my professional association and how these competencies may apply to ethical thinking and decision making.

_____ 8. Attend to and work to eliminate biases, prejudices, and discriminatory contexts in reviewing and interpreting my profession's ethical code.

_____ 9. Recognize characteristics or situations in which my limitations in cultural, personal, religious beliefs, and/or issues of identity development require assistance.

_____ 10. Have developed professional relationships with educators, administrators, and staff from backgrounds different from my own and maintain a dialogue regarding multicultural differences, similarities, and preferences and their potential impact on ethical thinking within a multicultural context.

guidelines promote dissonance reduction and deemphasize differences. The new rules, values, and guidelines promote an appreciation of differences as well as similarities and a renewed appreciation of ambiguity.

The counseling profession, for example, has taken a stance and has committed to recognizing the value of both similarities and differences among people and the subsequent impact of both factors on human nature, problem solving, and thinking. Many authors in the literature suggest that helping from a multicultural perspective is a force in itself. Some refer to multicultural counseling as the "fourth force" in counseling (Ivey et al., 1997; Pack-Brown et al., 1998; Pedersen, 1998). D'Andrea, Daniels, and Heck (1991) projected that the impact of multicultural counseling on counselor education in the 1990s would be as potent and encompassing as the influence of the client-centered movements in the 1950s and 1960s (p. 143).

Pedersen (1998) examines nine issues that constitute our knowledge about multiculturalism and its impact on the helping professions. He suggests that multiculturalism may be better known as the "fourth dimension" of the helping professions rather than the fourth force in psychology. As such, the multicultural dimension helps us understand that life experiences are dimensional, and multiculturalism plays a significant role in these dimensions. Pedersen suggests that we know the following:

1. Significant changes are occurring in the helping professions, and we as professionals disagree about the nature of the changes.

2. Multiculturalism is becoming a viable force in most cultures and continues to emerge in terms of a coordinated global perspective.

3. Some professionals use multiculturalism to rationalize oppression (e.g., reverse racism). Consequently, multiculturalism has received a bad reputation.

4. It may be premature to describe multiculturalism as the fourth force. Of critical importance, however, is that we know that multiculturalism has had a powerful impact on counseling, psychology, and social work.

5. In North America, multiculturalism is grounded in an individualistic approach to life. As such, there is struggle around recognizing and understanding a collectivistic approach to life.

6. Racial and ethnic differences within groups function like cultures around issues such as age, gender, and so on.

7. Cultural similarities among racial and ethnic populations more than likely exceed similarities across generations.

8. Multiculturalism changes the content of the way we think as well as the way we process our thoughts.

9. If culture is centrally placed in our thoughts, culture may well enhance the meaningfulness of traditional theories. A viable outcome of placing culture in the center of our thoughts may be that such multicultural helping is seen as a fourth dimension rather than a fourth force.

There are benefits related to a commitment to multiculturalism. One benefit is that formal education and training programs are offering, in varying degrees, counselors, psychologists, and social workers specific courses that address multiculturalism and its impact on providing more effective helping services to all they serve—so much so that receiving multicultural training is considered ethical behavior and those practicing without such education and training may find themselves in jeopardy of being accused of unethical behavior. Another benefit is that existing courses are beginning to intentionally address the realities of multiculturalism and diversity on the helping profession, professionals, and persons served. Yet a dilemma is that insufficient research has been done to ascertain what is effective in promoting cultural sensitivity, intentionality, competence, and, ultimately, ethical thinking within a multicultural context. Consequently, many who aspire to become culturally intentional and ethical educators, trainers, practitioners, and researchers struggle with knowing exactly what type of training is more effective than another. This struggle brings forth questions such as (a) what processes and what content promote ethical thinking? and (b) how are these processes and content applied to ethics in a multicultural context?

ACA, APA, NASW: 1980 to the Present

While determining appropriate answers to what processes and content promote ethical thinking and how these processes and content apply to ethics in a multicultural context, caution is advised about becoming overwhelmed (i.e., to the point of debilitation) by personal concern for people, the desire to be humane, the need to see all people as the same, and ethnocentrism. It is important to remember that when you are on solid multicultural and diversity ground, you are open to recognizing people in all their wholeness. That is, you are comfortable seeing the differences and similarities that make up the whole person. You understand that some people desire you to see and personally appreciate the differences and similarities that they culturally and individually bring with them. You appreciate the power that both differences and similarities bring to a person's life and life experiences. At the same time, you recognize the contributions that differences and similarities make to people's pain, struggles, and hurdles in life.

"Stand still" and see and experience the whole person. See people's differences and similarities. See how differences and similarities help and hinder people. Break the grip that is on you as a helping professional. Break the grip of saying or believing that people can be appreciated only if you see their similarities. Shake off the shackles that are keeping you from recognizing the beauty and value of differences stemming from cultural background and life experience. Do not let your ambition to see all people as the same become a cancer.

Educators, trainers, researchers, and students in the ACA, APA, and NASW are currently contending with questions related to process and content necessary for the promotion of ethical thinking within a multicultural context. At the core of their work has been and continues to be seeing how differences and similarities play out in the lives of people; breaking personal grips and shackles related to differences and similarities in people and subsequent helping implications; and dealing with their own "cancer." With these struggles come consequences that affect making basic strides forward. One struggle is associated with language. Members of professional associations are struggling with appropriate language to describe what they are talking about. Culture, cultural competence, and multicultural, for example, are concepts that have presented difficulty among educators, clinicians, and researchers, in that many definitions exist among professionals and within professional associations.

We define *culture* as comprising traditional ideas and related values, and as being the product of action. Culture is learned, shared, and transmitted from one generation to another generation. Finally, culture organizes life and promotes interpretation of existence. Thomas Parham frequently refers to culture as specific rules for living adopted by a group of people. To illustrate, respect is a value common to all cultures. Yet there are cultural dictates (rules) for showing respect. In White European American middle-class society, respect is displayed by direct eye contact: looking a person (regardless of age) directly in the eyes while interacting with that person. In the Latino culture, respect (according to age) is shown by indirect eye contact: A young person shows respect for an older person by engaging in indirect eye contact while interacting with that person.

Cultural competence frequently presents struggles for practitioners and practitioners-in-training. A working definition of *cultural competence,* in its broadest context, is the ability to effectively provide services cross-culturally. According to Cross (1988), cultural competence is a set of congruent behaviors, attitudes, and policies united within a system, agency, or among professionals that provide a means for working more effectively in cross-cultural situations. Professional associations have adopted the idea of cultural competence and identified specific competencies necessary for sensitive and appropriate work with multicultural and diverse populations. The Association for Multicultural Counseling and Development (AMCD) adopted a set of competencies that provide guidelines for effective work with diverse populations. Factors included in the AMCD competencies are awareness, knowledge, definition of terms, and racial identity development and skills. Accompanying these factors are specific behaviors and attitudes toward which professionals are to aspire as they manifest cultural competence in their work.

Historically, the term *multicultural* meant differences that exist among people according to race and ethnicity. As time has progressed, however, the contemporary definition of multicultural has become the differences that exist among individuals according to age, socioeconomic status, sexual orientation, gender, race, and ethnicity—so that today, many people believe multicultural and diversity to be synonymous. Yet there is an intense controversy among mental health professionals as to the advisability of perceiving these two terms as one. There are a great number of people who adamantly believe that multicultural still means race and ethnicity and that diversity means all other differences, such as gender, socioeconomic status, sexual orientation, and so on. A major problem emerging from this controversy over language is confusion as to what is meant when a particular term is used. When a professional association uses the term multicultural, are they talking about race, ethnicity, gender, or sexual orientation? When a professional association uses the term diversity, are they talking about human differences other than race and ethnicity? This confusion affects accurate communication and thinking. For instance, when reading and interpreting ethical codes in which the term multicultural is used, is the code referring to race and ethnicity, or is the code referring to all differences, such as race, ethnicity, gender, social economic status, sexual orientation, age, and so on?

As early as the 1980s, national professional associations began to struggle with language and concepts and the subsequent application thereof to ethical behavior. The ACA, APA, and NASW recognized the need to address ethical standards and issues from a cultural perspective. In fact, committees and subcommittees were formed to devote attention to drafting standards for cross-cultural training. Many professional associations approved and published revised standards in their journals. The following is a review of the current literature related to ethics within a multicultural context relative to the ACA, APA, and NASA ethical codes. Two questions provide the motivation for this review. The first question is: Are the ACA, APA, and NASW codes written primarily from a monocultural perspective (e.g., the Eurocentric worldview)? The second question is this: Are counselors, psychologists, and social workers engaging in culturally appropriate interpretations of their professional associations' ethical codes and subsequently competently practicing within a cultural context? Specific guidelines for professional conduct, discharge of duties, and resolution of moral dilemmas will be presented.

The ACA Code of Ethics

The preamble to the 1995 ACA *Code of Ethics and Standards of Practice* states clearly that counselors are expected to embrace a cross-cultural approach. Specific standards related to nondiscrimination and multicultural competence are woven throughout the code. Interestingly, prior to the 1995 version of the ACA code of ethics, numerous multicultural specialists discovered that the code was in need of serious rectification because of its inadequacies in addressing ethics within a multicultural context. However, many believe that with the 1995 revisions came the initiation of the rectification process. This process began with the preamble and included more specific statements about ACA's (a) commitment to multiculturalism and diversity as integral parts of ethical practice and (b) recognition that diversity and pluralism are social realities. Today, many authors in the literature question the commitment of or even the competence of persons reading and interpreting the ACA 1995 code, teaching about the code, and ultimately making decisions about applying appropriate skills required to bring to fruition the concept and action of ethics within a multicultural context.

Numerous counseling professionals and counseling students display ambiguity and concern for the many different ways that ethical codes may be perceived. To illustrate, over the past 10 years or more, a common voice of counseling students engaged in the process of reviewing and interpreting the ACA code of ethics has said, "It is great to review the ACA code of ethics because so many in the class respond in so many different ways when thinking about and interpreting the code." As students share their approval of this educational effort, many reveal that they (a) have not looked beyond the "face value" of the ACA *Code of Ethics and Standards of Practice* and/or (b) have trouble putting the code into a "real" situation. That is, though many believe that the ACA *Code of Ethics and Standards of Practice* is a great tool to use in guiding professional thinking, when they review and interpret the code, they often do so via individual interpretations that emanate (consciously or unconsciously) from their personal cultural backgrounds and experiences.

Multicultural and diversity components are directly addressed in seven of the eight major sections of the ACA (1995) *Code and Standards of Practice*:

Section A	The Counseling Relationship
Section A.2	Respecting Diversity
Section A.2.a	Nondiscrimination
Section A.2.b	Respecting Differences
Section A.5	Personal Needs and Values
Section A.5.b	Personal Values
Section A.6	Dual Relationships
Section A.6.a	Avoid When Possible
Section B	Confidentiality
Section B.1	Right to Privacy
Section C	Professional Responsibility
Section C.2	Professional Competence
Section C.2.a	Boundaries of Competence
Section C.2.f	Continuing Education
Section D	Relationships With Other Professionals
Section D.1	Relationships With Employers and Employees
Section D.1.g	Practices
Section D.1.i	Discrimination
Section E	Evaluation, Assessment, and Interpretation
Section E.2	Competence to Use and Interpret Tests
Section E.2.a	Limits of Competence
Section E.3	Informed Consent
Section E.3.a	Explanation to Clients

The APA Code of Ethics

During the 1980s, the APA experienced deep concerns about the inadequacies of preparation for culturally appropriate services offered by counseling psychologists. To address this concern, the Education and Training Committee of Division 17 of the APA presented a position paper to the APA Division of Counseling Psychology Executive Committee in September 1980, titled "Cross-Cultural Counseling Competencies." The paper was well received enough to be published in the association's official journal, *The Counseling Psychologist,* in 1982. This publication presented a rationale for the competencies and described the characteristics of culturally skilled counseling psychologists, under the subheadings of beliefs/ attitudes, knowledge, and skills. After that article, specific APA subgroups worked for many years to promote and enhance the quality of culturally intentional and ethical work offered by counseling psychologists.

Multicultural and diversity components are directly addressed in four of the six general principles suggested for psychologists in the APA *Ethical Principles of Psychologists and Code of Conduct* adopted by the APA representatives during their meetings in August 1992:

Principle A   Competence

Principle B   Integrity

Principle C   Professional and Scientific Responsibility

Principle D   Respect for People's Rights and Dignity

Multicultural and diversity components are directly addressed in four of the eight ethical standards suggested for psychologists in the 1992 code:

1.0   General Standards

1.04   Boundaries of Competence (includes 1.04.a)

1.08   Human Differences

1.09   Respecting Others

1.10   Nondiscrimination

1.11   Sexual Harassment (includes 11.11.a and 11.11.b)

1.12   Other Harassment

1.13   Personal Problems and Conflicts (includes 1.13.a, 1.13.b, and 1.13.c)

1.15   Misuse of Psychologists' Influence

1.17   Multiple Relationships (includes 1.17.a)

1.18   Barter (With Patients or Clients)

2.0   Evaluation, Assessment, or Intervention

2.04   Use of Assessment in General and With Specific Populations (includes 2.04.c)

2.05   Interpreting Assessment Results

3.0   Explaining Assessment Results

4.0   Therapy

4.05   Sexual Intimacies With Current Patients or Clients

7.0   Forensic Activities

7.01   Professionalism

Multicultural and diversity components are directly addressed in two of the five general principles of the 2002 version of the APA *Ethical Principles of Psychologists and Code of Conduct:*

Principle D   Justice

Principle E   Respect for People's Rights and Dignity

Multicultural and diversity components are clearly addressed in 3 of the 10 ethical standards suggested for psychologists:

2.0   Competence

2.01   Boundaries of Competence (2.01.b)

3.0   Human Relations

3.01   Unfair Discrimination

3.02   Sexual Harassment

3.03   Other Harassment

9.0   Assessment

9.02   Development and Use of Assessments (9.02.b, 9.02.c, 9.02.d, and 9.02.e)

9.06   Interpreting Assessment Results

The NASW Code of Ethics

The NASW *Code of Ethics* was approved by the 1996 NASW Delegate Assembly and revised by the 1999 NASW Delegate Assembly. The preamble states clearly that the fundamental mission of social workers is to enhance human well-being and help meet the basic human needs of all people, with particular attention to the needs and empowerment of people who are vulnerable, oppressed, or living in poverty. Social workers are charged to promote social justice and social change with and on behalf of all clients, regardless of the clients' differences and similarities. More important, the preamble clearly articulates guidelines around diversity and multiculturalism, in that social workers are to be sensitive to cultural and ethnic diversity. Furthermore, they are to strive to end discrimination, poverty, and other forms of social injustice in our society. These values are woven throughout the NASW standards.

NASW (1996) offers a set of six principles and accompanying values for social workers. Immediately following the principles are six ethical standards and accompanying subheadings. Two of the six NASW principles directly include multicultural and diversity components:

- Social workers challenge social injustice (value dignity and worth of the person).
- Social workers respect the interest, dignity, and worth of the person (value importance of human relationships).

Four of six ethical standards directly address multicultural and diversity factors:

1.0   Social Workers' Ethical Responsibilities to Clients

1.03   Informed Consent (includes 1.03.b)

1.05   Cultural Competence and Social Diversity (includes 1.05.a, 1.05.b, and 1.05.c)

1.06   Conflicts of Interest (includes 1.06.c)

1.09   Sexual Relationships (includes 1.09.a, 1.09.b, and 1.09.c)

1.10   Physical Contact

1.11   Sexual Harassment

1.15   Interruption of Services

2.0   Social Workers' Ethical Responsibilities to Colleagues

2.01   Respect (includes 2.01.b)

2.03   Interdisciplinary Collaboration (includes 2.03.a)

2.08   Sexual Harassment

4.0   Social Workers' Ethical Responsibilities as Professionals

4.02   Discrimination

6.0   Social Workers' Responsibilities to the Broader Society

6.01   Social Welfare

6.04   Social and Political Action (includes 6.04.a, 6.04.b, 6.04.c, and 6.04.d)

In reviewing the ACA, APA, and NASW preambles, it is clear that each professional association makes some reference to and recognizes the importance of culture as their members behave in ethical ways. Each specifies codes, principles, and/or values for their members to hold in esteem as they make ethical decisions and engage in ethical behavior. However, each association seems to directly specify information about the importance of and implications of culture only in certain sections of the code. This leaves the inclusion of culture and subsequent interpretations in unspecified areas up to those reading the code. Such a reality is dangerous given where professionals and professionals-in-training stand in their diverse positions on the importance of culture in areas such as education, training, and service delivery, and research design, implementation, and interpretation. More important, this reality is dangerous because demographic studies estimate that by the year 2030, members of racial ethnic minorities will make up the majority of the North American population. Given this projection, it will be highly likely that counselors, psychologists, and social workers will find themselves in positions in which they are counseling or providing helping services to clients and patients who are culturally different from themselves or who are dealing with differences affecting their personal lives in areas such as career choices, educational training and supervision, psychological and emotional maturity, and spirituality.

Exercise 2.2   Critical Incident

After reading the critical incident, respond to the following from the perspective of your professional association's code of ethics.

 1. What ethical principles, guidelines, or standards apply to this critical incident?

 2. From an ethical standpoint, what are potential multicultural and diversity considerations?

 3. What are potential mistaken views of the ethical principles, guidelines, or standards indicated in question 1?

Critical Incident

Dr. Thompson is a single African American male psychologist in his late 20s. He practices in a small, predominantly White college community in the East. Most of the relatively few African Americans in this community know one another, attend the same church, and socialize with one another. (See Exercise 2.2.)

Summary and Key Points

This chapter provided a brief overview of the literature on ethics within a multicultural context by focusing on the following three interrelated topics: (a) different orientations to morality and codes of ethics, (b) historical perspective, and (c) research and writings of selected professionals on the intersection of a multicultural orientation with practice and research.

Key points regarding the review of literature related to ethics within a multicultural context include the following:

- Culturally competent counselors, psychologists, and social workers understand and appreciate that cultural experiences and values undergird human behavior.
- Culturally competent counselors, psychologists, and social workers recognize and appreciate that human behavior is displayed within a cultural context.
- Culturally competent counselors, psychologists, and social workers understand the multidimensionality of humans and the subsequent role that

multiple human dimensions plays in the manifestation of cognitive, affective, physical, and spiritual behavior.

- Counselors, psychologists, and social workers should understand and appreciate that multicultural ethics mandates a solid knowledge base built on a historical context of the collective studies of philosophers and philosophical ethics over time.
- Four major schools of ethics have positioned multicultural ethics within a historical context: absolutism, relativism, intentionalism, and consequentialism.
- Educators, trainers, and leaders in counseling, psychology, and social work must be culturally competent in order to accurately contribute to and promote the perception of ethics within a multicultural context.
- Increasing numbers of counselors, psychologists, and social workers contend that helping from a multicultural perspective is a critical force in the helping professions.
- Counselors, psychologists, and social workers operating on solid multi-cultural and diversity ground are open to recognizing people in all their wholeness and are comfortable with both human differences and similarities.
- Language (e.g., *multicultural* and *diversity*) and inherent meanings and application thereof to ethical behavior has historically been and continues to be a challenge for counselors, psychologists, and social workers.
- Though multicultural and diversity components are directly addressed in the ACA, APA, and NASW codes of ethics, ambiguity and *concern* for the many different ways that ethical codes may be perceived has been and continues to be a *concern*.

3

Ethical Codes

Multicultural Explorations and Implications

Culturally skilled counselors understand how race, culture, ethnicity, and so forth may affect personality formation, vocational choices, manifestation of psychological disorders, help seeking behavior, and the appropriateness or inappropriateness of counseling approaches.

—Arredondo et al. (1996, p. 21)

A critical question associated with the concept of ethics within a multicultural context is this: Are there areas around identification of important sections within the American Counseling Association (ACA), the American Psychological Association (APA), and the National Association of Social Workers (NASW) ethical codes that have not been fully explored regarding their multicultural context and subsequent implications? In response to this question, some multicultural specialists have accused the professions (counseling, psychologists, and social workers) of engaging in cultural oppression by using unethical and harmful practices in working with culturally different clients (Ibrahim & Arredondo, 1986; Sue, 1995). In the past, professional organizations have been negligent in their work related to adopting ethical guidelines that are multicultural in scope. Advocates of multiculturalism believe that omission of such standards or failure to translate multicultural awareness into actual practice is inexcusable and represents a powerful statement of low priority and lack of commitment given to cultural diversity (Casas, 1984; Ibrahim & Arredondo, 1986).

Some multicultural specialists suggest that none of the major professional associations have developed or accepted standards that would serve to define competent cross-cultural work. Instead, these specialists contend that professionals and professionals-in-training are left with professional codes that warn against claiming professional qualifications exceeding those they possess and that recognize their boundaries of competence. Still others suggest that more emphasis needs to be placed on students' learning to (a) examine how their personal cultures influence their professional philosophies and behavior and (b) become aware of the "cultural baggage" they bring to their helping services.

This chapter discusses three factors that may contribute to areas within the ACA, APA, and NASW ethical codes that have not been fully explored regarding the multicultural context and subsequent implications. The first factor is cultural competence. The second factor is cultural bias. The third factor is worldview analysis. Each factor will be presented separately to provide principles that define ethical responsibilities of ACA, APA, and NASW members. The chapter concludes with a critical incident designed to assist the reader exploring his or her ethical code specific to multicultural implications.

Cultural Competence

Most in the literature agree that culture controls the lives of people and defines reality. At the same time, many agree that people may or may not be aware of the role that culture plays in their lives or even the lives of others, so that given one's level of awareness and understanding of the impact of culture on life and reality, counselors, psychologists, and social workers may or may not recognize the profound impact of culture. One consequence is that if a professional, professional-in-training, or professional association genuinely desires to practice in the best interests of those they serve, they may not be able to appropriately do so without an awareness of and knowledge about culture. Another consequence is that as professionals, professionals-in-training, and professional associations strive to act in the best interests of those they serve, they may struggle with engaging in culturally intentional helping services, values, and guidelines. That is, they will struggle with being able to anticipate and behave in a purposive rather than an accidental manner as they decide what helping actions and guidelines are appropriate for those they serve.

The intentional helping professional, professional-in-training, and professional association have many possibilities for effective service delivery, whether educational and training practices, supervision models, research design, or development of ethical codes. Ivey, Pedersen, and Ivey (2001) define intentional helping behavior as flexible, creative, continuously monitoring, and continuously building a repertoire of skills and strategies effective with individuals, groups, and families. Intentionality can be expanded to a cultural context, such that cultural intentionality is the ability of professionals, professionals-in-training, and professional associations to work with multiple and varying types of people with widely multicultural and diverse backgrounds. Of critical importance, however, is that cultural intentionality is built on a multicultural rather than a monocultural foundation.

Purposive Decision Making: Promoting Cultural Intentionality and Competence

Counseling or helping from a purposive rather than an accidental stance mandates that the helping professional focus on the task of making a decision for or with the person being served rather than just helping the person being served to make his or her own decision. A helper operating from a purposive approach seeks to facilitate effective and culturally appropriate problem solving. During the problem-solving process, the helper aspires to make good decisions based on the systematic collection of data gathered (a) while working with the client and (b) outside the helping arena and required to supplement data directly obtained from the client.

Pedersen and Hernandez (1997) refer to purposive decision making as decisional interviewing and offer four guidelines to promote effective decisional interviewing:

1. Decisional interviewing initiates with a problem in need of resolution or a decision that needs to be made.

2. Data relevant to the problem or decision are gathered.

3. Promising alternative solutions or decisions are identified and narrowed down in a priority ranking.

4. Solutions or decisions determined to be top priority are implemented in real-world situations.

Caution is advised when engaging in purposive helping; beware of cultural encapsulation. "We are all human beings," and "I do not see difference, I just see the person," though often meant as very positive and caring helping comments and approaches to life, suggest that the person making the comment is operating from a *self-referenced criterion*. Operating from a self-referenced criterion is cultural encapsulation. Culturally competent counselors, psychologists, and social workers recognize both the differences and similarities evident in people. They are aware that assuming that other people are like themselves and thus can be judged by the same criterion is incompetent and unethical behavior.

Pedersen and Hernandez (1997) offer guidelines to increase requisite awareness, knowledge, and skill for (a) appropriately engaging in decisional interviewing within a cultural context and (b) enhancing the helper's comprehension of the client's cultural context, thereby facilitating the helper's ethical decision making. Counselors, psychologists, and social workers are encouraged to increase the following aspects:

1. Multicultural awareness of their personal culturally learned and underlying assumptions, which are typically unexamined

2. Cultural knowledge, information, and most of all, accurate comprehension of the client's cultural context and understanding of the meaning that context has for the client

3. Appropriate skill for making appropriate changes at the right time in the right way

Professional associations are challenged to increase the consciousness of persons reviewing and revising ethical codes, standards, and principles so that these people recognize and respect the multicultural and diversity realities of the broader society and subsequent implications of how the codes are written. Furthermore, professionals and professionals-in-training are challenged to work harder (physically, psychologically, and emotionally) to increase their consciousness of how best to apply their professional associations' ethical standards and principles in ways that recognize, understand, and respect the values and gifts of multiculturalism and diversity. A framework for ethical considerations requires cultural competence.

Culturally Biased Assumptions

Cultural encapsulation in mental health is profound. The Basic Behavioral Science Task Force of the National Advisory Mental Health Council (NAMHC) (1996) summarized five areas in which cultural encapsulation is threaded throughout mental health services:

1. According to anthropological and cross-cultural research, diagnosis and treatment of mental illness are affected by cultural beliefs.

2. Culture gives meaning to one's world, and that meaning differs across cultures when diagnosing mental illness.

3. Research supports the idea that differences in how individuals express symptoms are affected by their individual cultural contexts.

4. Diagnoses that are culturally based vary according to the diagnostic categories specific to the majority culture.

5. The cultural profile of providers to clients is that providers are predominantly members of the majority culture and clients are predominantly members of minority cultures.

The NAMHC report suggests that mental health providers are encapsulated, as are their standard practices of mental health services. Given this reality, the question of how the services of encapsulated providers can be used for the benefit of clients from different cultural backgrounds becomes critical.

A culturally competent helping professional and profession possess requisite knowledge of people different from them. A critically important area of difference is related to thematic cultural values. Culturally competent helping professionals and their professional associations are aware of their personal and collective cultural values. They are aware of how these values affect the assumptions they make about human behavior, problem solving, decision making, and general interpretation of life. One way in which culturally competent helping professionals and their professional associations display their cultural competence is through culturally accurate and appropriate understanding of how their thematic personal and professional cultural values interact with the thematic cultural values of those they serve. The following is a series of questions to promote this awareness and knowledge:

1. What are my thematic personal and cultural values?

2. What are the thematic cultural values of my professional association?

3. Is it possible that I am aiding and abetting unethical behavior because of incongruence between my thematic personal and cultural values and those of the people I serve?

4. Is it possible that my professional association is aiding and abetting unethical behavior because of incongruence between the association's thematic cultural values and the thematic cultural values of people served by members of the association?

5. As a counselor, psychologist, or social worker, should I be concerned that by protecting myself by acting in accordance with the "guidelines and values" of my professional association, I might be contributing to limiting the potential of those I serve?

6. In protecting myself, what is my ethical obligation to my association and the people I serve when I notice a cultural incongruence in values espoused by my professional association and the multicultural and diverse populations we serve?

Adopting guidelines and values that are multicultural in scope and being able to accurately translate multicultural awareness into practice requires skill emanating from culturally appropriate training, experience, and study. One skill required to promote ethical thinking within a multicultural context is identification of basic assumptions inherent to the professional codes of ethics as well as the person(s) interpreting the codes. In his article "Ten Frequent Assumptions of Cultural Bias in Counseling," Pedersen (1987) identified specific assumptions of cultural bias in counseling that mental health providers have learned and, he asserts, can unlearn. Pedersen calls for the removal of automatic acceptance and use of traditional helping approaches and thinking with people who are not *born members* of the traditional society, for example, not born of the European American society. Pedersen (1988), in discussing the power of culturally biased assumptions, states, "These assumptions are usually so implicit and taken for granted that they are not challenged by fair-thinking, right-minded colleagues. The consequences of these unexamined assumptions are institutionalized racism, ageism, sexism, and other examples of cultural bias" (p. 39). The following are the 10 culturally biased assumptions that Pedersen discovered consistently emerge in the literature about multicultural counseling and development in educating counselors.

Assumption 1:
A Common Measure of "Normal" Behavior

People share a common measure of "normal" behavior and frequently presume that their descriptions of "normal" are universal. People's descriptions of what is considered normal behavior implies that one pattern of behavior is appropriate and that if that pattern of behavior is challenged, it signifies a deviation from the "norm." For example, in the European American culture, one way to show respect is to maintain direct eye contact while communicating. If direct eye contact is not evident, an interpretation of the indirect eye contact may be disrespect from, or abnormal behavior in, the person with whom you are interacting. On the other hand, when communicating with a professional or client from another culture, such as a person who self-identifies as Asian American and espouses traditional Asian beliefs and values, indirect eye contact during communication may be perceived as respectful and direct eye contact as disrespectful. In either case, if the helping professional is unaware of the cultural definitions of normal behavior across cultures, he or she is prone to justify and explain the behavior that is different from the professional's cultural norm as "abnormal." A consequence may be the protection of the status quo of normality from a skewed perspective (i.e., respect is exhibited with direct eye contact from a European American perspective, or respect is exhibited with indirect eye contact from an Asian American perspective).

Assumption 2: An Emphasis on Individualism

Individuals are the basic building blocks of society. Many codes of ethics impose the concept of individualism on the individual. They advocate concentrating on the individual so that ethical thinking and decision making are frequently encouraged from an individualistic (emphasis on individual values) approach to life. Of significance is that many cultures espouse a collectivistic (i.e., group, such as family) approach to life.

Assumption 3: An Emphasis on Definition of Problems

Professionals and professionals-in-training tend to define problems from a framework limited by the boundaries of their professions' academic discipline. Professional identities (e.g., counselor, psychologist, and social worker) tend to be separated, and artificial boundaries grounded in academic training are created and foster the emergence of assumptions that may hinder appropriate ethical thinking within a multicultural context. In reality, clients' problems are not solely inhibited by one or any of the artificial boundaries underscoring a profession and its professional association's framework. Yet professionals and professionals-in-training attempting to serve the best interests of multicultural and diverse clients marginally "intentionally" interact with each other on behalf of mutual clients (e.g., exchange questions and insights).

Pedersen (1987), in discussing the impact of culturally biased assumptions on counselors, states, "The self-imposed boundaries counselors in the United States place on their description of counseling are themselves culturally learned and must be relearned as counselors move from one culture to another" (p. 18).

Assumption 4: Dependence on Abstract Words

Others will understand professional and personal abstractions in the way they were intended when presented and/or reviewed. There is an assumption that regardless of cultural background, values, beliefs, and life experiences, practitioners and ACA, APA, and NASW practitioners-in-training will understand the words and abstractions of the profession in the way that those who created the ethical codes and standards of practice meant them to be understood. Many factors must be taken into account to determine how abstractions are perceived and interpreted. One factor is the *context* of the person reviewing and interpreting the code. High-context people (cultures) need reference to a context in order to discern meaning, and low-context people (cultures) presume that abstract concepts have meaning and carry this meaning from one context to another. For example, the abstraction of respect varies from culture to culture and context to context.

Assumption 5: Overemphasis on Independence

Many mental health professionals and professionals-in-training believe that one individual should not depend on another individual—to the degree that they assume that independence is valuable and dependence is not valuable, or is even undesired. The assumption that individuals should not depend on others and not allow others to depend on them is directly or indirectly threaded throughout professional codes of ethics. Yet many cultures place an emphasis on dependency and advocate that dependence is healthy and necessary for the promotion of successful relationships and life experiences. For example, a powerful African proverb is, "I am because we are, we are therefore I am." These words exemplify the conscious or unconscious motivation for large numbers of African Americans aspiring to live their lives driven by a value for cooperation and collective behavior. Historically within the African American community, it is often expected that family comprises immediate and extended family. "Extended" could mean biological members (e.g., cousins and grandparents) as well as members of the community (e.g., friends and neighbors).

Assumption 6: Neglect of the Client's Support Systems

There is a common perception among many mental health professionals and professionals-in-training that natural support systems, such as churches, families, and organizations, are not as important as the services provided by professional associations and their members. Because of this perception, natural support systems are often overlooked by professionals and professionals-in-training. If they are not careful, they may substitute Shostram's concept from the 70s—often referred to as the "purchase of friendship" through professional counseling services in formal contexts (Pedersen, 1987, p. 21)—for developing a collaborative relationship with natural support systems to provide the best mental health services to mutual populations (i.e., clients, individuals, or groups of individuals). Pedersen (1987) firmly suggests that, "The health of the individual is tied in many ways to the health of the supporting unit surrounding that individual. The counselor needs to include consideration of a client's natural support system in an effective treatment plan for counseling" (p. 21).

Assumption 7: Dependence on Linear Thinking

Using linear thinking and cause-and-effect relationships as tools to understand the world results in a monocultural view of how the larger society thinks and defines relationships. An important factor in linear thinking is dependence on measures to describe what is appropriate and inappropriate relative to a particular construct. Many ethnic minority populations, in fact, accept their effectiveness in life on faith or on some qualitative measure rather than by an objective measure that is proven through the empirical process, or nonlinear thinking. Pedersen (1987), in his discussion of cultural biases, suggests,

> Counseling has frequently erred in assuming that if a test, a book, or con-cept is accurately translated in terms of its content, the translated tool will be effective and appropriate. Consequently, in translating, it is important to change not just the content of a message for counseling but also the way of thinking through which that message is being expressed. Although counselors spend considerable time making sure that the content of their message is culturally appropriate, they spend less time adapting the underlying way of thinking behind the translated message. (p. 22)

Pedersen (1988) suggests that counselors and psychologists need to carefully consider the "underlying way of thinking behind the translated message" (p. 43) when working with clients from other cultures. For exam-ple, a counselor works to help a client diminish stress and offers an inter-vention that embraces a linear (if-then) perspective. The counselor says to a client, "If you listen to music when you are stressed, you will feel less stressed." The client is not able to grasp this idea, in part due to the cultural beliefs of the client. That is, the client comes from a culture that espouses the interrelatedness of all things. A more appropriate intervention may be helping the client to see how listening to music, working with the family, and meditating work collectively to both promote and diminish stress.

Assumption 8: Changing the Individual, Not the System

The thinking behind this assumption is that the client should change to fit in. Counselors need to recognize when counseling should be more activistic and change the system to fit the individual rather than trying to change the individual to fit the system. Counselors must differentiate between the best interests of clients and the best interests of the surround-ing social institutions. There is an ethical obligation to the client that requires counselors to protect clients' best interests even at the risk of offending social institutions. This assumption is especially harmful when working with those who have suffered from direct or insidious oppression.

Assumption 9: Neglect of History

Many helping professionals believe that "listening to a client's history is a practice of intellectualization and a waste of time." Others believe that it is important to address history in order to understand contemporary events. In many cultures, the connection between past and present history makes it necessary for counselors to clearly understand a client's historical context and understand his or her present behavior. We lose important data and helping behaviors when we neglect history. For example, via history, we can obtain a sense of what has worked and what has not worked as clients deal with problems. Remember that a person's problems can be directly affected by the internalized lessons of the past.

Assumption 10: Dangers of Cultural Encapsulation

Statements such as, "Helping professionals already know all of their assumptions" probably mean that these helping professionals do not believe their biases and appear to be closed. They never take responsibility for changing their biases or their closed behavior, which leads to inaccurate assumptions. Cross-cultural counseling is an attempt to integrate our assumptions with and coordinate them among contrasting assumptions of other persons from different cultures. This often complicates the helper's life and at the same time brings helpers closer to culturally defined reality. Pedersen (1987) says, "The primary argument for cross-cultural awareness in counseling has less to do with the ethical imperative of how counselors should relate to others and more to do with the accuracy and effectiveness of counseling as an international professional activity" (p. 23). Exercises 3.1 and 3.2 provide specific steps that can be used in developing skills for assessing culturally biased assumptions and promoting ethical thinking within a cultural context.

Worldview Analysis

Worldview is defined as the way an individual perceives the world and his or her relationship to the world. Mental health professionals and those they serve share many aspects of their worldviews with other people of the same cultural backgrounds. Consequently, a powerful parallel exists between studying and understanding culture and studying and understanding worldviews. Before counselors, psychologists, and social workers can understand the worldviews of others, they need to understand their own worldviews. This understanding is critically important as they read and interpret the principles, guidelines, and values underscoring their professional associations' codes of ethics; differing worldviews of helpers and their helpee's can present barriers to effective multicultural helping and accurate reading and interpretation of ethical codes.

Given an appreciation for this parallel, mental health professionals are better positioned to recognize how worldviews (personal and others) affect accurate interpretation of codes of ethics. A common question posed by practitioners-in-training and practitioners striving to understand the impact of diversity and multiculturalism in the field is this: How can I know about all the values, beliefs, and life experiences of the multitude of cultures that exist?

Exercise 3.1   Assessing Culturally Biased Assumptions

Ethics in a Multicultural Context: A Preliminary Journey

Instructions: Develop a case scenario applying information from a realistic situation you have experienced or witnessed. Follow the guidelines below to assist you in taking culturally intentional steps while assessing the possibility of culturally biased assumptions made by the characters in your scenario.

Step 1: Create a brief but realistic case scenario that reflects a situation in which a helping professional is believed to exhibit unethical behavior. Include the following in your initial scenario:

1. The professional identities of the people involved.
1.1. The cultural identity (multicultural and diversity dimensions) of the person reading and interpreting the code of ethics and making the accusation of unethical behavior.
1.2. The cultural identity (multicultural and diversity dimensions) of the person accused of engaging in unethical behavior.
2. The behavior of the professional believed to be exhibiting unethical behavior. That is, what did the person do?

The ethical code (share the essence of the code if you cannot remember the exact wording) that addresses the unethical behavior identified in equation question 2.

Step 2: Review your scenario and identify potential culturally biased assumptions specific to the following aspects:

1. Ethical code
    Potential culturally biased assumption(s)
2. Person reading and interpreting the code
    Potential culturally biased assumption(s)
3. Person potentially exhibiting unethical behavior
    Potential culturally biased assumption(s)

Step 3: Review the scenario in Step 1, taking into account the potential influence of implications specific to the influence of culturally biased assumptions.

Step 4: Rewrite the ethical code identified in Step 1 to reflect a more accurate presentation of ethical behavior as presented within a multicultural context.

Once the skill of assessing culturally biased assumptions has been developed, a next step to achieving ethical and culturally competent behavior is to identify ways to diminish cultural bias. Exercise 3.2 offers examples of diminishing cultural bias and encourages the reader to generate a personal strategy of his or her own.

Exercise 3.2   Culturally Biased Assumptions

Cultural Bias 1: People all share a common measure of "normal" behavior and frequently presume the universality of their descriptions.

How to Diminish Cultural Bias: Recognize that culture affects the definition of "normal" behavior and interpret appropriate and "normal" behavior as defined within the cultural context of those served.

Create a Personal Way to Diminish Cultural Bias: "As a counselor, social worker, or psychologist, I . . ."

Cultural Bias 2: Individuals are the building blocks of society.

How to Diminish Cultural Bias: Recognize the effectiveness of both an individualistic and a collectivistic approach to life as it relates to a multicultural helping foundation.

Create a Personal Way to Diminish Cultural Bias: "As a counselor, social worker, or psychologist, I . . ."

Cultural Bias 3: Problems are limited to and defined from a framework provided by academic training boundaries.

How to Diminish Cultural Bias: Recognize that problems are inhibited by academic training boundaries as well as the boundaries of mutual professions. Counselors, psychologists, social workers intentionally collaborate with and interact with each other on behalf of mutual clients.

Create a Personal Way to Diminish Cultural Bias: "As a counselor, social worker, or psychologist, I . . ."

Cultural Bias 4: Others will understand the abstract words we use in the way in which we intend our abstractions to be understood or reviewed.

How to Diminish Cultural Bias: Determine how personal and professional abstractions are perceived and interpreted. One way to do so is to determine the context of the person sending and receiving the abstraction.

Create a Personal Way to Diminish Cultural Bias: "As a counselor, social worker, or psychologist, I . . ."

Cultural Bias 5: Independence is valuable, and dependencies are undesirable. That is, one individual is not encouraged to depend on another individual if he or she is to be successful in life.

(Continued)

Exercise 3.2 (Continued)

How to Diminish Cultural Bias: Determine the cultural and personal appropriateness and effectiveness of dependence and independence on the lives of the people they serve.

Create a Personal Way to Diminish Cultural Bias: "As a counselor, social worker, or psychologist, I . . ."

Cultural Bias 6: Natural support systems (e.g., church, family, and organizations) are not as valued as the relationships and/or friendships developed in psychotherapy. Thus, these natural support systems are frequently overlooked.

How to Diminish Cultural Bias: Include consideration of natural support systems in effective treatment planning.

Create a Personal Way to Diminish Cultural Bias: "As a counselor, social worker, or psychologist, I . . ."

Cultural Bias 7: We depend on linear thinking (each cause has an effect, and each effect is tied to a cause) to promote understanding of the world around us. This type of thinking often directs us into thinking guided by the importance of things (e.g., measures to describe appropriate and inappropriate behavior).

How to Diminish Cultural Bias: Accurately consider the "underlying way of thinking behind the translated message." Strive to make sure that (a) the content of messages is culturally appropriate, and (b) the underlying way of thinking behind the translated message is adapted to the cultural foundation upon which the thought is built.

Create a Personal Way to Diminish Cultural Bias: "As a counselor, social worker, or psychologist, I . . ."

Cultural Bias 8: Changing the individual is more important than changing the system. This is a belief or value for a client fitting into the system in order to live life more fully.

How to Diminish Cultural Bias: Differentiate between the "best interests of those served" and the "best interests of social institutions providing services."

Create a Personal Way to Diminish Cultural Bias: "As a counselor, social worker, or psychologist, I . . ."

Cultural Bias 9: Neglect of history. Many mental health professionals believe that listening to history is a practice of intellectualization and a waste of time. On the other hand, other professionals believe history is important to understanding contemporary events.

(Continued)

Exercise 3.2 (Continued)

How to Diminish Cultural Bias: Recognize that a person's problems and/or issues can be directly affected by internalized lessons of the past. Use the connection between the past and the present as a tool to more clearly understand a historical context and present behavior.

Create a Personal Way to Diminish Cultural Bias: "As a counselor, social worker, or psychologist, I . . ."

Cultural Bias 10: Dangers of cultural encapsulation. Large numbers of mental health professionals know all their assumptions. They do not believe their biases, do not take responsibility for changing their biases, and often engage in closed behavior.

How to Diminish Cultural Bias: Integrate personal assumptions with and coordinate personal assumptions among contrasting assumptions of persons from different cultures.

Create a Personal Way to Diminish Cultural Bias: "As a counselor, social worker, or psychologist, I . . ."

SOURCE: Adapted from: Pedersen, P. (1987). Ten frequent assumptions of cultural bias in counseling. *Journal of Multicultural Counseling and Development, 15,* 16–24.

Understanding all values, beliefs, and life experiences is an unrealistic goal. A more reasonable goal is to have a grasp of formats for studying culture. Though this question may be new for counselors, psychologists, and social workers in that their emphasis on culture in the field is relatively new (approximately 30 years old), culture is not a new concept. Anthropologists have studied culture for many years. Their work can and has presented formats to facilitate the growth and development of counselors, social workers, and psychologists, particularly as professionals and professionals-in-training aspire to view ethics within a multicultural context. Of the many anthropological cultural researchers, Kluckhohn and Strodtbeck's 1961 findings on categories for viewing culture have been instrumental to mental health professionals (e.g., Ibrahim, 1987; Pedersen, 1988; Sue & Sue, 1999) working to promote cultural competence and sensitivity among the professionals and their professional associations. Kluckhohn and Strodtbeck summarized five primary areas for viewing culture:

1. How people view human nature (bad, good, or bad and good)

2. The relation of people to nature (in control of, subjugated to, or have respect for living in harmony with)

3. The temporal or time orientation of the cultural group (past, present, future, or a combination of these perspectives)

4. What people believe about human activity (doing, being, or being-in-becoming)

5. The relational orientation of people to other people (lineal, collateral, or individualistic)

In operating from an ethics within a multicultural context stance, it is necessary to assess ethical guidelines, principles, and values as cultural entities prior to interpreting and implementing ethical codes. One way to assess worldviews, beliefs, values, and perspectives inherent to a particular code may be accomplished by Ibrahim and Kahn's (1984, 1987) Scale to Assess Worldviews (SAWV). The SAWV is based on Kluckhohn's five existential categories. Using the five categories may assist counselors, psychologists, and social workers in understanding the inherent cultural values and assumptions of ethical codes and how these codes relate to cognitive and social perceptions and interactions with the world. The SAWV can also clarify potential issues and problems that might be inherent to a code. Thus, those reading and interpreting the code can better formulate interpretations that are more in-line with the worldviews of diverse cultures. Furthermore, those writing and revising the codes can formulate codes of ethics that are more meaningful to ethical thinking within a multicultural context.

One might go through a number of steps to ascertain the worldview of a particular code's principles, goals, or guidelines and its implications for determining ethical or unethical behavior:

1. Assess the worldview of the ethical code as it is written.

2. Assess the worldview of the reader-person reviewing and interpreting the code.

3. Assess the worldview of the professional whose behavior is called into question.

4. Determine how these three worldviews influence decision making specific to ethical and unethical behavior.

The following example demonstrates how one might use Ibrahim and Kahn's model to assess the worldview of an ethical code. For purposes of this illustration, the *Code of Ethics of the National Association of Social Workers,* approved by the 1996 NASW Delegate Assembly and revised by the 1999 NASW Delegate Assembly, was randomly chosen. The ethical principle, "Social Workers Challenge Social Injustice" was chosen. This principle emphasizes the value of dignity and worth of the person:

Social workers pursue social change, particularly with and on behalf of vulnerable and oppressed individuals and groups of people. Social workers' social change efforts are focused primarily on issues of poverty, unemployment, discrimination, and other forms of social injustice. These activities seek to promote sensitivity to and knowledge about oppression

---

Question 1: What is the character of *human nature* displayed in this principle? Is human nature perceived as good, bad, or both good and bad?

Response: Implied in this principle is a characterization of human nature as both good and bad. People are oppressed and vulnerable to something or someone that is bad. People are good, and one example of goodness is that social workers pursue social change and promote a better quality of life for all people.

Question 2: What is the modality of people's *relationships?* Is the relationship of people lineal, collateral, or individualistic?

Response: Implied in this principle is a collateral modality in that social workers work with and on behalf of individuals and groups of people.

Question 3: What is the *natural environment* and the relationship of people to nature?

Response: Implied in this principle is control over nature, particularly if the system (nature) oppresses and promotes social injustice. Another cultural perspective is that people strive to live in harmony with nature, particularly if the system already works to promote sensitivity to and omission of oppression.

Question 4: What is the *time orientation,* or temporal focus of human life? Is human life focused on the past, present, future, or a combination of the three?

Response: Implied in this principle is a present and future temporal focus in that the goal is to seek social change now and for the betterment of the future of those served.

Question 5: What is the *activity orientation,* or modality of human activity (self-expression)? Is human activity (self-expression) doing, being or being-in-becoming?

Response: Implied in this principle is a "doing activity" orientation. Social workers pursue, seek to promote, strive to ensure, and so on.

and cultural and ethnic diversity. Social workers strive to ensure access to needed information, services, and resources; equality of opportunity; and meaningful participation in decision making for all people. (p. 3)

The first step in assessing the worldview of the code using the Ibrahim and Kahn model is to ask a series of five questions. Each question is presented separately, and a possible response to the question is offered. Keep in mind that the response necessitates an intentional effort on the part of the reader to be as culturally sensitive and accurate as possible.

After the worldview of the professional association's code has been assessed, the next step is to assess the worldview of the person interpreting the code. The same five steps would be undertaken with questions and responses exemplary of the culture of the individual reviewing and interpreting the code. For example,

---

Question 1: How do I culturally and personally define the character of *human nature* displayed in my worldview? Do I more often than not view human nature as good, bad, or both good and bad?

Response: More often than not, across situations, I culturally and personally view human nature as both good and bad.

Question 2: How do I culturally and personally define people's *relationships?* In my worldview, is the relationship of people lineal, collateral, or individualistic?

Response: More often than not, across situations, I believe that relationships are individualistic. That is, people are responsible for their own behavior, have choices, and make up their minds as to what is best for them in life. If they are to succeed, they do so on the basis of their own behavior.

Question 3: How do I culturally and personally define *natural environment?* In my world, is the relationship of people to nature controlled, subjugated, or in harmony?

Response: More often than not, across situations, I believe that people need to take control of their lives. They need to identify what they need to do to ensure success, be that professionally or personally.

Question 4: How do I culturally and personally define *time orientation,* or temporal focus of human life? Is human life focused on the past, present, future, or a combination of the three?

(Continued)

Continued

Response: More often than not, across situations, I believe that the future is most important. To succeed in life, we must prepare for the future. We do so in ways such as saving money, making plans, and setting goals. The decisions we make today are based on where we want to be tomorrow.

Question 5: How do I culturally and personally define an *activity orientation,* or modality of human activity (self-expression)? Is human activity (self-expression) doing, being or being-in-becoming?
Response: More often than not, across cultures, I believe that people are defined by what they accomplish. Therefore, they need to work hard and produce.

After the worldview of the person reviewing and interpreting the professional association's code has been assessed, the next step is to assess the worldview of the professional whose ethical behavior has been called into question. Caution is advised here; that is, work must be done to (a) ascertain how the person self-identifies culturally, (b) review the literature or obtain formalized information on the thematic values of the identified culture, and (c) determine how the individual accepts or rejects his or her thematic cultural values. After such knowledge and understanding are obtained, the same five steps would be undertaken with questions and responses exemplary of the culture of the individual whose ethical behavior has been called into question. For example,

Question 1: How does culture affect the definition of character of *human nature* displayed in the helping professional's worldview? Culturally, is human nature good, bad, or both good and bad?
Response: After identifying how the person self-identifies culturally, reviewing thematic values of that culture, and determining how the individual accepts or rejects the cultural values, it is evident that the professional more often than not, across situations, culturally and personally views human nature as bad.

Question 2: How does culture affect the definition of people's *relationships?* Culturally, are relationships lineal, collateral, or individualistic?

Response: After identifying how the person self-identifies culturally, reviewing thematic values of that culture, and determining how the individual accepts or rejects his or her cultural values, it is evident that the professional, more often than not, across situations, culturally and personally views human relationships as collateral.

Question 3: How does culture affect the definition of *natural environment?* Culturally, are relationships of people to the natural environment perceived as controlled, subjugated, or in harmony?

Response: After identifying how the person self-identifies culturally, reviewing thematic values of that culture, and determining how the individual accepts or rejects his or her cultural values, it is evident that the professional more often than not, across situations, culturally and personally views nature as "subjugated to" people.

Question 4: How does culture affect the definition of *time orientation,* or temporal focus of human life? Is human life focused on the past, present, future, or a combination of the three?

Response: After identifying how the person self-identifies culturally, reviewing thematic values of that culture, and determining how the individual accepts or rejects his or her cultural values, it is evident that the professional, more often than not, across situations, culturally and personally views human life as being focused on the past. What happened in the past determines how one thinks and behaves in the present and in the future.

Question 5: How does culture affect the definition of *activity orientation,* or modality of human activity (self-expression)? Is human activity (self-expression) doing, being or being-in-becoming?

Response: After identifying how the person self-identifies culturally, reviewing thematic values of that culture, and determining how the individual accepts or rejects his or her cultural values, it is evident that the professional, more often than not, across situations, culturally and personally values self-expression as based solely on being. That is, humans are important because they were born and exist. They need to do nothing more to prove their self-worth.

After the assessment process, critical information is included in Table 3.1, "Worldview Assessment: A Trifocal Perspective Promoting Ethical Decision Making," to reflect differences and similarities in culture and worldview that affect how people interpret the world, their relationship to the world, and potential barriers to effective decision making in ethics within a multicultural context.

Table 3.1 Worldview Assessment: A Trifocal Perspective Promoting Ethical Decision Making

Categories	Ethical Code	Reader of Code	Professional in Question	Comments: Similarities and Differences
Human nature				
Relationships				
Natural environment				
Time orientation				
Activity orientation				

Critical Incident

Marta, a Mexican American female client in her early 30s, has been seeing Dr. Tinsdale, a White female therapist in her 50s, for several months for psychotherapy related to her history of sexual abuse. Dr. Tinsdale is an expert in violence against women and the only practitioner with this expertise in the rural community where they both live. Marta has shared with Dr. Tinsdale her knowledge that several other Mexican American women in her circle of close friends have experienced physical and sexual abuse of various kinds. Her friends have been inspired by Marta's journey toward greater self-respect through her work with Dr. Tinsdale. They want Dr. Tinsdale to facilitate a women's sexual abuse survivors' group in which they, Marta, and other Latinas could participate. Dr. Tinsdale is concerned about nondiscrimination as she begins to screen members for the survivors' group. (See Exercise 3.3.)

Summary and Key Points

This chapter focuses on three factors (cultural competence, cultural bias, and worldview analysis) that may contribute to areas within the ACA, APA, and NASW ethical codes that have not been fully explored regarding the multicultural context and subsequent implications. Counselors, psychologists, and social workers aspiring to practice ethical thinking within a multicultural context are challenged to ask and respond to this question: Are there areas around identification of important sections within my

---

Exercise 3.3   Critical Incident

After reading the critical incident, complete the following:

1. Identify one ethical principle, guideline, or standard representative of your professional association's code of ethics that you believe applies to the critical incident.

2. Complete Table 3.1, identifying the thematic cultural values inherent to (a) the ethical principle, guideline, or standard chosen in question 1, (b) your worldview, and (c) the worldview of the clinician in the critical incident. What are your insights? What are the implications for ethical behavior within a multicultural context?

---

association's ethical code that have not been fully explored regarding multicultural context and subsequent implications?

Key points regarding multicultural explorations and implications for ethical codes include the following:

- Some multicultural specialists believe that counseling, psychology, and social work engage in cultural oppression by using unethical and harmful practices in working with culturally "different" clients.
- Though many agree that culture controls people's lives and defines reality, many also agree that counselors, psychologists, and social workers may or may not be aware of the role of culture in their lives, the lives of others, and the helping professions.
- Consequences emerge when professionals and professional associations work to "act in the best interests of clients" without consideration for the impact of culture. One example is an inability to appropriately "act in the best interest of the client" due to a lack of awareness and knowledge of the interplay between the cultural values and worldviews of clients, helpers, and professional associations.
- Without appropriate cultural awareness, knowledge, and skills, counselors, psychologists, and social workers are inhibited in their ability to anticipate and behave in a purposive rather than an accidental manner.
- Counselors, psychologists, and social workers are cautioned to beware of cultural encapsulation (i.e., focusing only on the reality that all people are human beings and not recognizing both human differences and similarities).
- Culturally intentional and competent counselors, psychologists, and social workers are aware of the impact of their personal and professional values on assumptions about human behavior, problem solving, decision making, and interpretation of life.

- Pedersen (1987) identified 10 culturally biased assumptions that counselors, psychologists, and social workers might use to monitor their ethical thinking within a cultural context.
- The parallel between worldview and culture is powerful, and counselors, psychologists, and social workers must understand their own worldviews in order to accurately read and interpret the principles, guidelines, and values underscoring their professional associations' codes of ethics.

Section II

Overview

If there is one guideline for this section of the book, it is to question everything. The fact that ethical codes exist is the result of guidelines and concerns that arise within a particular context within a particular cultural environment. One outcome of the existence of these codes is that their existence becomes the norm. Future revisions are often based on the assumptions that underlie the original. Changes are guided by experiences, professional, legal, and civil, that are found to be inadequate. The underlying assumptions fade into the background and are seldom exposed to the scrutiny of the adequacy of specific individual aspects of the ethical codes.

Many authors propose that the basis for ethical codes should be identified major moral principles. Furthermore, these authors advocate that principles such as beneficence, nonmaleficence, autonomy, fairness, and fidelity are important. MacDonald (2001), in *A Guide to Moral Decision Making,* defines morality as a shared system of rules that modify human behavior in social situations. Of significance is that human behavior can be justified if at least two factors are present: (a) others see an action as reasonable, and (b) there are better reasons in favor of the behavior than there are against the behavior. Morality, according to MacDonald, is not a separate, special domain needing to be consulted only on rare occasions. Rather, moral issues surround us all the time. Moral theory, in fact, seeks to introduce a rationality into our moral deliberations. Though no formula for moral decision making appears to exist, moral decision making involves a number of elements. For example, when engaging in moral decision making, one must have knowledge of the following:

1. Specific moral dimensions involved

2. Parties involved

3. The relationships of the parties involved

4. Values inherent to the issue(s)

5. Specific benefits and/or burdens inherent to the issue(s)

6. Legal or organization rules

Opotow (1990) discusses moral exclusion and specifies two critical factors that affect the incidence of moral exclusion. The first is conflict, ranging from war to competition for jobs and money. The second is unconnectedness, in which individuals' perceptions of relationships are affected by realities such as dissimilarity, uncommon goals, and differences in belief. Of significance is that Coser (1956), Leventhal (1979), and Staub (1987), in Opotow (1990), suggest that these factors reinforce group boundaries, change information processing strategies, and alter choice specific to rules of justice.

The extent to which these moral principles are relevant within a multicultural context is a critical question for individual counseling professionals and their professional associations charged with developing and maintaining ethical codes. From this question emanate numerous additional questions. How culture bound are the major moral principles identified? Are these principles universal? Are the principles exhaustive? Would the principles be weighted differently by different practitioners, clients, and/or cultures? The issue of competence is fundamental to practicing counseling in a manner that provides the necessary conditions for the major moral principles to be met. Regardless of the theoretical or practice orientation of the counselor, only through practicing competently will he or she be able to avoid doing harm (nonmaleficence), provide the conditions that allow the client to make a personal choice (autonomy), within an environment that meets the expectations for the relationship that is agreed upon by the counselor and client (fidelity), in a way that recognizes the client's unique situation, background, and culture (fairness), and helps bring about a positive outcome for the client (beneficence). Competence is the basis for moral and ethical practice.

Section II of this book addresses competence within a cultural context and is based on the a document titled *Operationalization of the Multicultural Counseling Competencies* (Arredondo et al., 1996), approved by the Association for Multicultural Counseling and Development (AMCD), which advocates a three-dimensional model of cultural competency: awareness, knowledge, and skills. Chapter 4 provides an overview of AMCD's three-dimensional approach to multicultural counseling competence. In general, the concept of difference, the pervasiveness of the influence of culture, emotional knowledge, cultural bias, and the development of an ethical multicultural framework are discussed in this chapter.

Following the overview of the AMCD model of multicultural competence, Chapters 5 and 6 focus on a specified dimension of multicultural competence. Each chapter has a dual focus: (a) practicing competently and (b) applying the chapter's topic to the ACA, APA, and NASW ethical codes. Chapter 5 provides an in-depth discussion of Dimension 1: awareness. This discussion emphasizes the person rather than the professional. Important issues related to the person include the influence of (a) difference, (b) the "self" and cultural assumptions, and (c) the pervasiveness of the influence of culture. The chapter concludes with application of awareness using the ACA, APA, and NASW ethical codes. Chapter 6 provides an in-depth discussion of Dimensions 2 and 3: knowledge and skills. Important issues in this chapter include becoming a helper within a multicultural context, adapting learned skills and counseling theory to work ethically within a client's cultural framework, developing a plan of action to assist in "moving from awareness to action," and ethical decision making within a cultural context.

4

Confused? Try Thinking in a Competent and Multicultural Context

When clients come for counseling, they invest a great deal of trust and reliance in their counselors. The client's role in the therapeutic relationship, which involves dependency, self-disclosure, vulnerability, and expectations of finding relief and solutions to problems in a safe environment, underscores the counselor's obligation to provide competent services.

—Remley & Herlihy (2001, p. 135)

Mental health professionals such as counselors, social workers, and psychologists are charged to practice within areas in which they are competent and to determine the limits of their competence and to practice accordingly. Competence is threaded throughout the fabric of professional practice. Credentialing (i.e., identification of mental health professionals by occupational groups), for example, whether in the form of certification or licensure, mandates specific accomplishments and accompanying implications for assessing the competence of individuals. Training is another area of professionalism requiring competence. Competent trainers are deemed so because of formal education and supervised experience, state and national professional credentials, and appropriate professional experience. Even students, though they are neophytes in the profession, are expected to be competent and to display specific competencies prior to graduation.

Cultural competence is a critical area of competence mandating that professionals practice within areas in which they are competent, determine the limits of their competence, and practice accordingly is the area. Numerous professionals and leaders within professional associations agree that recognizing multiculturalism and diversity is requisite to cultural competence and ethical practice. In fact, many will go so far as to say that if a practitioner, educator, researcher, or student is untrained and incompetent to work with culturally diverse clients, professionals-in-training, and supervisees, the professional may well be practicing unethically if he or she provides services to culturally diverse populations. However, the idea of working within a culturally competent context is often confusing, particularly for those who believe that, "Human beings are human beings, and to be a competent professional, you respect all people and treat everyone the same."

Competence is the minimum standard for mental health professionals. Professionals and professionals-in-training are charged by their professional associations to understand and carefully interpret requisite awareness, knowledge, and skills needed to act in a competent manner. Of significance is competence specific to working within a multicultural and diverse society. This chapter presents and discusses competence within a cultural context. First, the foundation for building competence comprises the multicultural competencies developed by the Association for Multicultural Counseling and Development (AMCD). Next, a multicultural framework is offered to facilitate the development of competence and addresses (a) the concept of difference on ethical thinking, (b) the pervasiveness of the influence of culture within ethical thinking, and (c) the impact of emotional knowledge on ethical thinking. The chapter concludes by viewing competence as specified within the ethical codes of the American Counseling Association (ACA), the American Psychological Association (APA), and the National Association of Social Workers (NASW), within a cultural context.

Competence Within a Cultural Context

The core of ethical responsibility across professions is to do nothing to harm the client or the society. More and more members of the ACA, APA, and NASW are embracing the idea that ethical responsibility mandates recognition of the individual and the cultural differences and similarities existing among the helping professional and those served by such professionals. In fact, it is common knowledge that to engage in ethical behavior, one needs to develop multicultural and diversity "lenses" in order to accurately see differences and similarities reflective of race, ethnicity, culture, gender, and so on. Of equal importance is the development of multicultural and diversity "hearing aids" that facilitate hearing values as having cultural foundations. These values are not to be heard as right or wrong, only as having cultural foundations. How these issues relate to competence

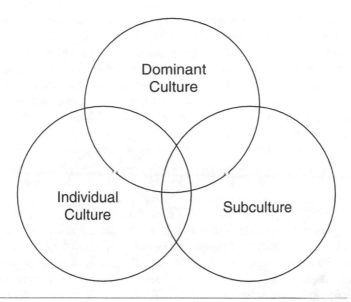

Figure 4.1   The Point of Intertwining: A View Through Trifocal Lenses

is of critical importance. The development of multicultural and diversity lenses and hearing aids is grounded in the definition and application of competence. And yet it is unrealistic to expect counselors, social workers, or psychologists to know all there is to know about all multicultural and diverse populations. However, practicing within a cultural context mandates at the very least that such professionals and professionals-in-training build a helping foundation that is grounded in the cultural worldviews and life experiences of those they serve. Critical to building on this foundation are the influence of the worldviews and life experiences of individuals and groups being served and the impact of the dominant culture on these populations. To better illustrate this trifocal view of helping, the following diagram is offered in Figure 4.1.

Each circle represents a specific dimension of worldviews, life experiences, and values that capture the essence of living within a pluralistic society. Each circle is multidimensional. Each has multiple circles within it. Yet at some point the circles overlap, and it is at the point of intertwining that realities of life are manifested for individuals and groups of individuals living within a tripartite world.

The first circle represents the dominant culture. Dominance can take on many forms, such as race and ethnicity, gender, socioeconomic status, and sexual orientation. Within the first circle are values, worldviews, and life experiences specific and common (which we will refer to as *thematic* from this point on) to dominance. For example, if dominance takes the form of ethnicity (European American) and race (White), thematic values from an ethnic perspective include individualism and competition. A thematic life experience from a White European American perspective includes privilege (i.e., general societal benefits given because of a natural membership within a dominant culture). That is, for a White (racial) and European American (ethnic) person within a racist society such as the United States of America, privilege manifests itself in (a) positions of power related to jobs (e.g., the majority of counselors, social workers, and psychologists are White European American) and (b) visual and frequent representation in the media (magazines and television more often than not reflect White European Americans in commercials, programs, etc.).

The second circle represents the subculture (i.e., the cultural heritage) of the person being helped and living within the dominant culture. For example, a client may be Chinese American. This person has subcultural values, life experiences, and a worldview reflective of the Chinese culture. As a Chinese American, thematic Chinese values might include dependence on relationships and appreciation for family. A thematic life experience might include personal and group struggles associated with (a) being perceived (based on physical characteristics) as a member of "the model minority" within the European American dominant culture and (b) being expected to excel in areas such as math and science.

The third circle represents the individual culture of the person being helped. This person lives within and/or is guided by the rules, norms, and general guidelines and perceptions of the dominant culture. In addition, this person has a subcultural heritage and ancestry that underscore the person's values, beliefs, and general worldview. Furthermore, this person has individual values, life experiences, and a worldview reflective of the person as an individual. However, the values, life experiences, and worldview of the individual are affected by the individual's subculture and by perceived or real-life realities associated with the dominant culture. For example, continuing with the Chinese American illustrated in the second circle, the individual, though Chinese American, may appreciate the subcultural values of dependence and family but not appreciate math or science as a career path. Yet the probable general perception of members within the dominant culture (e.g., White European American counselors, social workers, or psychologists) of the Chinese American client, based primarily on the person's visual characteristics, is that the Chinese American client is a member of the "model minority" and will excel in math and science—though in fact, the Chinese American client wants to become a mental health professional. The reader is reminded to be cautious about generalities due to issues of assimilation and acculturation. At the same time, the reader is reminded that themes do exist within cultural groups and are passed from generation to generation and thus must be taken into consideration.

The three circles overlap. It is at the point of overlap that counselors, psychologists, and social workers (be they practitioners-in-training or practitioners) must be competent if they are to provide helping services that facilitate the maturation and enhance the quality of life of the individuals and groups being served. However, competence, though important, is difficult to define and demonstrate and thus often creates confusion. Remley and Herlihy (2001) state,

> Counselor competence is an important concept, even though it is difficult to define from an ethical viewpoint and difficult to demonstrate in a court of law. It is best viewed as being based on performance and as existing along a continuum from gross negligence to maximum effectiveness. (p. 149)

Numerous issues surround counselor competence and the subsequent difficulties in both defining and demonstrating competence ethically and legally. Remley and Herlihy (2001) highlight 18 key points related to difficulties for counselors. The following points were chosen from the 18 because they appear to have a more visible and direct connection to culture and competence:

1. Though possibly difficult to do, counselors are charged to practice within their boundaries of competence.

2. The development of cultural competence begins with training and education. Counselor educators and supervisors hold the initial responsibility for producing competent practitioners.

3. Upon graduation from academe and other training systems and assuming the role of practitioner, counselors determine their own competence.

4. When unable to provide competent services, counselors must know when it is appropriate to refer clients and how to do so.

5. Counselors with marginal to no experience with particular client populations and concerns must carefully determine how to stretch their boundaries of competence.

6. Counselors of today must possess intercultural counseling competence. (See Exercise 4.1).

To complete Exercise 4.1, the reader and others attempting to practice ethics within a multicultural context must possess specific cultural characteristics and competencies. The AMCD adopted a set of competencies to facilitate this process. The ACA and a number of ACA divisions have adopted or endorsed these competencies as guidelines for cultural competence.

Exercise 4.1   Clarifying Professional Competence Within a Cultural
                    Context

Instructions: To personalize the key points offered by Remley and
Herlihy and make them professionally meaningful, complete the
following steps:

Step 1: Restate each point and substitute your name and your
profession in appropriate places. For example, the first point reads:

*Counselors, though it is possibly difficult to do, are charged to
practice within their boundaries of competence.*

The first point restated reads:

*I, Taylor, a social worker, though it is possibly difficult for me to
do, am charged to practice within the boundaries of competence as
specified by the NASW.*

Step 2: Reflect on Step 1 and identify potential cultural implications specific to each statement.

For example, you might ask yourself, what possible culturally
bound variables (values, life experiences, beliefs, and attitudes)
between yourself and those you serve might affect your practicing
within your professional boundaries of competence?

AMCD Multicultural Competencies

Some scholars, clinicians, students, and educators define cultural competence as the ability to effectively provide cross-cultural services. Others
define cultural competence as harmonious behaviors, attitudes, and policies
integrated to empower a system, agency, or professional to work more
effectively in cross-cultural situations. The AMCD, a division of the ACA,
has been a pioneer (for approximately 30 years) in the centrality of culture
and multiculturalism to the counseling profession. The AMCD has and
continues to provide leadership for the counseling profession in major
sociocultural and sociopolitical domains.

The AMCD adopted and published a living and evolving document
titled *Operationalization of the Multicultural Counseling Competencies*
(Arredondo et al., 1996), more commonly referred to as the *Competencies*.
The foundation for the *Competencies* was built on the vision of AMCD
president Thomas Parham (1990–1991) and other AMCD past presidents
and leaders. The 1992 AMCD Professional Standards and Certification
Committee, under the leadership of the 1991 to 1992 AMCD president
Clemmie Solomon, worked on issues of cultural competence. A by-product

of this work was a manuscript, *Multicultural Counseling Competencies and Standards: A Call to the Profession,* written by Sue, Arredondo, and McDavis (1992). The 1994 to 1995 Professional Standards and Certification Committee, under the leadership of AMCD president Marlene Rutherford Rhodes, was charged to provide additional clarification to the revised *Competencies* and to specify enabling criteria for the creation of ways of operationalization. Work on the *Competencies* continued under the leadership of the 1995 to 1996 AMCD president Sherlon Brown, and the monograph titled *Operationalization of the Multicultural Counseling Competencies* was published in January 1996.

Through the *Competencies,* AMCD challenged colleagues and readers to answer the question, "Through whose lenses am I looking?" This question would serve as a guide to thinking and practice leading to culturally respectful and relevant diagnosis, intervention, curriculum development, outcome studies, and other helping behaviors. The fundamental thesis was that AMCD believed that the *Competencies* would support the processes that value individuals and enable institutions to make the environmental changes necessary for the provision of excellence through culturally appropriate and accurate awareness, knowledge, and skills.

Difference, Culture, and a Multicultural Framework

Difference, the pervasiveness of the influence of culture, emotional knowledge, cultural bias, and the development of an ethical multicultural framework are requisites for a broader understanding of the inescapable impact of ethical thinking within a multicultural context. Today, *cultural diversity* and *cultural pluralism* are common terms used to describe perceptions and life experiences of the global society in which we live. Inherent to this culturally diverse global society are multiracial, multiethnic, multilingual, and multicultural roots and variations.

Mental health professionals are cautioned about seeing "all people as people" (personal ethnocentrism) and looking only for similarities to determine the best practice for persons served. When counselors, psychologists, and social workers are really on sound and competent ground, they recognize people in their wholeness. That is, they recognize both the similarities and differences in themselves as well as in those served. Of equal importance is that counselors, psychologists, and social workers appreciate the power that both differences and similarities have in life and in the helping professions. As mental health professionals move toward cultural competence and competency, they are advised to ask a series of questions to facilitate their forward movement. Those questions include, but are not limited to, the following:

- How comfortable am I personally and professionally with the idea of difference?
- Do I see and hear differences when I am working? Why or why not?
- What makes seeing similarities important to me as a person and professional?
- What makes similarities powerful in my approach to mental health practice?
- What are basic similarities and differences in human beings?
- How are similarities and differences helping and/or hindering the people I serve?
- What powers do similarities and differences bring to the helping relationship, process, and outcome?

Counselors, psychologists, and social workers (practitioners-in-training and practitioners alike) are encouraged to break the grip that motivates personal beliefs and statements such as, "People can best be helped and appreciated by seeing and attending to their similarities." Counselors, psychologists, and social workers are challenged to shake off the shackles keeping them from recognizing the beauty, power, and value of differences stemming from life experiences and cultural backgrounds. Finally, counselors, psychologists, and social workers are encouraged to disallow personal or professional ethnocentricity to become cancerous to their effectiveness with the differences brought to them by multicultural and diverse individuals and groups served.

Two of the principle components of ethics within a multicultural context are *axiology* and *epistemology*. Any culture has its way of identifying what is valued (axiology). Any culture has its way of knowing and understanding (epistemology). Axiology and epistemology are stepping-stones to accuracy and appropriateness in writing, interpreting, acting on, and enforcing ethical codes. The extent to which counselors, psychologists, and social workers are able to hear and understand the cultural, social, and historical foundations of axiology and epistemology will affect their abilities to make culturally appropriate ethical decisions and engage in culturally accurate ethical thinking. Thus, professional development around cultural competence becomes critical in promoting and enforcing ethics within a multicultural context.

When mental health professionals and professionals-in-training consider the idea of gender, for example, it becomes apparent that though gender cuts across cultures, there are similarities and differences in the female and male gender that are guided by the culture in which the individual was raised. As mental health practitioners and practitioners-in-training make decisions about how best to provide services in the best interests of the female and male persons with whom they work, gender is a critical dimension of the individual. Furthermore, a client's predominate cultural orientation tends to guide the way in which the person conceptualizes "self" (Arredondo et al., 1996; Helms & Cook, 1999; Pack-Brown,

Whittington-Clark, & Parker, 1998). For example, when the predominate cultural orientation is collectivistic, the person tends to conceptualize "self" within a complex conglomeration of social roles and contexts. In fact, the person is prone to describe "self" and/or personal problems through the eyes of other people or situations in which he or she finds him- or herself (Helms & Cook, 1999). Of significance is that most people (helper and helpee alike) bring to the helping environment an appreciation of conformity to their cultural socialization. Table 4.1 presents a comparison of select African American and European American worldview factors as seen through the lenses of the female gender.

As seen in Table 4.1, on one hand, similarities cut across gender relative to values (axiology) and include cooperation, community, and self-in-relation. On the other hand, a predominate cultural orientation dictates meaning and interpretations of values, such that the cultural foundation influences how the value is manifested behaviorally, psychologically, and emotionally. For many African American females, there is a predominate cultural orientation for self-in-relation. From an Afrocentric orientation, the underlying meaning of self is self as a member of the group. This value is often manifested in statements such as, "I am because we are," meaning, "I am valued and important because I am an extension of my race, ethnicity, and gender." From a Eurocentric orientation, the underlying meaning of self is self as an individual. But research has shown that for European American women, the underlying meaning of self is self as a member of the group. As a result, many European American women, though they value self-in-relation, often view self as an extended self and couch the meaning in the Eurocentric belief that, "I am an individual (unique) female," and, "I think, therefore I am." Thus, the female factor (gender) becomes important to many European American females without regard to race or ethnicity.

When mental health professionals carefully watch for and listen to gender within a multicultural context, they listen with cultural hearing aids and observe through cultural lenses. They recognize and appreciate the extensiveness of culture as it is woven throughout the fabric of human life. A by-product of hearing with cultural hearing aids and observing with cultural lenses is the potential for more accurately helping within the life experiences and cultural contexts of those served. Counselors, psychologists, and social workers who understand the impact of culture are better positioned to think ethically within a multicultural context.

Moral Principles of Three Codes of Ethics: The View Within a Cultural Context

The major moral principles of an ethical code (Herlihy & Corey, 1996; Pedersen, 2000; Thompson, 1990) represent a level of values aimed at a

Table 4.1	Selected Gender and Racial Worldview Factors	
Through Whose Lenses?		
A Bicultural Worldview Analysis		
Gender Worldview	*Thematic Values*	*Cultural Worldview*
African American females		Afrocentric
Axiology (what is valued)	Cooperation, emotional vitality, community, self-in-relation, direct/open behavior, nonverbal and verbal expression	
Epistemology (how one knows)	Feelings (experience: African Americans and women)	
Concept of self	Extended self (I am because we are. Racial and gender factors are important)	
Needs in relationships	We care (relate) We understand (connect) We appreciate each other	
European American females		Eurocentric
Axiology (what is valued)	Cooperation, open emotions, community, self-in-relation, direct/controlled behavior, verbal and nonverbal expression	
Epistemology (how one knows)	Feelings, experience (other women)	
Concept of self	Extended self (I think, therefore I am. I am because we are. Female factors are significant)	
Needs in relationships	We care (relate) We understand (connect) We appreciate each other	
SOURCE: Collins (1990); Pack-Brown, Whittington-Clark, and Parker (2002).		

higher standard of behavior. This standard of behavior is sometimes referred to as *virtue ethics* or *aspirational ethics*. The goal of practicing under virtue or aspirational standards challenges the person reading and interpreting the standards to meet the spirit behind establishing ethical codes for practice rather than for the literal meaning of a given code (Herlihy & Corey, 1996; Pedersen, 2000). By aspiring to virtue or aspirational ethics, counselors, psychologists, and social workers would therefore be guided by a higher order of values but not necessarily by the guidelines of a *mandatory ethics* (Herlihy & Corey, 1996) or *normative ethics* specified in a particular written code. Freedom to meet the spirit behind established codes of ethics allows counselors, psychologists, and social workers to identify and evaluate the major moral principles within the specific cultural context of the client (Pedersen, 2000). The guiding moral principles and subsequent ethical behaviors would then be assessed within a client's cultural context. This type of assessment is critical because a client's cultural context is where the presenting concern or problem exists.

Major moral principles are less evident upon review of existing ethical codes. One reason for this is that existing codes tend to reflect normative ethics (Thompson, 1990) or *principle ethics* (Jordan & Meara, 1990, in Pedersen, 2000). At best, existing codes are guided by major moral principles, but more often than not, existing codes result from the efforts of mental health professions (e.g., ACA, APA, NASW) to promote ethical guidelines for practice. Thus, existing codes tend to reflect more descriptive norms addressing minimal acceptable practices identified by a group of professionals. Of significance is that these professionals have been commissioned by their professional associations (e.g., ACA, APA, NASW) to identify acceptable practice rather than to implement the major moral principles. Most often, the starting point in reviewing and interpreting ethical codes is with the existing code. Yet if the starting point is the code as it currently exists, persons reading and interpreting the code, unless culturally competent and sensitive, will reflect the codes' original assumptions as the foundation for ethical thinking and implementation of principles.

A Multicultural Framework: Ethical Thinking and Decision Making in a Multicultural Context

Thus far in this chapter, we have presented and discussed competence within a cultural context. We have advocated the foundation of building competence to be the 1996 multicultural competencies developed and approved by the AMCD. From this point on, we offer a framework for ethical thinking and decision making in a multicultural context. We will then review competence as specified within the ethical codes of three professional associations, ACA, APA, and NASW. Each review will be addressed separately and within a cultural context. Our goal is to identify major moral principles that guide practice (i.e., minimal acceptable practices) and then propose recommendations for implementation of the major moral principles using the proposed framework for ethical thinking and decision making.

Given the past and present struggles associated with ethics and multiculturalism, we acknowledge that one starting point in reviewing and interpreting ethical codes is with the existing code. However, we offer a culturally competent and sensitive framework that is an alternative foundation, created to promote ethical thinking and implementation of principles within a multicultural context.

What is ethics within a multicultural context? Essentially, ethics in a multicultural context is a process of implementing major moral principles guiding a code of ethics according to the worldviews, values, and life experiences of multicultural and diverse groups. To accurately engage in ethics in a multicultural context, specific cognitive and affective behaviors are necessary and are grounded in (a) guidelines/standards of development and practice for mental health professionals considered essential for culturally appropriate interpretations of an existing ethical code and (b) personal ability and skill to identify and correct culturally troublesome aspects of current ethical codes. This framework articulates attitudinal and trait-based statements/characteristics for three developmental stages: (a) beliefs and attitudes, (b) knowledge, and (c) skills in three domains for interpretation and implementation of ethical principles within a multicultural context. These skills are as follows:

1. Awareness of one's own beliefs and attitudes, knowledge, and skills needed for effective reading, interpreting, and implementation of the existing ethical code.

2. Understanding of beliefs and attitudes as well as personal knowledge held about the worldviews of professionals from cultures different from one's own.

3. Ability to provide ethical and culturally relevant interpretations through appropriate intervention strategies and techniques for thinking and implementation of the existing code.

Though the framework is built on the foundation of the AMCD multicultural competencies and was written for counselors, as readers review the quotes from Arredondo et al. (1996), they are advised to substitute the name of their profession (e.g., psychologist, social worker) in the place of "counselor."

Awareness of Personal Assumptions, Values, and Biases

Beliefs and Attitudes

"Culturally skilled counselors are aware of how their own cultural background and experiences have influenced attitudes, values, and biases about psychological processes" (Arredondo et al., 1966, p. 11).

The first stage of development in the process of operationalizing ethics in a multicultural context is to focus on one's personal awareness and personal characteristics. The awareness of culturally skilled counselors, psychologists, and social workers cognitive and emotional experiences of "self" is critically important to the way they view others similar to or different from "self." Equally important is the way in which mental health professionals regard their personal attitudes and beliefs, biases, and assumptions about their own cultural heritages. Finally, it is important for culturally skilled counselors, psychologists, and social workers to be aware of beliefs and attitudes about their emotional experiences with cultural differences. This awareness will enhance their abilities to effectively read and appropriately interpret the challenges of cultural differences implied in or explicit to a code of ethics.

Knowledge

"Culturally skilled counselors have specific knowledge about their own racial and cultural heritage and how it personally and professionally affects their definitions and biases of normality/abnormality and the process of counseling" (Arredondo et al., 1996, p. 12).

Counselors, psychologists, and social workers make content-based statements that build on the characteristics of self-awareness and are influenced by personal thoughts and feelings of individual counselors, psychologists, and social workers. The knowledge held by mental health professionals is attained through multiple life experiences, be they with people similar to or different from "self," or through knowledge gained from formal and informal academics.

Skills

Culturally skilled counselors seek out educational, consultative, and training experiences to improve their understanding and effectiveness in working with culturally different populations. Being able to recognize the limits of their competencies, they (a) seek consultation, (b) seek further training or education, (c) refer out to more qualified individuals or resources, or (d) engage in a combination of these. (Arredondo et al., 1996, p. 14)

Skill statements are grounded in personal and professional developmental opportunities for counselors, psychologists, and social workers. As readers of ethical codes and watchdogs over the ethical behavior of their respective professions, these professionals at the very minimum are able to recognize their own limits and are open to seeking consultation, further training, or education to ensure that they engage in appropriate ethical thinking and implementation within a cultural context.

Understanding the Worldview
of Culturally Different Colleagues

The second stage of development in the process of operationalizing ethics in a multicultural context is to gain knowledge about the population(s) served. This stage underscores the development of a knowledge base built on the cultural values and life experiences that enrich accurate professional cross-cultural interactions, worldview interpretations, and cross-cultural thinking between and among counselors, psychologists, and social workers. The responsibility is placed on the person reading and interpreting a particular code of ethics to be aware, knowledgeable, and skilled about his or her multicultural and diverse colleagues. Counselors, psychologists, and social workers who understand a worldview outside their own are continuously engaging in the task of self-awareness and knowledge building about self.

Beliefs and Attitudes

"Culturally skilled counselors are aware of their stereotypes and preconceived notions that they may hold toward other racial and ethnic minority groups" (Arredondo et al., 1996, p. 19).

Counselors, psychologists, and social workers are reminded of the importance of understanding colleagues and other professionals (who share cultural heritages different from their own) from multivariate perspectives obtained through learning methodologies such as formal education and information emanating from personal experiences. In addition, mental health professionals are reminded that regardless of professional affiliation, all people have personal biases and assumptions about difference, whether in the form of race, ethnicity, gender, sexual orientation, or culture. A requisite to effective ethical thinking and implementation of ethical codes within a cultural context is accurate understanding of both similar and diverse worldviews.

Knowledge

"Culturally skilled counselors understand how race, culture, ethnicity, and so forth may affect personality formation, vocational choices, manifestation of psychological disorders, help seeking behavior, and the appropriateness or inappropriateness of counseling approaches" (Arredondo et al., 1996, p. 21).

A person's environment (whether sociopolitical or socioeconomic) influences his or her attitudes and behaviors, particularly those held about others with whom he or she interacts. Counselors, psychologists, and social workers have been trained regarding human behavior and development of the people they serve. These mental health professionals are reminded to apply the same knowledge to those with whom they work.

Skills

"Culturally skilled counselors become actively involved with minority individuals outside the counseling setting (e.g., community events, social and political functions, celebrations, friendships, neighborhood groups, and so forth) so that their perspective of minorities is more than an academic or helping exercise" (Arredondo et al., 1996, p. 23).

The courage to change, to think, and to feel within a cultural context is an active, interactive process. Counselors, psychologists, and social workers cannot learn about other professionals in abstractions. Cultural differences, if handled comfortably and appropriately, mandate a "realistic" perspective and view of life and subsequent approach to life within a particular cultural context. Issues, conditions, values, beliefs, and other life realities that are part of multicultural and diverse mental health professionals' lives cannot be ignored when reading, interpreting, and implementing ethical codes. To ignore them would constitute unethical behavior and heighten the possibility of inaccurate ethical thinking.

Developing the Skill of Ethical Thinking in a Multicultural Context

Counselors, psychologists, and social workers are challenged in this stage to assess the depth of (a) their critical understanding of existing ethical codes and the codes' cultural limitations and (b) the importance of respecting thematic historical and cultural life experiences, attitudes, and values of colleagues who are similar to and different from themselves. Developing appropriate thinking and implementation strategies involves ethical monitoring and definition of ethical behavior by culturally sensitive counselors, psychologists, and social workers.

Beliefs and Attitudes

"Culturally skilled counselors respect clients' religious and/or spiritual beliefs and values, including attributions and taboos, because they affect worldview, psychosocial functioning, and expressions of distress" (Arredondo et al., 1996, p. 25).

Counselors, psychologists, and social workers today are more than ever challenged to look beyond an ethnocentric perspective of codes of ethics and definitions of ethical behavior. Ethnocentric codes of ethics of the ACA, APA, and NASW are based on an individualistic system promoting self as the building block of society. Though counselors, psychologists, and social workers have been challenged (via revisions of ethical codes and formal and informal training), there remains an ongoing struggle around ethics in a multicultural context from cultural and linguistic perspectives.

Knowledge

"Culturally skilled counselors have a clear and explicit knowledge and understanding of the generic characteristics of counseling and therapy (culture bound, class bound, and monolingual) and how they may clash with the cultural values of various cultural groups" (Arredondo et al., 1996, p. 25).

Skills

Culturally skilled counselors are able to engage in a variety of verbal and nonverbal responses. They are able to send and receive both verbal and nonverbal messages accurately and appropriately. They are not tied down to only one method or approach to helping, but recognize that helping styles and approaches may be culture bound. When they sense that their helping style is limited and potentially inappropriate, they can anticipate and modify it. (Arredondo et al., 1996, p. 27)

The true test of cultural competence lies at the thinking, interpretation, and implementation levels. The skills statements in this section underscore the complexity of being "culturally skilled and competent" and ethical. Consider such statements as developmental guidelines promoting accurate and ethical thinking within a multicultural context. An important point is that culture cuts across all aspects of life and in so doing is an inescapable and critical factor in identifying ethical and unethical behavior and interpreting ethics more in-line with culture and life experiences.

Review of the ACA, APA, and NASW Ethical Codes in a Cultural Context

A more comprehensive review of the ACA, APA, and NASW ethical codes as viewed within a cultural context will be presented in Section III. In the final section of this chapter, we lay a foundation for using a proposed framework to review ethical codes. To facilitate communication, we apply the framework to the ACA, APA, and the NASW codes. We begin with the preamble of each professional association (see Chapter 1). Next, we assess the preamble, focusing on one of three stages of multicultural competence (awareness, knowledge, or skill). Finally, we apply the preamble for each professional association to the framework of promoting ethical thinking within a cultural context.

ACA Code of Ethics

The American Counseling Association is an educational, scientific and professional organization whose members are dedicated to the enhancement of human development throughout the life span. Association members recognize diversity in our society and embrace a cross-cultural approach in support of the worth, dignity, potential, and uniqueness of each individual.

The specification of a code of ethics enables the association to clarify to current and future members, and to those served by members, the nature of the ethical responsibilities held in common by its members. As the code of ethics of the association, this document establishes principles that define the ethical behavior of association members. All members of the American Counseling Association are required to adhere to the *ACA Code of Ethics and Standards of Practice. The ACA Code of Ethics and Standards of Practice* will serve as the basis for processing ethical complaints initiated against members of the association. (ACA, 1995, p. 1) (See Exercise 4.2)

APA Code of Ethics: Developing and Implementing Worldview Assessment and Knowledge Formation

Mental Health Professionals'
Awareness of the Worldviews of Others

Psychologists are committed to increasing scientific and professional knowledge of behavior, people's understanding of themselves and others, and the use of such knowledge to improve the condition of individuals, organizations, and society. Psychologists respect and protect civil and human rights and the central importance of freedom of inquiry and expression in research, teaching, and publication. They also strive to help the public in developing informed judgments and choices concerning human behavior. In doing so, they perform many roles, such as researcher, educator, diagnostician, therapist, supervisor, consultant, administrator, social interventionist, and expert witness. This Ethics Code provides a common set of values upon which psychologists build their professional and scientific work.

This Ethics Code is intended to provide specific standards to cover most situations encountered by psychologists. It has as its primary goal the welfare and protection of the individuals and groups with whom psychologists work and the education of members, students, and the public regarding ethical standards of the discipline.

The development of a dynamic set of ethical standards for a psychologist's work-related conduct requires a personal commitment to a lifelong effort to act ethically; to encourage ethical behavior by students, supervisees, employees, and colleagues; and to consult with others concerning ethical problems. Each psychologist supplements, but does not violate, the Ethics Code's values and rules on the basis of guidance drawn from personal values, culture, and experience. (APA, 2002, p. 1)

Knowledge: Worldview of
Colleagues With Different Cultural Heritages

Counselors, psychologists, and social workers who understand the worldviews of colleagues different from themselves and the worldview of the code of ethics they are reading are better positioned to identify ethical behavior

Exercise 4.2   Awareness: Personal Awareness of One's Own Cultural
                    Values and Biases

Instructions: To assist in the process of ethical thinking within a
cultural context, the following questions are offered to help ascertain
the influence of personal attitudes, values, and biases on psychological
processes involved in ethical thinking and implementation within a
cultural context. Ask and respond to each question individually and
as honestly and thoroughly as possible.

Beliefs and Attitudes

"Culturally skilled counselors, psychologists, and social workers
are aware of how their own cultural background and experiences
have influenced attitudes, values, and biases about psychological
processes" (Arredondo et al., 1996, p. 11).

1. How do I self-identify ethnically? What is my predominant cultural
   heritage?

2. What are thematic (common) cultural experiences that have influenced my personal attitudes, values, and biases about how people
   similar to and different from me think about and process the world?

3. What impact do my ethnicity, thematic cultural experiences, personal and cultural values, and beliefs have on how I think about and
   interpret the ACA preamble?

Knowledge

"Culturally skilled counselors have specific knowledge about
their own racial and cultural heritage and how it personally and
professionally affects their definitions and biases of normality/abnor-
mality and the process of counseling" (Arredondo et al., 1996, p. 12).

1. What do I know about my own racial and cultural heritage?

2. How does what I know about my racial and cultural heritage affect
   my definitions and biases regarding what is considered normal or
   abnormal behavior? What impact does my knowledge of my own
   racial and cultural heritage have on defining ethical and unethical
   behavior as prescribed by the ACA *Code of Ethics and Standards of
   Practice?*

(Continued)

Exercise 4.2   (Continued)

Skills

"Culturally skilled counselors seek out educational, consultative, and training experiences to improve their understanding and effectiveness in working with culturally different populations. Being able to recognize the limits of their competencies, they (a) seek consultation, (b) seek further training or education, (c) refer out to more qualified individuals or resources, or (d) engage in a combination of these" (Arredondo et al., 1996, p 14).

1. What educational, consultative, or training experiences have I participated in during the last month to improve my understanding an effectiveness in working with culturally difference populations?

2. What are 1–2 limits of my cultural competency at this juncture in my professional career include?

3. Given the limits identified in number 2, who is available and competent to assist me in developing culturally competent helping skills?

---

within a cultural context. Exercise 4.3 is designed to promote ethical thinking within a cultural context using knowledge of the worldview of the ethical code and the person believed to be engaging in unethical behavior.

NASW Code of Ethics: Developing and Implementing the Skill of Ethical Thinking in a Multicultural Context

The primary mission of the social work profession is to enhance human well-being and help meet the basic human needs of all people, with particular attention to the needs and empowerment of people who are vulnerable, oppressed, and living in poverty. An historic and defining feature of social work is the profession's focus on individual well-being in a social context and the well-being of society. Fundamental to social work is attention to the environmental factors that create, contribute to, and address problems in living.

Social workers promote social justice and social change with and on behalf of clients. "Clients" is used inclusively to refer to individuals, families, groups, organizations, and communities. Social workers are sensitive to cultural and ethnic diversity and strive to end discrimination, oppression, poverty, and other forms of social injustice. These activities may be in the form of direct practice, community organizing, supervision, consultation, administration, advocacy, social and political action, policy development and implementation, education, and research and evaluation. Social workers seek to enhance the capacity of people to address

Exercise 4.3   Knowledge: A Precursor to Ethical Thinking

Instructions: To assist in the process of ethical thinking within a cultural context, the following questions are offered to help ascertain the influence of knowledge of the worldviews (thematic values, life experiences, attitudes) of culturally different colleagues and subsequent implications for culturally sensitive and appropriate interpretations of ethical and unethical behavior between and among counselors, psychologists, and social workers. Ask and respond to each question individually and as honestly and thoroughly as possible.

Beliefs and Attitudes

"Culturally skilled counselors are aware of their stereotypes and preconceived notions that they may hold toward other racial and ethnic minority groups" (Arredondo et al., 1996, p. 19).

1. What are my stereotypical reactions to colleagues who are different from me? For example, as a man, when I hear or read about women who directly and firmly share their thoughts and feelings, do I silently say to myself, "That woman is aggressive!"

2. Am I able to differentiate between the thematic and individual values, beliefs, and attitudes of my heritage and individuals from the same cultural heritage? That is, if I share a cultural heritage with another colleague, do I recognize that though we have a common heritage, we may differ due to other human dimensions and life experiences in areas such as (but not limited to) gender, socioeconomic status, sexual orientation, and age? For example, as an Asian American woman in her late 50s who came to the United States approximately 10 years ago, I value religious and mystical traditions as tools to facilitate interpreting psychological problems. That is, I value interpreting problems within a religious framework. At the same time, my Asian American male 30-year-old colleague who was born in the United States values interpreting psychological problems within a cognitive framework. He values interpreting problems as a by-product of the way people think.

3. As a psychologist, what impact do my stereotypes and preconceived notions have on how I think about and interpret the APA preamble and code of ethics?

4. As a psychologist, what impact do my stereotypes and preconceived notions have on how I think about and interpret ethical behaviors as prescribed by the cultural contexts of my colleagues and those they serve?

(Continued)

Exercise 4.3   (Continued) **Knowledge** "Culturally skilled counselors understand how race, culture, ethnicity, and so forth may affect personality formation, vocational choices, manifestation of psychological disorder, help-seeking behavior, and the appropriateness or inappropriateness of counseling approaches" (Arredondo et al., 1996, p. 21). 1. Am I able to describe and cite examples of how a psychological intervention may or may not be appropriate for a specific population based fundamentally on, but not limited to, age, culture, ethnicity, gender, language, and sexual orientation? Describe and cite one or two examples. 2. Am I able to appropriately and within a cultural context describe at least one traditional theory of personality development, the cultural populations on which the traditional theory was developed, and how the traditional system relates or does not relate to at least one other culturally different population? 3. As a psychologist, what impact does my ability to describe and cite examples of the cultural appropriateness of a particular psychological intervention have on how I think about and interpret the APA preamble and code of ethics? 4. As a psychologist, what impact does my ability to describe and cite examples of the cultural appropriateness of a particular psychological intervention have on how I think about and interpret ethical and unethical behaviors as prescribed within the cultural contexts of my colleagues and those they serve? **Skills** "Culturally skilled counselors become actively involved with minority individuals outside the counseling setting (e.g., community events, social and political functions, celebrations, friendships, neighborhood groups, and so forth) so that their perspective of minorities is more than an academic or helping exercise" (Arredondo et al., 1996, p. 23). 1. What are 3 to 5 multicultural and diverse experiences in which I have participated within the past 2 to 3 years? For example, I have participated in (a) a Greek ethnic community meeting, (b) an Asian New Year's celebration, and (c) attended an Islamic religious service. *(Continued)*

Exercise 4.3   (Continued)

---

2. What experiences and/or activities have I planned within the last 3 months to help me contradict my negative stereotypes and preconceived notions about people who are similar to and different from myself?

3. As a psychologist, what impact has my involvement or lack of involvement in multicultural and diverse life experiences had on how I think about and interpret the APA preamble and code of ethics?

4. As a psychologist, what impact has my involvement or lack of involvement in multicultural and diverse life experience had on how I think about and interpret ethical and unethical behaviors as prescribed within the cultural contexts of my colleagues and those they serve?

---

their own needs. Social workers also seek to promote the responsiveness of organizations, communities, and other social institutions to individuals' needs and social problems. (NASW, 1996, p. 1)

Skill: Ethical Thinking in a Multicultural Context

Counselors, psychologists, and social workers who have a keen and accurate (a) awareness of their personal and cultural assumptions, values, and biases and (b) understanding of the worldviews of culturally different colleagues are better positioned to exhibit and use skills that foster ethical thinking within a multicultural context. Exercise 4.4 is designed to promote the use of skills to enhance ethical thinking within a cultural context.

Critical Incident

Dr. Sam Martson is the only counselor in a rural community in the West. He has just begun his practice in this area and has until recently lived his entire life in New York City. Dr. Martson enjoys big city life but was drawn to the rural community because he wanted a challenge and wanted to provide helping services to people he believed had little to no access to mental health services due to their geographic location. Furthermore, he believed that a new environment might help broaden his personal and professional life perspective.

Dr. Martson was educated in a large eastern university and had befriended a number of people in his program from rural communities. He became intrigued by his friends' personal experiences in classes and stories

---

Exercise 4.4   Skills: Enhancing Ethical Thinking in a Cultural
Context

To assist in the process of ethical thinking within a cultural context,
the following questions are offered to help identify and use requisite
skills needed to more accurately identify ethical and unethical helping behavior as perceived within a multicultural context.

Beliefs and Attitudes

"Culturally skilled counselors respect clients' religious and/or
spiritual beliefs and values, including attributions and taboos,
because they affect worldview, psychosocial functioning, and
expressions of distress" (Arredondo et al., 1996, p. 25).

1. What aspects of spirituality relate to ethical and unethical behavior?

2. Who are the religious and spiritual leaders that provide guidance to
   the various multicultural and diverse populations that I serve?

3. What relationship do those I serve have with the leaders identified
   in question 2?

4. As a social worker, what impact does my skill in identifying
   religious and spiritual leaders within the communities I serve and
   subsequent relationships of those I serve with these leaders have on
   how I interpret the NASW preamble and ethical code?

Knowledge

"Culturally skilled counselors have a clear and explicit knowledge and understanding of the generic characteristics of counseling
and therapy (culture bound, class, and monolingual) and how they
may clash with the cultural values of various cultural groups"
(Arredondo et al., 1996, p. 25).

1. What historical, cultural, and racial contexts of traditional social work
   theories and interventions are evident in the NASW code of ethics?

2. What cultural values, beliefs, and assumptions are made about
   individuals and groups within the NASW code of ethics?

3. How do the values, beliefs, and assumptions in question 2 contrast
   with values, beliefs, and assumptions of culturally different social
   workers and clients?

(Continued)

Exercise 4.4   (Continued)

4. What influence do historical, cultural, and racial contexts of traditional theories and interventions have on my interpretation of the NASW preamble and ethical code within a multicultural context?

Skills

"Culturally skilled counselors are able to engage in a variety of verbal and nonverbal responses. They are able to send and receive both verbal and nonverbal messages accurately and appropriately. They are not tied down to only one method or approach to helping, but recognize that helping styles and approaches may be culture bound. When they sense that their helping style is limited and potentially inappropriate, they can anticipate and modify it" (Arredondo et al., 1996, p. 27).

1. What is one example of interpreting an existing NASW code within the context of another culture? Rewrite the existing code to reflect an interpretation made within a multicultural context.

2. What is one example of a helping behavior identified as unethical in the existing NASW code that may be identified as ethical when viewed within a cultural context?

3. How might I apply different verbal and nonverbal helping responses to a colleague who is engaging in unethical behavior? Cite one example.

4. As a social worker, what impact do my skills in using a variety of verbal and nonverbal responses have on my promoting ethical behavior among my colleagues?

---

they shared during social times together. During his academic training, Sam noticed that few of his professors provided training about the influence of culture on the helping professions. In fact, most talked about traditional approaches to helping and general respect for all clients as the foundations for clinical service and promotion of change in clients. Though Dr. Martson was aware that his program marginally addressed difference, he did not consider it a problem, in part because he believed that to be a good clinician, he needed primarily to respect people, look for similarities to connect with people, ask questions when unsure or confused, and treat everyone the same way. (See Exercise 4.5.)

Exercise 4.5   Critical Incident

Instructions: The following are some questions for consideration as you think about the role that culture plays in ethical thinking, interpretation, and behavior.

1. Review the guidelines specific to dual relationships in your professional code of ethics. What cultural and ethical considerations may affect ethical behavior in Dr. Martson's case?

2. Based on what you know about Dr. Martson's worldview and value system, what are two potential biases Dr. Martson may have relative to working in a rural community?

3. Given your response to question 2 above, assume that Dr. Martson is a professional colleague of yours (e.g., you are both psychologists). Given Dr. Martson's new professional focus, how might his view of difference affect his interpretation of the code of ethics reflective of your professional association (e.g., APA code of ethics, if a psychologist)?

4. Identify one code within your professional code of ethics that addresses multiculturalism or diversity as exemplified within the Dr. Martson critical incident. Interpret this code within a cultural context. For example, think about how geography, gender, education, and so on may affect a more accurate interpretation of the identified code from the perspective of Dr. Martson's worldview and the value systems of the people served by Dr. Martson.

Summary and Key Points

The AMCD provides a three-dimensional approach to multicultural counseling competence. This chapter provides an in-depth discussion of awareness. The first dimension of cultural competence emphasizes the person rather than the professional. Specific areas related to the person include (a) difference, (b) self and cultural assumptions, and (c) pervasiveness of the influence of culture.

Key points regarding confusion around ethical thinking in a competent and multicultural context related to the dimension of awareness include the following:

- Large numbers of counselors, psychologists, and social workers agree that multiculturalism and diversity are requisites to cultural competence and ethical practice. Yet this idea is often confusing and influences ethical thinking within a cultural context.

- Increasing numbers of counselors, psychologists, and social workers embrace the belief that ethical responsibility mandates recognition of individual and cultural differences and similarities among helping professionals and the people they serve.
- Various issues (some of which are culturally based) surround competence, and difficulties exist related to the definition and demonstration of ethical and legal perspectives.
- The monograph *Operationalization of the Multicultural Competencies,* adopted and published by the AMCD in 1996, continues to challenge readers to recognize the "lenses" they look through as they engage in helping behaviors. The monograph is a tool that counselors, psychologists, and social workers may use to assist them as they engage in ethical thinking within a cultural context.
- Axiology (values) and epistemology (knowing and understanding) are principle components of *any* culture; they are stepping-stones that counselors, psychologists, and social workers can use to accurately write, interpret, act on, and enforce ethical codes.
- Major moral principles exist and affect ethical thinking, reading, and interpretation but are less evident within existing codes of ethics due to the reflection of normative ethics. Thus, counselors, psychologists, and social workers are challenged to explore the cultural implications of existing codes.
- Applying ethics in a multicultural context is a process of implementing major moral principles guiding a code of ethics according to the worldviews, values, and life experiences of multicultural and diverse populations.
- Culturally skilled counselors, psychologists, and social workers are aware of their cognitive and emotional experiences of "self" and their impact on their views of differences and similarities in others in accurately reading and interpreting ethical codes.
- Culturally skilled counselors, psychologists, and social workers possess a knowledge base built on cultural values and life experiences that enrich, not confuse, their ethical thinking.
- Culturally skilled counselors, psychologists, and social workers are skilled in (a) assessing their personal understanding of ethical codes and inherent cultural limitations and (b) respecting common historical and cultural life experiences, attitudes, and values that are both different from and similar to their own.

5

Awareness

The First Stage of Ethical Thinking in a Multicultural Context

Counseling has frequently erred in assuming that if a test, a book, or concept is accurately translated in terms of its content, the translated tool will be effective and appropriate. Consequently, in translating, it is important to change not just the content of a message for counseling but also the way of thinking through which the message is being expressed. Although counselors spend considerable time making sure that the content of their messages is culturally appropriate, they spend less time adapting the underlying way of thinking behind the translated message.

—Pedersen (1987, p. 22)

The task facing practitioners and practitioners-in-training aspiring toward cultural competence in their helping behavior, particularly their interpretations of existing ethical codes of professional associations, is how to translate ideals related to multiculturalism and diversity into purposive, competent ethical thinking and practice. This task is of critical importance when practitioners and practitioners-in-training recognize fundamental goals of competent and effective ethical and culturally intentional mental health services. One such goal is clarification of the roles of cultural diversity in the origin, expression, and resolution of problems in general. Another goal is clarification of the roles of cultural diversity in the origin, expression, and interpretation of professional associations' codes of ethics. A third goal is facilitating colleagues' understanding of the impact of multiculturalism and diversity on helping behaviors, so they can better understand their professional behavior within the cultural context in which those behaviors occur.

Many mental health students and supervises seek help in developing their professional competence because of known or unknown problems that evolve from issues related to areas such as racial history, ethnic socialization, social class experiences, gender identity, and sexual orientation. Of significance is that mental health practitioners also struggle with their professional competence for the same reasons. Robinson and Howard-Hamilton (2000) suggest that people seek help because of life realities specific to the convergence of their multiple identities (e.g., race, ethnicity, and gender). Both practitioners and practitioners-in-training experience the impact of this convergence.

The concept of multiple identities may be equated with an iceberg. Ninety percent of the identity of practitioners and practitioners-in-training lies "beneath the water." Without purposive behavior on the part of counselors, psychologists, and social workers, it may be difficult to see and understand a colleague who is culturally and individually different, because only the "tip of the iceberg" is visible. However, with exploration, it becomes easier to see the multiple identities of colleagues who are culturally different from and similar to one's self. Within this new vision, it becomes easier to (a) see how multiple identities affect the core of a colleague, (b) understand what makes a colleague who he or she is, (c) determine how the colleague defines his or her problems, and (d) recognize and appreciate the influence of cultural differences on how a colleague thinks and feels. Of significance, however, is that before practitioners and practitioners-in-training can accurately view and interpret the "iceberg" and multiple identities of others, counselors, psychologists, and social workers must have a clear view and perception of self within the context of the iceberg (see Exercise 5.1).

The purpose of Chapter 5 is to provide an in-depth discussion of Stage 1: awareness of self. This discussion highlights (a) the person and then the professional, (b) the approach to differences by the mental health practitioner or practitioner-in-training, (c) the self and thematic cultural assumptions, and (d) the pervasiveness of the influence of culture on the individual's multiple identities.

The Person and Then the Professional

The professional and ethical issues thus far described in this book present barriers to ethical thinking among and between counselors, psychologists,

Exercise 5.1 Uncovering Personal Dimensions of the Iceberg

Sometimes it is easier to begin looking at "self" through the lenses of friends or colleagues who know you well (internally and externally). Ask a friend or colleague to provide the following information to you. Ask that person not to engage in deep thought, just to share what initially comes to mind when asked these questions. Have your colleague or friend complete the following statement:

"When I visualize what I know about you and equate that vision with an iceberg . . ."

1. What I see when I look at the top of the iceberg as it relates to you is . . .

2. What I see when I look beneath the surface, at the rest of the iceberg, as it relates to you is . . .

After your friend or colleague has responded to the above questions, ask yourself the following questions:

1. What have I learned from the perceptions of one who knows me well, externally and internally?

2. How might this knowledge affect my ability to engage in ethical thinking and decision making in a multicultural context?

and social workers of multicultural and diverse backgrounds. These same professional and ethical issues call for building a framework to facilitate understanding the person as he or she prepares to engage in ethical behavior and monitor the ethical behavior of others. As a precursor to professional and ethical practice, practitioners and practitioners-in-training are challenged to be aware of their own cognitive and emotional behaviors as exhibited within a multicultural context. Such awareness and understanding will foster the development of personal skills needed to operationalize Stage 1 of achieving cultural competence and ultimately promote the ethics of both the mental health profession and its professionals. That is, awareness of self and multiple identities by counselors, psychologists, and social workers is the first step to enhancing personal accuracy of culturally appropriate thinking and decision making specific to their professional associations' codes of ethics.

The following framework is offered to facilitate the process of enhancing self-awareness: the person first and then the professional.

A Framework Promoting Self-Awareness
to Facilitate Understanding the
Cultural Behavior of Others

Key guidelines for this framework are described in the following section.

Primary Guideline for Ethical Behavior

Given the reality of multiple interpretations of professional codes of ethics, it is critical that counselors, psychologists, and social workers find ways to make initial mental, emotional, and physical connection with "self." They need to be aware of their personal beliefs, attitudes, biases, stereotypes, life experiences, and worldviews and the subsequent influence thereof on personal ethical thinking and decision making. Three questions are significant in enhancing personal awareness: (a) What is my worldview? (b) how am I a product of my cultural conditioning? and (c) are my worldview and cultural conditioning reflected in my ethical thinking and decision making, particularly when cultural difference is evident? Competence is promoted when answering these questions according to accurate personal beliefs and attitudes, knowledge, and skills.

The following reflect sample characteristics of culturally skilled mental health professionals working within three dimensions (beliefs and attitudes, knowledge, and skills) to enhance their personal awareness.

Personal Awareness of Worldview,
Cultural Conditioning, and Reflections

Beliefs and Attitudes

"As a culturally skilled counselor, psychologist, or social worker I . . ."

1. Have moved from being culturally unaware to being aware and sensitive to my cultural heritage and to valuing and respecting (within a cultural context) cultural differences of my colleagues.

2. Am aware of how my cultural background and experiences, attitudes, values, and biases influence my cognitive, emotional, and physical behaviors.

3. Am comfortable with cognitive, emotional, and physical differences that exist between myself and colleagues who are from different multicultural and diverse populations.

Knowledge

"As a culturally skilled counselor, psychologist, or social worker I . . ."

1. Have specific knowledge about my racial and cultural heritage and how it affects my interpretations of ethical and unethical behavior.

2. Know how oppression, racism, sexism, and other social discriminations affect me and my attitudes, beliefs, and feelings associated with my multiple identities (e.g., age, gender, race, ethnicity) and my perception of personal benefits from individual, institutional, and cultural racism.

3. Am aware of my social impact on my colleagues and know my personal communication style and how it may clash with or facilitate ethical thinking and decision making within a multicultural context.

Skills

"As a culturally skilled counselor, psychologist, or social worker I . . ."

1. Seek educational, consultative, and training experiences to enhance my understanding and effectiveness in working with culturally different colleagues and implications for culturally accurate ethical thinking.

2. Am constantly seeking to understand myself as a racial and cultural person.

•   *Promote personal awareness* via movement (a) from being culturally unaware to being culturally aware and sensitive; (b) toward awareness of the affect of cultural background and experiences, attitudes, values, and biases on cognitive, emotional, and physical behaviors; and (c) toward enhanced comfort with cognitive, emotional, and physical differences between "self" and culturally different colleagues.

To date, the American Counseling Association (ACA), the American Psychological Association (APA), and the National Association of Social Workers (NASW) have not developed or accepted standards that would define competent ethical thinking and decision making within a multicultural context. Counselors, psychologists, and social workers are left with professional codes that (a) warn against claiming professional qualifications exceeding those possessed by the practitioner and (b) challenge the practitioner to recognize personal boundaries of competence. Yet without specific guidelines as to what competence looks like, it becomes difficult, if not impossible, to assess or achieve competence.

Given the historical nature and struggles associated with multiculturalism and diversity in the mental health profession, counselors, psychologists, and social workers need to explore their personal senses of multiculturalism and diversity prior to addressing the maturation of their professional associations in this area. One reason for this personal exploration is to assist them in discerning what belongs to the struggles of the association and what belongs to the individual counselor, psychologist, or social worker.

As they work toward attaining the goal of discernment, it is critically important that counselors, psychologists, and social workers be personally aware of multicultural and diversity realities within the specific context of their own lives. As they develop personal sensitivity to the effects of multiculturalism and diversity on their own perceptions of ethical and unethical behavior, practitioners and practitioners-in-training are challenged to factor the variable of cultural intentionality into their ethical thinking and decision making. In so doing, they are better able to focus on their multiple identities and then the identities of their colleagues. Counselors, psychologists, and social workers are challenged to avoid discounting their personal cultural values, worldviews, and life experiences and how these contexts and subsequent dynamics affect ethical thinking.

Table 5.1 is presented to facilitate the process of culturally intentional and purposive ethical thinking and decision making, with an emphasis on the impact of multiple identities and cognitive and emotional behaviors. By emphasizing five basic contexts, the table provides a foundation for understanding the cultures in which the reader and the reader's colleagues formulated their multiple identities: (a) family, (b) social systems, (c) demography, (d) status, and (e) life experiences. The reader is reminded that once this fundamental information is a conscious part of his or her personal thinking, he or she is better positioned to understand the impact of this awareness on personal worldview, particularly as it relates to interpreting and upholding a code of ethics.

• *Promote knowledge via listening with a multicultural ear for underlying assumptions and values* emanating from (a) personal racial and cultural heritages and their affect on interpretations of ethical and unethical behavior; (b) how oppression, racism, sexism, and other social discriminations affect personal attitudes, beliefs, and feelings associated with one's multiple identities (e.g., age, gender, race, ethnicity); (c) perceptions of personal benefits from individual, institutional, and cultural racism; and (d) personal social impact on colleagues, personal communication style, and potential clashes with or facilitation of ethical thinking and decision making within a multicultural context.

The reader is advised that cultural knowledge about self emphasizes one's perceptual flexibility, increasing possibilities for identifying alternative assumptions and definitions about problems. That is, the person hears and sees the similarities and differences related to how he or she as well as others experience the world. The person takes that knowledge into consideration as he or she makes assumptions and uses that knowledge to enhance his or her personal perceptual flexibility.

Awareness of the multicultural and diversity dimensions of self has the potential to ensure that mental health practitioners and practitioners-in-training

Table 5.1	Awareness: Personal Assessment to Promote Ethical Thinking in a Multicultural Context

I am aware of the following general contexts of my life. I am aware of the common attitudes and beliefs, thoughts and feelings, and stereotypes and biases that emanated from each of the general contexts.

General Personal Life Contexts	*No*		*Somewhat*		*Yes*	
My general family context						
1. Is nuclear.	1	2	3	4	5	6
2. Is heterosexual.	1	2	3	4	5	6
3. Is gay or lesbian.	1	2	3	4	5	6
4. Is matriarchal.	1	2	3	4	5	6
5. Has a history of matriarchy.	1	2	3	4	5	6
6. Is patriarchal.	1	2	3	4	5	6
7. Has a history of patriarchy.	1	2	3	4	5	6
8. Is adoptive.	1	2	3	4	5	6
9. Values the extended family.	1	2	3	4	5	6
10. Is multicultural (race and ethnicity).	1	2	3	4	5	6
My general social systems context reflects that I						
1. Value English as the first language.	1	2	3	4	5	6
2. Value speaking multiple languages.	1	2	3	4	5	6
3. Am female.	1	2	3	4	5	6
4. Am male.	1	2	3	4	5	6
5. Am lesbian	1	2	3	4	5	6
6. Am gay.	1	2	3	4	5	6
7. Value religion.	1	2	3	4	5	6
8. Value spirituality.	1	2	3	4	5	6
9. Am a member of an oppressed race.	1	2	3	4	5	6
10. Am a member of the dominant race.	1	2	3	4	5	6
My general demographic context reflects that I						
1. Am an elder (55 years or older).	1	2	3	4	5	6
2. Am middle-aged (35–54 years).	1	2	3	4	5	6
3. Am a young adult (20–34 years).	1	2	3	4	5	6
4. Am a North American native.	1	2	3	4	5	6
5. Am a North American migrant.	1	2	3	4	5	6
6. Was raised Christian.	1	2	3	4	5	6
7. Was raised other than Christian.	1	2	3	4	5	6
8. Was raised in the Midwest, USA.	1	2	3	4	5	6
9. Was raised in the South, USA.	1	2	3	4	5	6
10. Was raised in the North, USA.	1	2	3	4	5	6
My general status context reflects that						
1. My past socioeconomic background was poor.	1	2	3	4	5	6

(Continued)

Table 5.1   (Continued)

General Personal Life Contexts	No		Somewhat		Yes
2. My past socioeconomic background was middle class.	1	2	3	4	5	6
3. My past socioeconomic background was wealthy.	1	2	3	4	5	6
4. My present socioeconomic class is working poor.	1	2	3	4	5	6
5. My present socioeconomic class is upper middle class.	1	2	3	4	5	6
6. My present socioeconomic class is upper class.	1	2	3	4	5	6
7. I have a bachelor's degree.						
8. I have a master's degree.	1	2	3	4	5	6
9. I have a Ph.D.	1	2	3	4	5	6
10. *I affiliate with the following groups:*						
10.1. A multicultural fraternity.	1	2	3	4	5	6
10.2. A multicultural sorority.	1	2	3	4	5	6
10.3. A multicultural athletic team/group.	1	2	3	4	5	6
10.4. A multicultural social group.	1	2	3	4	5	6
My general life experiences context reflects that I						
1. *Have encountered major physical issues*						
1.1. In general.	1	2	3	4	5	6
1.2. With people of a different race.	1	2	3	4	5	6
1.3. With people of a different ethnicity.	1	2	3	4	5	6
1.4. With people of a different gender.	1	2	3	4	5	6
2. *Have encountered major emotional issues*						
2.1. In general.	1	2	3	4	5	6
2.2. With people of a different race.	1	2	3	4	5	6
2.3. With people of a different ethnicity.	1	2	3	4	5	6
2.4. With people of a different gender.	1	2	3	4	5	6
3. *Have experienced discrimination or prejudice*						
3.1. In general.	1	2	3	4	5	6
3.2. With people of a different race.	1	2	3	4	5	6
3.3. With people of a different ethnicity.	1	2	3	4	5	6
3.4. With people of a different gender.	1	2	3	4	5	6

use best practices. Of importance is *best practice* as defined within a professional association's code of ethics and how that code relates the concept of best practice to the backgrounds, cultures, and heritages of multicultural and diverse populations. It is important for counselors, psychologists, and

Table 5.2   Differentiation in a Cultural Context: A Model

| | *Thematic Assumptions* | |
Code of Ethics	*Code*	*Personal*

social workers to strive toward two goals: (a) an enhanced awareness of underlying assumptions and values of their professional associations' code of ethics and (b) mindfulness of the multiplicity of assumptions and values involved in intentional culturally ethical thinking. The skill of differentiation is necessary to achieve these goals. At the very least, individuals must be able to differentiate personal assumptions from assumptions inherent to those of their professional association's code of ethics. The goal is to know what is "yours" and what is someone else's. (See Table 5.2 and Exercise 5.2.)

• *Build skills* via thinking in a culturally competent context built on a foundation of (a) educational, consultative, and training experiences and (b) personal understanding of the multicultural and diverse identities of self. A pillar of this foundation is one's personal approach to difference.

Approach to Difference

Similarities and differences are critical elements to thinking in a multicultural context. Both elements facilitate the process of accurately seeing, understanding, interpreting, and thinking as counselors, psychologists, and social workers intentionally determine ethical behavior. Historically, multiple media (education programs, in-service training, consultations) have emphasized the role of similarities in providing competent and sensitive helping services. For example, it is not uncommon for counselors, psychologists, and social workers to share that one of the most important helping tools they have is that of identifying commonalties and similarities with persons served. However, less attention has been given to the role of differences as a tool to facilitate the delivery of competent and sensitive helping services.

If you ignore similarities, you eliminate the possibility of common ground across differences. If you ignore differences, you impose the strongest

Exercise 5.2   Differentiating Personal Assumptions From Association
                    Assumptions

Table 5.2 offers a model to assist in the differentiation process. Review your professional code of ethics and identify and write a specific ethical guideline of interest or immediate applicability to you. Then ask yourself, "What assumption am I making as I read this guideline?" As you respond to the question, focus on how your cultural background is influencing your personal response. Note: This request may be easier for some people than others, but stay with the struggle and discomfort of the task. Conclude with studying the guideline and identifying one assumption that is inherent to the guideline as it is written.

To illustrate, a counselor might select Section A.1.c of the American Counseling Association (1995) *Code of Ethics and Standards of Practice*.

The ethical guideline reads,

> Counselors and their clients work jointly in devising integrated, individual counseling plans that offer reasonable promise of success and are consistent with abilities and circumstances of clients. Counselors and clients regularly review counseling plans to ensure their continued viability and effectiveness respecting clients' freedom of choice. (p. 2)

As the counselor responds from personal awareness of her or his cultural heritage on personal and current thinking, the counselor's *personal assumption is* that the family is a critical part of important life decision making. Regardless of age, if a person is going to be successful in life, he or she must have the family's blessings and support, and that choice is a family matter, not an individual one.

One assumption of my professional association is that viable and effective measures are characterized by increasing one's freedom of choice. This assumption is more in-line with an individualistic worldview than a collectivistic worldview.

Processing Questions

1. What assumptions do I hold that help me better understand my culturally learned behaviors?
2. What assumptions do I hold that hinder me from better understanding my culturally learned behaviors?
3. What insights have I gained?
4. What implications for my ethical thinking in a multicultural context are evident in this exercise?

cultural norms on everyone. The reader is advised to recognize and use the benefits of similarities in his or her work. This section, however, addresses difference as a helping tool, in part because of the reality that the helping professions and helping professionals continue to struggle with the benefits of this approach.

Many practitioners and practitioners-in-training, when asked about their comfort with difference, will readily indicate that they feel comfortable with the issue. Yet if you listen and watch carefully when they are talking about or actually interacting with difference, the message changes. For example, you may hear a statement from a colleague such as, "I feel comfortable with difference." In the course of conversation, you hear your colleague say, "It took a lot for me to muster up the strength to ask a client what it was that she might not like about me being a man and she (the client) being a woman." Inherent in this statement is a level of discomfort with difference. Or you may be with a colleague who says, "I am comfortable working with men." The two of you enter an elevator. You and your colleague are going to the eighth floor. The elevator stops at the seventh floor. A Hispanic male enters the elevator; you look at your friend and notice that she begins to move away from him. At first, you think your friend is just making space for him to enter the elevator. However, you notice that ever so gently, your friend puts her purse out of sight. When you get to your destination, you share your observations with your colleague, and she says she was unaware of her behavior. Inherent in her behavior is the possibility of discomfort with difference. Of significance is that it is often easier to see and hear such discrepancies in others. Yet being able to enhance one's ability to recognize similar discrepancies in one's "self" is critically important as well. In fact, many scholars acknowledge that this self-awareness is the first step to cultural competence and as such positions one to better meet the challenges and demands of Stages 2 (knowledge of others) and 3 (skills development).

The literature is full of definitions and interpretations of difference and how people approach difference as it relates to multiculturalism and diversity. The following are a few of the more frequent approaches to difference:

1. *Ignore difference.* Act as if difference does not exist. An example of this approach to difference is, "If people would just stop paying attention to difference, I believe this world would be a better place to live in."

2. *Move difference to a point of homogeneity.* Act as if people are all the same based on their humanness. An example of this approach to difference is, "I believe that because we are all human beings, we all bleed red blood, we all feel, we all eat, and we are all going to die. People are people."

3. *Fear difference.* Experience and perceive people who think and feel differently than you to be deviant, up to no good, or abnormal. An

example of this approach to difference is, "I think that people who are interdependent are immature."

4. *Appreciate difference.* See difference and recognize its goodness and potential as a tool to promote change and maturation. An example of this approach to difference is, "I know that I come from a culture that appreciates a collectivistic approach to life and that my colleague comes from a culture that appreciates an individualistic approach to life. Our individualistic and collectivistic approaches to life are beneficial to us and will affect our interpretations of a particular code of ethics."

Exercise 5.3 is designed to help readers assess themselves in order to foster the development of personal and professional skills related to seeing, perceiving, and acting on difference as a tool to facilitate ethical thinking within a multicultural context, rather than thinking in a monocultural and ethnocentric context. The premise for the exercise is that immersion in a culture (different from one's own) will facilitate the modification of attitudes, beliefs, and assumptions more readily than just reviewing the literature or reading a book about differences within a cultural and personal framework. In addition, the modification may be more in-line with the worldview, beliefs, and assumptions of those coming from different cultural contexts.

Critical Incident

Marc is a 27-year-old Navajo man in his second year in psychology at a prestigious medical school in the Northwest. Marc wants to give something back to his Navajo community and plans to use his degree to help make a difference in addressing the mental health problems of his community. Marc is enrolled in an introductory ethics class, and his professor has assigned the students to work in groups and interpret their profession's ethical code. Marc's group consists of four people, one man who self-identifies as White and of Italian descent, a woman who self-identifies as Black and African American, and another woman who self-identifies as White and American. They each share an interpretation of the code, and all but Marc interpret from an individualistic worldview. Marc is frustrated and feels as if he is incompetent because of his inability to appreciate the individualist view of the code. (See Exercise 5.4.)

Summary and Key Points

This chapter provides an in-depth discussion of Stage 1: awareness of self. Highlights include (a) the person and then the professional, (b) the practitioner's and practitioner-in-training's approaches to difference, (c) "self"

Exercise 5.3   Awareness: A Self-Assessment of My Personal Approach
                    to Difference

Instructions: Reflect upon your life, life experiences, and worldview and
respond to the following statements as honestly as you possibly can:

  1. I have attended the following multicultural-related activities within
     the past 6 months. Name the specific activity and the focus of the
     activity. For example, I attended the ABC forum on advocacy for
     cultural competence.

  2. Within the past year, I have developed a professional relationship
     with the following mental health professionals who are different
     from me in terms of (name the person relative to each of the
     following dimensions) . . .
     2.a. Race (e.g., Black, Brown, White)
     2.b. Ethnicity (e.g., German American, Asian American)
     2.c. Gender (female, male)
     2.d. Sexual orientation (e.g., gay, lesbian, bisexual)
     2.e. Religion (Christian, atheist)
     2.f. Other difference(s)

  3. I have attended the following formal training sessions (e.g., sessions
     emphasizing multiculturalism and diversity work within a particular
     content area during my attendance at a professional conference,
     whether state or national level) designed to help enhance skills in
     recognizing personal limitations to working with difference.
     3.a. Name of the formal training session. For example: The title of
          the workshop I attended was "Ethics in a Multicultural Context."
     3.b. Name of the presenter(s) and their expertise in cultural compe-
          tence. For example: John Doe implemented the presentation I
          attended. John is president of the ABC professional associa-
          tion, which is a division of the ACA. The mission of ABC is
          promoting cultural competence with "X" professionals . . .
     3.c. Name of the professional conference and indicate whether state
          or national. For example: I attended the 2002 ACA, APA, or
          NASW national conference.
     3.d. Identify two issues you learned about yourself relative to your
          potential limitations around working with difference. State the
          form of difference that feeds into your limitation. For example:
          I am not comfortable working with women who are aggressive
          and am intimidated when in their presence. If I am not careful,
          I often defend my abilities and myself when in their presence.
     3.e. Identify two issues you learned about yourself relative to skills
          you currently possess specific to working with difference.
          For example: I am able to identify cultural values thematic to
          African Americans and women. I can actively listen with the
          inclusion of culture and worldview as factors important to what
          and how I hear.

Exercise 5.4   Critical Incident

Instructions: Assume that you are a consultant and Marc's group has come to you for assistance with their struggle associated with understanding that ethical practice requires multicultural awareness, knowledge, and skills. However, the first step in becoming culturally competent is awareness of self. As their consultant, complete the following statements as a means of helping the students develop in Stage 1 of cultural competence: self-awareness.

1. Two possible ethical concerns evident in your group are . . .

2. Marc does or does not appear to have a working knowledge of himself as a person, because . . .

3. To assist in understanding the impact of one's "person" and personal approach to differences in possible interpretations of the code, I recommend that your group . . .

---

and thematic cultural assumptions, and (d) the pervasiveness of the influence of culture on the individual's multiple identities. Some key points regarding the awareness stage of cultural competence and thinking within a multicultural context include the following:

- A fundamental step in integrating cultural competence with ethical decision making in a multicultural context is translating ideals related to multiculturalism and diversity into purposive, competent, and ethical thinking, practice, and problem solving.
- Counselors, psychologists, and social workers possess multiple identities, some of which are more visible than others, that affect the total person. All identities need to be considered as awareness is developed to enrich thinking and translation of ethical codes.
- Counselors, psychologists, and social workers should be aware of personal beliefs, attitudes, biases, stereotypes, life experiences, and worldviews and their impact on ethical thinking and decision making.
- Counselors, psychologists, and social workers engaging in ethical thinking in a multicultural context become personally aware via a commitment to intentionally move from cultural unawareness to cultural awareness and sensitivity.
- Given the historical nature and struggles of multiculturalism and diversity in counseling, psychology, and social work, practitioners and practitioners-in-training must explore their personal issues before addressing their professional associations' issues around ethics in a multicultural context.

- Listening with a multicultural ear for underlying assumptions and values promotes cultural knowledge about self and others.
- "Self"-knowledge increases perceptual flexibility and identification of alternative assumptions and definitions about problems.
- A critical skill for the enrichment of personal awareness is the identification of one's personal approach to difference.
- Difference, when viewed appropriately, is a tool to facilitate the delivery of competent and sensitive helping services.
- "Self"-awareness is the first step to cultural competence and positions counselors, psychologists, and social workers to better meet the challenges and demands of gaining knowledge about others and developing culturally competent helping skills such as more accurate ethical thinking.
- Counselors, psychologists, and social workers are encouraged to constantly challenge their personal approaches to difference and the subsequent impact on helping and ethical thinking.

6

Knowledge and Skills, Stages 2 and 3

Ethical Thinking and Decision Making in a Multicultural Context

The need for culturally competent mental health services has never been greater as increasing numbers of diverse clients seek psychological services. According to APA's "Guidelines for Providers of Psychological Services to Ethnic, Linguistic, and Culturally Diverse Populations" (APA, 1993), "Psychological service providers need a sociocultural framework to consider diversity of values, interactional styles, and cultural expectations in a systematic fashion. They need knowledge and skills for multicultural assessment and intervention" (p. 35).

This statement underscores the need for practitioners to understand the psychological impact of social, political, and economic factors when working across racial and ethnic populations. Knowledge of, familiarity with, and perhaps most important, appreciation of the values and cultural expectations of diverse groups minimize the risk that the Eurocentric underpinnings of therapist training programs will be imposed on clients.

Although cultural understanding is essential, it is also critical that practitioners move beyond intellectual understanding and "book knowledge" about their clients' sociocultural realities to the acquisition of concrete multicultural skill. Knowledge and skill in treating diverse clients effectively are the second and third factors, after self-awareness, for competent ethical practice in a cultural context. The purpose of this chapter is to identify specific knowledge and skills required for cultural and ethical competency.

Precounseling: Becoming a
Helper Within a Multicultural Context

Clinical, counseling, and social work training programs typically have at least one course, often required, in multicultural counseling. Multicultural therapy education for graduate students is a relatively recent phenomenon in the mental health field. Prior to the 1980s, cross-cultural counseling and therapy courses were offered in many programs but typically focused on understanding the mental health and pathology patterns of cultures outside North America. In the late 1970s, when attention turned to cultural groups within the United States, fairly simplistic treatment paradigms were initially formulated.

The early multicultural therapy literature often was marked by stereo-typic presentations of diverse populations in which formulaic approaches to treatment with ethnic/racial groups were prescribed. For example, Black and Latino Americans were said to respond best to behavioral approaches, American Indians to spiritually based approaches, and Asian Americans to holistic treatment. While the early literature was a necessary beginning to the examination of cultural constructs, the complexities and heterogeneity of Black, Latino, Asian, and Indian client populations failed to be adequately recognized and explored.

What was needed was research that revealed a range of psychological responses, developmental processes, and adaptive strategies within racial groups. Rather than conceptualizing members of a given racial population in a one-size-fits-all manner, the mental health fields needed more complex paradigms. The need was met with the advent of developmental models of racial identity; that is, through early writing purporting that within racial groups existed diverse worldviews accompanied by a complex array of intrapsychic and external coping strategies for responding to discrimination, bigotry, and racism. The research in this area, launched by Cross (1991), Parham (1989), and Jackson (2001), infused into mental health scholarship the reality that not all Blacks, Latinos, Asians, and Indians are alike; that is, no one treatment approach is suitable for all members of a given population due to the vast heterogeneity within racial groups.

It would be interesting, before continuing our discussion of cultural heterogeneity, to pause for a moment and consider the ethical implications of the one-size-fits-all approach. Despite research refuting the efficacy of this approach (Landrine, 1995), we contend that the practice of grouping individuals according to designated racial categories and then affixing psychological and behavioral norms and patterns to the group as a whole continues. One need only to peruse most multicultural counseling and psychotherapy texts to find evidence that populations continue to be grouped according to race, as represented by chapter titles and content. In fairness, these textbooks often contain statements cautioning against regarding the populations as homogeneous. However, the structure and organization of these texts conveys a message in itself that we feel may be confusing and misleading.

What are the ethical implications of the one-size-fits-all method of multicultural counseling? One question we think can and should be raised is this: Are practitioners constrained from operating in an ethical manner when multicultural theory is itself limited? This raises a second question: Is it unethical to practice in a racist manner (i.e., a one-size approach to clients of a given racial group) when theory encourages such an approach? Should practitioners be held responsible for unethical practice when treatment paradigms for multicultural counseling may themselves be flawed and inadvertently encourage unethical practices? We urge thoughtful discussion of these troubling questions.

Despite the proliferation of multicultural counseling and therapy research in recent years, this knowledge base has not trickled down to competency-based clinical and counseling training programs (Arredondo & Arciniega, 2001; Sue & Sue, 1999). Surveys of graduates of counseling programs consistently reveal a sense of inadequacy with regard to multicultural competency (Bernal & Castro, 1994). One problem is the failure of training programs to adequately prepare students to address the complexity of cultural phenomena. These limitations are understandable given the relatively recent emergence of multicultural therapy as a legitimate area of theory and research. A less tolerant view of the problem of the scarcity of competency-based training we would urge you to consider is that the quality of your multicultural training is a direct by-product of racism in the mental health professions, one consequence of which is the underrepresentation of people of color in counseling, psychology, and social work. This underrepresentation has a profound impact on your preparation and skill in working with diverse clients. Please turn to Exercise 6.1 for an activity that elaborates on this perspective.

Returning now to our discussion of cultural heterogeneity, a decade of multicultural counseling scholarship existed before stereotypic conceptualizations of people of color were replaced with more complex paradigms. Racial identity development theory was among the first areas to add richness and complexity to our understanding of persons of color. As stated above, the research on racial identity revealed within-group variability with regard to race, a critical contribution to the understanding of race as a multidimensional variable. As a result of this groundbreaking research, we now appreciate that racial identity is more fluid than fixed; that is, it may change during the course of an individual's life. We also recognize not only

---

Exercise 6.1   Training Environment Visualization

Imagine for a few moments that people of color control the mental health disciplines and training programs. That is, Black, Latino, American Indian, and Asian American men and women . . .

Hold all the positions of power at your graduate institution

Determine the content of your graduate curriculum

Supervise all your clients

Control the agencies where you did your internship

Run the professional ethics boards

Conduct almost all the mental health research and write all the major theories you studied in graduate school

Control the licensing process in your field

Control virtually every aspect of graduate education and postgraduate training

Though there are a few White faculty and supervisors, people of color dominate the profession. Despite the good intentions and self-defined cultural sensitivity of those in control, mental health education and training center on the psychology of people of color. White psychology is a fairly new subspecialty but is given relatively little attention in graduate curricula and training programs. The implicit message is that if one is a good practitioner, one will be able to work just as effectively with White ethnic populations, despite their cultural differences, as with clients of color. In small groups, discuss the following questions:

1. What are your guesses about why Whites are underrepresented in this hypothetical mental health world?

2. What is the impact of the relative absence of White faculty?

3. How might significant inclusion of White faculty and supervisors change graduate training?

Assume for the purpose of this scenario that most graduate students in psychology, counseling, and social work are students of color. Assume further that treatment populations are primarily made up of clients of color, although this reality is changing rapidly as

(Continued)

Exercise 6.1   (Continued)

White ethnic populations increase. Many graduate students are appropriately concerned about their ability to treat the growing numbers of White ethnic clients seeking or referred for mental health treatment. The people of color in control of the profession recognize that White ethnic groups are increasingly represented among treatment populations but are uncertain how to meet the challenges that accompany the changing population. Remember that much skepticism remains about the need to advance theory and research specific to White clients. Despite Whites having a history of subordination to people of color and a multitude of psychological issues arising from their disempowered status, the prevailing one-size-fits-all philosophy mitigates examination of White people's issues. With this in mind, discuss the following questions:

1. What ethical issues are raised by the dominance of people of color in the mental health professions?

2. What are the ethical problems with the one-size approach to treating White clients?

3. How do you explain what appears to be complacency on the part of those in control about advancing more complex research on White culture?

4. How would more advanced research on Whites benefit practitioners?

---

that members of the same racial group may be at various places along the continuum of identity development, but that the same individual may manifest behaviors associated with different stages at the same point in his or her life depending on the social context at a given moment. This notion seriously challenges the wisdom and ethics of the one-size approach and has huge implications for psychotherapy assessment and treatment. To add yet another dimension to the complexity of racial heterogeneity, the emerging research on multiracial identity suggests that several processes of identity development may occur simultaneously for individuals with multiple racial heritage (Wijeyesinghe, 2001; Williams, 1999). Clearly, ethical multicultural practice calls for knowledge and skill in all these areas.

The advent of racial identity development theory coincided with the emergence of feminism and feminist psychology theory and research. Together, this body of theory and research has further chipped away at existing homogeneity-based approaches to treating clients of color. Questions about the interface between race and gender began to raise the possibility that one's racial identity development and sense of self might be influenced by one's location on the gender hierarchy. That is, women of color experiencing "double oppression" in mainstream culture, by virtue of their disempowered status with respect to both race and gender, might actually be forced to develop stronger coping strategies than individuals experiencing only one form of oppression (Comas-Diaz & Greene, 1994). These explorations raised—and continue to raise—important questions about the ethics of treatment models that fail to adequately account for gender differences within racial groups (Brown & Root, 1990; Comas-Diaz & Greene, 1994; Landrine, 1995).

In summary, it is important for counselor, therapist, and social worker training programs to move beyond simplistic paradigms that unwittingly stereotype clients of color. Considerable research is now available addressing the psychological complexities of minority racial group status. We urge students and practitioners to become very familiar with the research on racial identity development, both monoracial and multiracial, and issues associated with gender diversity within racial groups.

Adapting Learned Skills and Counseling Theory to Work Ethically Within a Client's Cultural Framework

Recent research suggests that multicultural counseling competence rests in part on actual exposure during clinical training to members of different racial and ethnic groups (Diaz-Lazaro & Cohen, 2001; Merta, Stringham, & Ponterotto, 1988; Mio, 1989; Mio & Morris, 1990). Diaz-Lazaro and Cohen (2001) summarized existing theory and research by stating that, "Cross-cultural contact may have a positive influence on the reduction of negative attitudes toward members of culturally different groups and thus also on the development of multicultural counseling competencies" (p. 44).

Diaz-Lazaro and Cohen's (2001) study is the first quantitative examination of the relationship between cross-cultural contact and multicultural counseling competencies. Results reinforce the notion that cross-cultural contact plays a significant role in developing multicultural counseling competency. Their study makes a good case for the integration of actual multicultural contact in counselor training programs. One way I (CBW) have done this in my own multicultural counseling classes is to require students to provide service to a program or agency that serves a racial population with which the student is relatively unfamiliar. Students are asked to keep journals and share their experiences with others in the class throughout the semester. See Exercise 6.2 for a detailed description of this course activity.

Multicultural counseling awareness, knowledge, and skill acquired through these and other training activities are basic ingredients for ethical and competent practice. We would argue that the adaptation of these skills to actual practice is shaped significantly during the course of clinical and counseling supervision. Bernard and Goodyear (1998) defined *supervision* as an evaluative relationship between a senior and junior member of the counseling profession whose purpose is to "enhance the professional functioning" of the supervisee" (p. 4). Thus, supervision is a relationship in which the supervisee role is as an apprentice, one who is learning the tools of the trade from an experienced "master." In the sociocultural climate in which therapy is practiced today, the master, or supervisor, has an ethical obligation to assist the supervisee in developing multicultural competence.

It is our premise that ethical and competent multicultural practice is guided by ethical and competent supervision that attends to cultural factors. Although considerable attention has been given to cultural competence in the counseling arena, an area that has been addressed far less frequently is multicultural competence in supervision. A basic feature of competent supervision of cultural issues is the supervisor's ability to facilitate explorations of racial and ethnic differences, both between supervisee and client and between supervisee and supervisor (Estrada, Frame, & Williams, 2002). However, scholarship in this area points decisively to the virtual absence of racial exploration in supervision (Lappin & Hardy, 1997).

That the multicultural aspects of supervision have remained largely unexplored may be explained in part by O'Byrne and Rosenberg's (1998) sociocultural analysis of supervision. These authors describe supervision as a process whereby the supervisee is acculturated into the profession of counseling. They characterize counseling as a "culture" with a common language, rites of passage (e.g., "apprenticeship" to an "elder"), and defined socialization practices. As previously discussed, this culture of counseling has only recently begun to shift and broaden its perspective to include client variables such as race, ethnicity, class, gender, sexual orientation, disability, and spirituality. Although cultural variables have begun to be acknowledged, "The focus remains scattered, superficial, and marginalized" (Lappin & Hardy, 1997, p. 42). This is the case especially with regard to supervision (Lappin & Hardy, 1997). The message is clear: The opportunity to develop and implement multicultural skills in supervision is largely missed.

What makes this oversight especially troubling is the fact that in most cross-racial supervision dyads, the supervisor is White and the supervisee

Exercise 6.2   Cultural Service Project

A critical component of multicultural counseling competence is direct exposure to stigmatized populations during graduate training. This service project provides an avenue for students to participate in direct cultural service. The objective is to acquire experience with a cultural group through professional service.

Choosing a Setting

Choose a setting that serves a population that is stigmatized. See the following pages for suggestions. [Note to reader: I include with this assignment a list of more than 30 agencies in the urban area surrounding the counselor training program in which I teach. The list includes agency or program title, contact person, phone number, and a brief description of the ethnic/racial composition of the population served. I update the list every semester.] The population should be one with which you have had little personal and/or professional contact. Choose a setting that is relevant for your future counseling work. For example, school counseling students may want to contact local schools. Students planning to work with young children may wish to contact day care centers, elementary schools, libraries, or bookstores that offer story times. Students interested in college settings may want to contact one of the university programs for students of color, international students, or Gay, Lesbian, Bisexual, and Transgender (GLBT) students. Also, keep churches in mind as possibilities. Many of them have meal delivery programs, youth activities and events, and other community services.

Initiating the Contact

The settings listed vary in terms of the time commitment they prefer. Some require a commitment on your part of 40 hours over the course of the semester, while others will lend themselves to fewer hours. Some of the clients served by these agencies may require considerable time with you before trust can be established. Please be respectful of their needs. Be very clear about your availability when you make the initial contact with the program. It is also helpful if you can be flexible in terms of your availability. For example, some agencies may prefer you to be available 3 hours per week for a few weeks to work on a special project. Others may need you for only an hour a week. These are the sorts of issues you will have to discuss with them. Also, be aware that some of these programs require training sessions for service providers.

(Continued)

Exercise 6.2 (Continued)

Documentation

Keep a journal of your service activities. Your entries should include dates and times and corresponding activities and impressions. Type and submit your journal at the end of the semester, along with a three-page summary of your service. Your summary should include: (a) description of setting, (b) description of population, (c) service(s) you provided, (d) what you learned and how it relates to the counseling role, (e) whether you would recommend this site to other students and why or why not, and (f) feelings, reactions, and other process comments. Include in this last part your initial impressions and how they may have changed over time. Finally, attach a signed verification sheet to your log and summary.

Class Presentation and Discussion

Describe your cultural service projects and what you learned with others in the class. Be specific about what you learned about yourself and your cultural competence as a result of your involvement with the client population you chose.

is a person of color (Goodyear & Guzardo, 2000). According to Goodyear and Guzardo (2000), in cross-racial supervisory relationships, social power differences between supervisee and supervisor create potent interpersonal dynamics that should be examined (p. 492). To ignore racial and cultural differences in supervision is tantamount to ignoring the proverbial elephant in the room. When this occurs, conversations about racial dynamics between supervisees and their clients may also be compromised.

Estrada et al. (2002) provide several recommendations for incorporating racial, ethnic, and other cultural variables in supervision. Their first recommendation is for supervisors to create a safe environment for discussing racial issues. This task presupposes supervisors' own comfort exploring racial issues, which may or may not be the case. If it is not, supervisors are urged to seek their own consultation or supervision. Discussion in supervision of the supervisee's and supervisor's racial differences, experiences with racial issues, their developmental stages with regard to racial identity, and implications of these factors for both the supervision relationship and treatment of particular ethnic clients is a building block toward ethical practice.

A second strategy for building competence is for the supervisee and supervisor to assess their multicultural awareness, knowledge, and skill levels. Several instruments are available for cultural self-assessment, including the Multicultural Awareness, Knowledge, and Skills Survey (MAKSS) (D'Andrea, Daniels, & Heck, 1991). Racial identity development measures (Helms, 1990; Helms & Cook, 1999) may also be used as springboards for disclosure and discussion of supervisors' and supervisees' developmental journeys toward racial consciousness. The third strategy the authors suggest is active learning about the cultural contexts of ethnic clients. This may include the sorts of activities described at the beginning of this section, which immerse supervisors and supervisees in cross-cultural settings.

Film viewing is an immersion strategy that can help students explore their cultural competence. One advantage to film viewing and discussion is the opportunity to explore one's comfort (or discomfort) level about different cultures within the safety of the classroom or supervision setting. Viewing films as a part of multicultural training can be a powerful strategy for uncovering hidden biases and beliefs about cultures other than one's own. I (CBW) would rather students and supervisees watch a film and talk honestly about their reactions so that we can work together to dismantle their biases rather than unconsciously impose them in their work with actual clients.

Many excellent films are available that depict ethnic cultures from the perspective of filmmakers who are members of the culture. Examples are Amy Tan's *The Joy Luck Club,* about Chinese American culture; *Smoke Signals,* based on a Sherman Alexie novel about American Indian culture; *My Family,* about Mexican American culture; and the film *Daughters of the Dust,* which tells the story of a community of African American women. Exercise 6.3 uses the John Singleton film *Baby Boy* to set up a series of activities designed to uncover hidden biases that may negatively affect treatment. Part I of the exercise facilitates examination of reactions to the film. Part II sets up practice dyads based on characters in the film as a method for developing multicultural counseling skill. Similar exploratory and practice exercises can be set up based on novels exploring cultural themes. Table 6.1 provides a list of novels I (CBW) have found effective for multicultural training.

Plan of Action: Moving From
Awareness and Knowledge to Action

Competent multicultural training for clinicians includes courses in theory and research, exposure to diverse populations, and supervision that facilitates exploration of relevant cultural variables in treatment. When

Exercise 6.3   Moving From Theory to Skill

Film viewing has been suggested as an effective tool for multicultural education and training (Williams, 1999). African American director John Singleton's film *Baby Boy* (Columbia, 2001) offers rich material for multicultural skill building. *Baby Boy* can be described as a contemporary coming-of-age story about Jody, a young African American male living in Los Angeles.

Part I: Self-Reflection

For the purpose of this exercise, we recommend that you view the film with other people and note their reactions as well as your own. After viewing the film, jot down a few notes in response to these questions:

1. How would you describe the culture depicted in the film?

2. What are the interaction styles of the main characters: Jody, Jody's girlfriend Yvette, Jody's mother, and her boyfriend Melvin? What are their emotional styles?

3. How do you find yourself responding to the characters in the film? Note specifically how you *feel* about them. How did others viewing the film with you react to the characters?

4. What has been your experience with the culture depicted in the film?

5. How does your experience affect the way you view and respond to the characters?

6. Did you have any judgments about the characters? If so, how does your own culture, race, ethnicity, gender, or age affect your evaluation of the people in the film?

7. How would you describe the values reflected by the characters? In what ways are they similar to and different from Eurocentric values?

Part II: Role Play

Role play is often used in multicultural training because of its power in assisting students to recognize their strengths and weaknesses and acquire competence through practice (Pedersen, 1995). Ask for volunteers to role-play Jody, Yvette, Jody's mother, and Melvin. Assume these characters seek individual counseling for problems they're having in coping with their situation. Set up a series of dyads in which students role-play the characters and counselors.

Exercise 6.3   (Continued)

Ask the role players and student observers to take note of what strategies seem particularly effective and ineffective in working with these "clients." It is helpful to tell students not to be afraid of making mistakes and that often it is through our mistakes that meaningful learning takes place. Process students' thoughts and feelings in both the client and therapist roles. Suggestions for discussion questions following the role play include the following:

1. What was most challenging to you in the therapist role? Client role?

2. What personal qualities helped you to connect with the client?

3. Did the role play reveal any blind spots or prejudices? How did these affect your ability to work with your client?

---

clinicians' formal training has ended, many avenues are available for ongoing development of multicultural skills. These include attending seminars and workshops, staying abreast of multicultural research, seeking consultation, and participating in informal supervision groups with other practitioners. Since multicultural therapy theory and research continues to grow rapidly, the ethical practitioner will be one who remains an active consumer of new information and tested skills. The ethical practitioner also is one who continues to look inside him- or herself for cultural biases and works to eliminate them.

At this point, turn to Exercise 6.4. A series of questions is posed as a way of helping you to take stock of your recent professional development activities related to multicultural counseling. We encourage practitioners to avail themselves of at least one of these activities every month. Although there is as yet insufficient data confirming the positive effect of professional development in multicultural counseling on ethical practice, we believe that active engagement in post–degree training in multicultural counseling has great value.

Engaging in thoughtful reflection about one's therapeutic relationship with clients also enhances ethical multicultural practice. When ethical questions or dilemmas arise, it is helpful to have a procedure in place to address these dilemmas. Consulting ethics codes may be a helpful first step, but because these codes are not designed to solve specific ethical dilemmas, they may fall short of providing the answers the practitioner is seeking. Certainly seeking and documenting the advice of colleagues, supervisors, or multicultural experts is good practice. In many states, "community standards" is the measure against which counselors' decisions and actions are

Table 6.1   Cultural Reading List

African American

The Autobiography of Malcolm X
Mama, Terry McMillan
Coffee Will Make You Black, April Sinclair
Their Eyes Were Watching God, Zora Neale Hurston
The Bluest Eye, Toni Morrison
The Color of Water, James McBride
Invisible Man, Ralph Ellison
A Choice of Weapons, Gordon Parks
Having Our Say, Sarah & Elizabeth Delany

Asian/Asian American

The Joy Luck Club, Amy Tan
The Woman Warrior, Maxine Hong Kingston
The Kitchen God's Wife, Amy Tan
The Hundred Secret Senses, Amy Tan
Snow Falling on Cedars, David Guterson
Memoirs of a Geisha, Arthur Golden

Latino

How the Garcia Girls Lost Their Accents, Julia Alvarez
One Hundred Years of Solitude, Gabriel Garcia Marquez
The House on Mango Street, Sandra Cisneros
The House of the Spirits, Isabel Allende

American Indian

Black Elk Speaks, John Neihardt
The Broken Cord, Michael Dorris
The Bingo Palace, Louise Erdrich
The Manly-Hearted Woman, Frederick Manfred
Grand Avenue, Greg Sarris
A Yellow Raft on Blue Water, Michael Dorris

Table 6.1   (Continued)

Women

The Women's Room, Marilyn French

Journal of a Solitude, May Sarton

The Company of Women, Mary Gordon

Talk Before Sleep, Elizabeth Berg

The Bell Jar, Sylvia Plath

She's Come Undone, Wally Lamb

The Deep End of the Ocean, Jacquelyn Mitchard

Jewel, Bret Lott

The Poisonwood Bible, Barbara Kingsolver

Lesbian/Gay

In Her Day, Rita Mae Brown

The Education of Harriet Hatfield, May Sarton

Loving Her, Ann Allen Shockley

The Mayor of Castro Street, Randy Shilts

Ruby Fruit Jungle, Rita Mae Brown

Fried Green Tomatoes, Fanny Flagg

Stone Butch Blues, Leslie Feinberg

---

weighed. Thus, documentation of consultation with colleagues is wise when confronting ethical dilemmas.

Counseling, clinical, and social work ethics committees also are sources of guidance. Their functions include educating members and answering inquiries about ethical courses of action in specific circumstances (Williams, 2001). Members' inquiries are typically responded to in a very timely manner, making these committees a valuable resource for the clinician facing a dilemma.

Models for ethical decision making have been proposed to help practitioners think through the dilemmas they face. These dilemmas often arise suddenly, without warning, requiring practitioners to "think on their feet." For example, suppose Maria, a client of color from a collectivistic culture,

---

Exercise 6.4   Professional Development in Multicultural Counseling

---

Mark the activities in the list below that you have engaged in during the past month:

I recognized a prejudice I have about certain people. _____

I talked to a colleague about a cultural issue. _____

I sought guidance about a cultural issue that arose in therapy. _____

I attended a multicultural training seminar. _____

I attended a cultural event. _____

I attended an event in which I was a racial minority. _____

I reflected on my racial identity and how it affects my work with clients. _____

I read a novel about a racial group other than my own. _____

I read a chapter or an article about multicultural issues. _____

I sought consultation or supervision about multicultural issues. _____

I talked to a friend or associate about how our racial difference affects our relationship. _____

I challenged a racist remark—my own or someone else's. _____

---

begins to think of you as "family" and asks you to attend her graduation and family celebration afterward. The question comes unexpectedly. Your mind races for a reply that, on one hand, conforms to ethical sanctions against dual relationships and, on the other hand, is responsive to your client's genuine valuing of her relationship with you as an esteemed "mentor." You search for a way to balance these factors with your knowledge that the client's cultural context embraces multiplicity in relationship roles. Western counseling norms of strict relationship boundaries are not emphasized in your client's culture.

Ethics experts have recommended several steps as helpful in working through ethical dilemmas. Welfel (1998), for example, proposed an ethical decision-making model consisting of the following nine steps:

Step 1: Develop Ethical Sensitivity

This implies that counselors have "done their ethics homework" (Welfel, 1998, p. 25); that is, they have the background knowledge in ethics through graduate study and familiarity with the ethics codes needed to make decisions, possibly under pressure.

Step 2: Define Dilemma and Options

Counselors must be able to clearly state the dilemma, first for themselves and later in possible consultations with others. Writing it down may be helpful at this point. What are all the possibilities for responding to the dilemma?

Step 3: Refer to Professional Standards

Counselors should review the ethics code for sections that apply directly to the ethical issue facing them. It may be the case that counselors are misinformed about what the codes actually state. Reviewing the actual language in the code can be a tremendous help to counselors as they try to clarify the issue at hand.

Step 4: Search Out Ethics Scholarship

Casebooks, articles, and other resources should be consulted. Ideally, therapists do so on an ongoing basis to heighten their familiarity with common ethical dilemmas and solutions. Such knowledge can serve them well in situations in which they must respond "on the spot." These resources can be very helpful as counselors begin to map out appropriate responses to ethical dilemmas they encounter.

Step 5: Apply Ethical Principles to the Situation

According to Welfel (1998), "The counselor who reaches Step 5 without clearly resolving his or her ethical dilemma must now conduct a more intensive analysis of the issues and rely on the philosophical literature and then on consultations with trusted colleagues" (p. 32).

Step 6: Consult With Supervisor and Respected Colleagues

Counselors are urged to share their dilemmas with trusted colleagues for several reasons, not the least of which is to help them feel less alone as they struggle to determine the best course of action. In addition, consulting colleagues can shed new light on or offer alternative ways of viewing a dilemma. Importantly, consultation and documentation thereof helps to establish "community standards," that is, the action other professionals would take or have taken in similar circumstances.

Step 7: Deliberate and Decide

At this point, counselors identify the action they will take, the pros and cons, and decide how to implement their decisions.

Step 8: Inform Supervisor, Implement and Document Actions

Counselors must now follow what they have determined to be the best course of action. Documentation of one's decisions, whom one consulted, the dates, content, and outcome of the consultations, the action taken, and reasons for the choices that were made are critical steps in the process.

Step 9: Reflect on the Experience

Welfel (1998) poses several questions intended to help counselors reflect on decisions they made in a way that will help them in future situations. One of the questions is key: Did I attend to the ethical dimensions of the situation as soon as they arose? This question provides a good starting point for a more specific discussion of ethical decision making within a multicultural context.

Ethical Decision Making
in a Multicultural Context

Using Welfel's steps as a framework, ethical decision making within a multicultural context necessitates several additional considerations. First, counselors must be knowledgeable about the culture(s) of their clients to anticipate situations in which ethics codes potentially conflict with non-Eurocentric cultures. Steinman, Richardson, and McEnroe (1998) stated that "until a situation is identified as a possible problem" (p. 18), the process of ethical decision making cannot begin. Though this may sound obvious, it has important implications for multicultural counseling. Counselors who have firsthand experience with or, at the very least, well-grounded knowledge of the client's culture—and how the culture varies from Eurocentric patterns—are in a better position to respond appropriately when ethical dilemmas arise. Below are three specific ethical considerations when working with clients from non-Eurocentric cultures.

Step 1: Anticipate Potential Conflicts

Ethical decision making within a multicultural context begins with enough awareness and knowledge about diverse cultures to recognize areas of potential conflict between the cultural worldview underlining professional codes and that of diverse clients. This point cannot be emphasized enough. Without adequate professional and personal preparation to work with culturally different clients, counselors run the risk of believing they are behaving ethically—when in fact they are discounting the significance of the client's culture and its impact on the treatment process. This is, in itself, an ethical violation. The task, then, is to balance cultural sensitivity and knowledge with ethical action.

The better acquainted the counselor is with the culture of the client, the more prepared he or she will likely be to handle ethical predicaments that may arise. When working with clients from cultures with which the practitioner is unfamiliar, we suggest several strategies counselors can undertake. Whenever possible, these options should be pursued prior to the first therapy session. The options include the following:

- Meet with an expert knowledgeable about the culture. Discussion of cultural patterns, norms, beliefs, and how they might arise in the therapy process would undoubtedly heighten your preparedness.

- Read about the culture. Much has been written on culture within the mental health fields and related disciplines such as sociology, history, and political science. Do not overlook these related areas, as historical and political factors profoundly affect the life experiences and relationships of many people of color.

- Cultivate friendships with people from other cultures. Rather than relying exclusively on outside expertise, develop ongoing relationships with diverse people and engage them in meaningful conversations about their experiences.

- Participate in self-awareness opportunities. Ongoing self-examination vis-à-vis issues of race, ethnicity, and culture can help you monitor your own countertransference. Look for workshops, conferences, and local seminars that address these issues and add your name to their mailing lists.

Step 2: Assess Cultural Sensitivity of Ethics Code

Mental health practitioners are expected to know and adhere to their ethics code. However, practitioners are usually not expected or required to demonstrate knowledge about their codes' sensitivity to diverse cultures. In the scenario with Maria, some practitioners might automatically respond in a manner consistent with what they believe their ethics code dictates; that is, they might explain to Maria that their participation in her graduation events would constitute a dual relationship, which would be against professional ethics. Although this may appear to be good practice, it may in fact not sufficiently take into account Maria's cultural assumptions and practices and the therapeutic impact of declining her invitation on the basis of a set of written "rules."

The ACA, APA, and NASW ethics codes contain statements cautioning about dual relationships. Section A.6.a of the ACA (1995) code of ethics advises that, "Counselors make every effort to avoid dual relationships with clients that could impair professional judgment or increase the risk of harm to clients." The code provides several examples of such relationships, including familial, social, business, and close personal relationships with clients.

Section 3.05 of the APA (2002) code, "Multiple Relationships," cautions psychologists against "entering into a multiple relationship if the multiple relationship could reasonably be expected to impair the psychologist's objectivity, competence, or effectiveness." Psychologists are expected to consider the potential for harm or exploitation of the client or impairment of the psychologist's objectivity.

The first section of the NASW (1996) code of ethics details the responsibilities of social workers to their clients. Subsection 1.06c states that, "Social workers should not engage in dual or multiple relationships with clients or former clients in which there is a risk of exploitation or potential harm to the client." This section also states that these relationships may be simultaneous or consecutive.

It is clear that none of the codes prohibits dual relationships outright. Instead, each clarifies its stance with the proviso that counselors avoid the risk of exploiting or otherwise harming their clients if they engage in dual relationships. Indeed, the APA code (2002) states, "Multiple relationships that would not reasonably be expected to cause impairment or risk exploitation or harm are not unethical" (Section 3.05a). Complicating this issue are the ethics codes' stances on cultural competence. Each of the codes contains statements similar to that in the preamble of the ACA (1995) code of ethics, that members are to "embrace a cross-cultural approach in support of the worth, dignity, potential, and uniqueness of each individual." It is clear that practitioners' familiarity with the language of the ethics codes is a necessary component of arriving at an ethical decision. In the case of Maria, knowledge of the specific language of the code prompts additional questions for the counselor to ask him or herself:

> Is there a risk of harm or exploitation if I attend Maria's events?

> Do I risk harming Maria if I do not attend?

> What decision, attending or not attending, would best respect Maria's dignity?

> How can I respond in a way that reflects Maria's worth as an individual and as a client about whom I care?

Step 3: Balance Culture and Ethical Codes

In the case of Maria, several responses to her request are possible, not all of which are sensitive to both her culture and ethical principles. Below are several options, with brief discussions of the extent to which each balances culture with consideration of professional ethical codes.

1. Explain to Maria that the professional ethics codes do not permit your participation in her graduation events. This is an example of a response emanating from a Eurocentric perspective without consideration of Maria's cultural practices. It is not a culturally sensitive response. It begs the question, Who is being protected—the practitioner or the client?

2. Ask Maria to share with you why it would be important to her for you to attend. This response is more culturally sensitive than the first but nevertheless emanates from a Eurocentric perspective. Inherent in questioning Maria's motives is the assumption that her request merits scrutiny.

3. Ask Maria to share with you how it would feel to her if you did or did not attend. Similar to Response 2, this one suggests that her request must be analyzed without sharing why. The problem is not as much the response itself as the timing of it. That is, it might be better to genuinely thank Maria for the invitation before exploring her reactions to your options.

4. Accept Maria's invitation to attend because you believe not doing so would deeply offend her and risk the therapeutic alliance. This is an example of a practitioner perhaps more concerned with political correctness than with balancing culture with ethical standards. An immediate acceptance appears not to adequately weigh the costs and benefits of agreeing to attend.

5. Explain your dilemma to Maria and tell her you wish to consult with a colleague from her ethnic background before you make a decision. This response begins to address the issue of weighing cultural factors against ethical constraints. Also, it appropriately places the dilemma in the therapist's hands; that is, it positions the dilemma as one embedded in ethical constraints rather than in Maria's request. However, in suggesting a consultation, the practitioner fails to draw on Maria's wisdom.

6. Tell Maria you feel honored to be asked but that her invitation presents a dilemma for you. We recommend that therapists preface their response to requests like Maria's with a culturally sensitive statement such as this. This particular response not only places the problem squarely in the therapist's hands but also demystifies the therapist's decision-making process by sharing the dilemma with the client. This shows respect for the client's wisdom. It may be appropriate to follow this response with Response 3.

Summary and Key Points

Knowledge of the worldviews, values, behavioral patterns, and perspectives on mental health of traditional ethnic cultures is a cornerstone of culturally competent treatment. Coupled with skillful supervision that is sensitive to ethnic and racial nuances in both the suppervisory process and the relationship between the supervisee and client, mental health practitioners are in an optimal position to think through ethical dilemmas related to their work with culturally diverse clients.

Key points in this chapter include the importance to practitioners of the following:

- Recognizing the cultural complexity of clients rather than imposing simplistic cultural descriptions that often stereotype members of an ethnic group
- Knowledge about clients' racial identity development status as part of their complexity
- Encouraging supervisors to explore racial and cultural differences in supervision and counseling processes
- Continually monitoring their own cultural assumptions while regularly availing themselves of opportunities to increase their multicultural competence
- Applying culturally inclusive ethical decision-making processes as ethical questions and dilemmas arise

Section III

Overview

Proposing thoughtful, culturally competent, and ethical approaches to clinical and counseling practice, supervision, and training has been the focus of this book. Ethics codes of the ACA, APA, and NASW, criticized for their culturally encapsulated frameworks (Ivey, 1987; LaFromboise, Foster, & James, 1995; Pedersen, 1995; Sue, Arredondo, & McDavis, 1992), have undergone periodic review and revision. These codes, as discussed in previous sections of this book, now explicitly state the need for sensitivity to issues of race, ethnicity, culture, gender, sexual orientation, and other stigmatized dimensions of human experience. The codes address the need for cultural competence in a range of professional activities and settings, including supervision, practice, and research.

The heightened awareness of the importance of cultural considerations in mental health practice provides a basis upon which culturally competent, ethical decision-making models may be constructed. We have argued in this book that few concrete guidelines exist for addressing common ethical dilemmas from a multiculturally competent stance. Codes of ethics cannot meet this challenge, as they must necessarily be broad based; they can offer guidance but cannot and should not be relied upon to solve practical ethical dilemmas involving cultural issues. So, where can counselors and clinicians turn for concrete assistance with addressing ethical dilemmas in a culturally responsive manner?

The remainder of the book is intended to address the need for a decision-making framework and concrete guidelines for ethical problem solving in a multicultural context. The six chapters in this section address areas of ethics codes that in our experience have repeatedly posed unique cultural dilemmas for practitioners. These areas are dual relationships (Chapter 7), unintentional cultural bias (Chapter 8), client welfare (Chapter 9), bartering for services (Chapter 10), fostering dependency (Chapter 11), and practicing beyond one's competence (Chapter 12). Our selection of these areas is not intended to suggest that these are the only areas of practice in which ethical dilemmas related to cultural differences arise. Rather, these six areas appear to us to raise especially unique challenges for practitioners wishing to respond both to ethical guidelines and to the cultural context of their work with clients. Our intention is to sort of "think out loud," that is, to reveal steps involved in discerning the key issues and resolving the dilemmas posed in the critical incidents.

We begin each chapter by highlighting sections of the ACA, APA, and NASW ethics codes relevant to the practice area under discussion. Thus, for the area of dual relationships, relevant sections from each of the professional ethics codes are presented to remind readers of the standards against which ethical practice is measured. The discussion that follows explores potential problems between the principles set forth in the codes and cultural patterns often at odds with these ethical principles. Each discussion is capped with questions for reflection and discussion. Undoubtedly, it is obvious from everything we have written that we place a high value on critical thinking and questioning. We believe that it is important for practitioners, especially at the training stage, to take nothing for granted. That is, we believe it is healthier to question our beliefs, the values underlying our profession and ethics codes, and the interplay among these factors and the needs of the clients we serve than to merely comply with codes of conduct and standards of practice.

Critical ethical dilemmas are presented in each chapter as vehicles for questioning, analyzing, and discussing ethics in a multicultural context. We have made a point of including information about the racial and/or ethnic backgrounds of the key characters in the scenarios, as well as additional relevant cultural information, such as sexual orientation, socioeconomic status, gender, and age. Our emphasis on these cultural factors does not mean that we are minimizing other significant cultural variables, such as physical ability, religious or spiritual orientation, and educational background. Indeed, we address these factors in follow-up questions and encourage students to actively consider the impact of all potentially relevant cultural factors in their discussions of the incidents.

Threads of several incidents that appear in this section were presented earlier in the book. The incidents are more fully elaborated on in the next six chapters and presented in the context of the ethical dilemmas they pose. Three of the critical incidents presented in the following chapters were sent to experts in multicultural counseling and psychotherapy, who were asked to respond in a way that shows a balance between ethical and cultural issues. In our selection of multicultural experts, we strove for heterogeneity with regard to race/ethnicity, gender, and professional affiliation. As a result, the experts whose responses appear in the following chapters reflect differences in racial and ethnic background, gender, sexual orientation, and professional identity. We want students and practitioners to get a sense of how multicultural experts process information about ethical dilemmas and how they might respond to actual ethical incidents. Toward that end, we asked experts to respond to a specific set of questions reflecting key areas of ethical multicultural practice. The questions, which appear in Chapter 7, involve hearing the client's story with a "cultural ear": identifying contextual issues that affect treatment, identifying relevant ethical questions and considerations, being mindful of differences and similarities between Eurocentric and multicultural perspectives on the incident, and proposing appropriate courses of action that take into consideration each of these points.

Our intention is for the questions and experts' responses to serve as a springboard for classroom discussion of ethical incidents presented in each chapter. The ethical incidents are intended to stimulate discussion that builds upon the decision-making processes and courses of action proposed by the experts. We encourage instructors to use the questions following each incident as a basis for classroom discussion. These incidents are also designed for use as examples for applying the decision-making model that we proposed in the previous chapter for ethical thinking within in a multicultural context. Finally, we include several exercises in these chapters. These exercises are designed to further develop students' capacities to think critically and ethically about cultural dilemmas.

7

Dual Relationships

ACA Code

Section A.6.a of the 1995 ACA code of ethics advises that, "Counselors make every effort to avoid dual relationships with clients that could impair professional judgment or increase the risk of harm to clients." The code provides several examples of such relationships, including familial, social, business, and close personal relationships with clients.

APA Code

Section 3.06 of the 2002 APA code, "Conflict of Interest," cautions psychologists about "taking on a professional role when personal, scientific, professional, legal, financial, or other interests or relationships could reasonably be expected to impair their objectivity, competence or effectiveness."

NASW Code

The first section of the 1996 NASW code of ethics details the responsibilities of social workers to their clients. Subsection 1.06.c states that, "Social workers should not engage in dual or multiple relationships with clients or former clients in which there is a risk of exploitation or potential harm to the client." This section also states that these relationships may be simultaneous or consecutive.

* * *

The counseling, psychology, and social work professions have their bases in Eurocentric norms and values. We have emphasized this point throughout the book and continue to do so because recognition of the culturally encapsulated nature of our professions and their codes of ethics is essential to competent multicultural practice. That is, it is critical that helping professionals are cognizant that the ethics codes reflect a particular cultural worldview, with its attendant values. Hope Landrine (1995), an African American feminist psychologist, raised the often overlooked issue of the importance of naming European American culture as a culture. Her point, with which we wholeheartedly agree, was that to inspect "other" (read non-European, non-White) cultural norms and patterns and fail to do so for European/White culture was to perpetuate the racist idea that White culture is normative, or given.

With Landrine's point in mind, part of our purpose has been to point out areas of the ACA (1995) *Code of Ethics and Standards of Practice*, the APA (2002) *Ethical Principles of Psychologists and Code of Conduct*, and the NASW (1996) *Code of Ethics* that reflect Eurocentric values. For example, the valuing of detachment over attachment, distance over closeness, and objectivity over influence are evident in these ethics codes' admonitions against dual relationships and reveal a cultural bias toward bounded as opposed to more fluid relationships.

We are not suggesting that it is wrong to operate from a cultural perspective. Indeed, it is impossible not to; each and every one of us operates from a cultural perspective. A fundamental aspect of being human is that we reflect the values we learn from the culture(s) that has shaped us—which is the very point we are emphasizing. The task of examining and exposing the underlying Eurocentric cultural assumptions inherent in the codes of ethics of the mental health professions is to name these codes as *culturally embedded* rather than *universally applicable*. Just as Afrocentric or feminist values fail to address the realities and identities of many of the clients with whom we work, so too do Eurocentric values and the ethical guidelines and professional practices based upon them. The failure of any one of these orientations to apply to all clients does not make it fundamentally wrong, only inappropriate under certain circumstances. It is this last point that we wish to illuminate in the critical ethical incidents that follow.

Pedersen (1995) cautioned counselors to examine the bias inherent in definitions of relationships that fail to incorporate the possibility that for many cultures, fluidity, engagement across hierarchical lines, and interdependence are more normative than strict relational boundaries. The ethics code sections on dual relationships rest on an assumption that more objective, impartial, and detached relationships between counselors and clients are more therapeutic. The inverse of this assumption is that closer involvement in the lives of the people we help necessarily mitigates sound professional judgment. These assumptions are culturally biased.

By challenging these assumptions, we are not suggesting that involvement in our clients' lives outside of the office environment is always productive from a professional standpoint. Instead, we are proposing that Western assumptions of individuality and clear relational boundaries underlying mental health ethics codes and practices be critically examined for cultural embeddedness rather than adhered to without question. Such an examination may assist counselors in identifying the benefit to some clients of beliefs and assumptions stemming from non-Western cultural norms. These assumptions include the belief in the healing effects of close personal relationships with influential community leaders and healers such as trusted elders, tribal healers, or family pastors from whom people frequently seek spiritual guidance (Sue & Sue, 1999). Traditional healers typically have been very involved and influential in the lives of the people in their communities. Their healing practices are not isolated to sanctioned institutional settings, but cross over into families' homes and everyday lives.

Most mental health professionals in North America, White and non-White, have been and continue to be trained in Western mental health paradigms, even as sociocultural demographics reveal that the population of people of color is surpassing that of Whites in many regions. This demographic shift gives rise to challenges to the dominant Western cultural paradigm underlying the mental health professions. As White and non-White practitioners work increasingly with clients of color whose worldviews are not consonant with Western frameworks, critical questioning is needed of the appropriateness of what have been deemed to be normative mental health practices. Such questioning, as we have suggested throughout this book, can lead to new ways of thinking about the practice of mental health and the ethical codes that guide these practices. Rather than regarding the sanction against dual relationships as if it were set in stone, we are advocating what we consider to be a healthy process of reexamining this assumption.

The first step in culturally inclusive ethical decision making is for practitioners to ask themselves critical questions. For example, therapists-in-training can begin to ask themselves questions such as the following and share their thoughts in discussion with colleagues.

Questions for Reflection and Discussion

1. What is my comfort level with personal self-disclosure in psychotherapy? How will I respond to a client who has a need to know me on a more personal level before he or she can trust me? How does my definition of appropriate interpersonal boundaries in therapy correspond with my client's efforts to establish trust in a manner consistent with his or her own cultural practices?

2. How do I respond to a client who asks me to help a family member with a dilemma? How do I respect and respond to this client's trust in me while at the same time practice in a manner that adheres to my professional ethics code?

3. What have been my own experiences with therapists I trusted and respected? What enabled these therapists to help me work through my problems? What steps or processes were involved in my learning to trust my therapist? What kinds of interactions with my therapist would have attenuated the therapy relationship?

4. How are relationships defined in different cultures? To whom do people go for help? How are culturally based healers effective with those they help? Are there procedures these healers use that could be integrated into Western approaches to therapy?

5. Have I ever chosen to work with a therapist whose race or ethnic background was different from mine? If so, were aspects of the therapy positively affected by our differences? Were aspects of the therapy negatively affected by our differences? Did we find a way to work through problematic aspects of our differences? If not, why not? If so, what made this possible? Is it the case that contrasting styles of relationship affected the therapy process?

6. Do the ethics codes' cautions against dual relationships work more as protection for the practitioner or the client?

Two critical ethical incidents follow. These incidents are based on real cases (with identifying information disguised) we have seen or worked with in supervision and consultation. Threads of some of the cases appearing in this and subsequent chapters were presented in earlier chapters as exercises for critical thinking about ethical issues. The incidents in this chapter are more fully drawn to reveal dilemmas regarding dual relationships. Table 7.1 contains the questions multicultural experts were asked to respond to in their analyses of incidents that appear in subsequent chapters. We present the questions here to challenge students to address them as they discuss the following incidents.

Ethical Dilemma 1

Dr. Frank Thompson, a single, African American male therapist in his late 20s, practices in a small, predominantly White college community in the East. Most of the relatively few African Americans in this community know one another, attend the same Methodist church, and socialize with one another. Because the community is small, Frank frequently finds himself at church and social gatherings with current and former clients. Frank

---

Table 7.1   The Client's Story

Discuss the importance of accurately hearing the client's story; that is, what are we hearing when we listen to the details of this ethical incident case with a "cultural ear?" How do our own ethnic and cultural backgrounds affect our hearing of the case? What avenues of exploration of the client's story open up when culture becomes a focal point?

Cultural Considerations

What are the questions therapists need to be asking about the cultural issues suggested in the incident? What might therapists want to explore about their own and/or the client's cultural background that would affect their handling of this incident? Are the cultural backgrounds of other people involved in the incident relevant?

Ethical Concerns and Questions

What are the important ethical issues to consider in the incident? Which ethics codes might have been violated? Do cultural elements affect how ethics codes might apply in this incident? Are the ethical questions or issues different when culture fails to be considered?

Monocultural and Multicultural Perspectives

How are Western/monocultural and multicultural perspectives similar and different when applied to this incident? How do Western mental health education, training, and practice aid and/or hinder in examining the incident from a multicultural perspective?

Options for Appropriate Action

What are some options for ethical thinking and behavior in this incident? What does it look like when culture and ethics are brought into balance? What does it look like when they are not?

---

has always made it a point to explain to his clients that due to ethical constraints, he cannot socialize with them when he encounters them in these settings.

Frank is seen in his community as an expert in African American psychology. He is frequently called on to consult with local college personnel about racial and cultural issues and often offers workshops on these topics.

Some of his clients are former workshop attendees, and many are actively involved with the college's efforts to increase its cultural diversity. In fact, some of his current clients have heard about his workshops and have expressed an interest in attending. Frank, not long out of graduate training and well aware of proscriptions against dual relationships, has discouraged his clients from enrolling in his workshops. He also has been careful to avoid actively interacting with his clients when he sees them at church or in other settings in the community.

However, Frank is finding it increasingly difficult to maintain these boundaries. He has begun to question the practicality of compartmentalizing his personal and professional life. He does not want to discontinue his consultation with the college, his involvement with his church, or his interest in community issues. However, he is unsure of how to balance what presently appear to him to be competing needs for a satisfying lifestyle, an active professional life, and real relationships with members of the Black community.

Frank grew up in a large, predominantly Black community, also in the East. He enjoyed active involvement with an extended family of aunts, uncles, cousins, and others not biologically related to him but considered family members. His father was a civic leader and his mother a librarian. Community leaders such as pastors, city council members, and teachers were frequently at his house engaging with his parents in lively debates about politics and race relations. People helped each other financially, emotionally, and spiritually as needed. Frank became drawn to the mental health profession as a way to personally contribute to the legacy of support and close interpersonal connection he experienced growing up.

Questions for Classroom Discussion

1. How has Frank's cultural upbringing contributed to his present dilemma?

2. How are professional ethics and cultural realities at odds in the incident?

3. What are some key questions you might wish to ask Frank to guide his decision making?

4. How would you advise Frank if he sought your consultation; that is, what is the next step Frank should take?

Ethical Dilemma 2

Marta, a Latina client in her early 30s, has been seeing Dr. Tinsdale, a White female therapist in her 50s, for several months for psychotherapy related to Marta's history of sexual abuse. Dr. Tinsdale is an expert in violence against women and the only practitioner with this expertise in the rural community in the Northwest where they live. Marta has shared with

Dr. Tinsdale her knowledge that several women in her circle of friends have experienced physical and sexual abuse of various kinds. Marta's friends are mostly Latina and Black. Each of these women, like Marta herself, struggles with issues of self-acceptance and trust. Marta's friends have listened to and been inspired by Marta's journey toward greater self-respect through her work with Dr. Tinsdale. They and Marta would like Dr. Tinsdale to facilitate a women's sexual abuse survivors' group in which they, Marta, and others could participate.

Dr. Tinsdale, sympathetic to Marta's request, is very interested in facilitating such a group. However, she is concerned about maintaining relational boundaries with Marta and wonders about possible complications in facilitating a group in which Marta is a member while seeing Marta individually. Also, Dr. Tinsdale isn't sure whether treating Marta's friends constitutes dual or multiple relationships. She recognizes that if she decides not to offer the group, these women will not get the help they desire because there are no other practitioners available with Dr. Tinsdale's expertise. Dr. Tinsdale feels torn between ethical constraints and the very real needs of the women who are seeking her help.

Questions for Classroom Discussion

1. What are the ethical questions and concerns in this incident?

2. Of what significance is the fact that Marta and her friends are mostly women of color seeking assistance from a White therapist? Would your thinking about how to handle Dr. Tinsdale's dilemma be different if Marta and her friends were White?

3. Would Dr. Tinsdale experience her dilemma differently if she were Latina? How does her race potentially affect her view of the ethical dilemma?

4. Let us assume that Dr. Tinsdale has had no experience with Latina clients prior to treating Marta. Let's also assume that race and ethnicity have not been explored in Marta's therapy because gender issues have been given priority. How does this information affect your thinking about the ethical issues involved in this case?

5. Is there a reasonable potential for harm or exploitation of Marta or her friends if Dr. Tinsdale decided to start the group?

Dr. Tinsdale seeks your consultation about how she should proceed with the request to run a group on violence against women. She tells you that she considers herself a radical lesbian feminist but has not disclosed this to Marta or to anyone else in the community. How does this information affect your thinking about this case?

Apply the three multicultural decision-making steps presented in Table 7.1. How might Dr. Tinsdale have prepared herself for the possibility that this dilemma would arise? How can culture and ethical guidelines be balanced in this case?

Classroom Exercises

1. Ask each student to think of a hypothetical example of an *ethical* dual relationship with multicultural elements. Have students share and discuss their examples.

2. Set up a role play based on one of the two ethical incidents above. Give students the opportunity to practice various responses to situations in which dual relationships are involved.

Summary and Key Points

The concept of dual relationships and the mental health codes and practices emanating from them are culturally embedded. In this chapter we challenge students to examine the cultural assumptions underlying proscriptions against dual relationships.

The following are key points for practitioners to consider:

*   Their own definitions of healthy versus unhealthy boundaries in relationships
*   Cultural contexts in which these definitions are shaped
*   The possibility that non-Western cultural formulations of relationships are as valid as Western ones when applied appropriately in mental health work
*   Circumstances under which different (i.e., non-Western) relational practices on the part of therapists may be advised when working with various clients
*   How flexible they are willing to be when the welfare of the client is best served by therapist self-disclosure

8

Unintentional Cultural Bias

ACA Code

Section A.2.a of the ACA (1995) code states, "Counselors do not condone or engage in discrimination based on age, color, culture, disability, ethnic group, gender, race, religion, sexual orientation, marital status, or socio-economic status."

APA Code

The general principles of the 2002 APA code include the statement (Principle E),

> Psychologists try to eliminate the effect on their work of biases based on [age, gender, gender identity, race, ethnicity, culture, national origin, religion, sexual orientation, disability, language, and socioeconomic status], and they do not knowingly participate in or condone activities of others based upon such prejudices.

NASW Code

The NASW (1996) code states,

> Social workers should act to prevent and eliminate domination, exploitation, and discrimination against any person, group, or class on the basis of race, ethnicity, national origin, color, age, religion, sex, sexual orientation, marital status, political belief, mental or physical disability, or any other preference, personal characteristic, or status.

* * *

All mental health codes of ethics include statements prohibiting practitioners from engaging in deliberate acts of racism, sexism, homophobia, and other forms of bias and discrimination. Although it is likely that most mental health practitioners do not engage in overt acts of discrimination, it is often less clear when discrimination is more indirect. Mental health codes fail to address the myriad ways in which unintentional bias may be exhibited. Ridley (1995) discussed numerous examples of covert racism in counseling and therapy. Practitioners being overconfident in their clinical judgment, attributing paranoia to clients who do not easily disclose to them, over-identifying with the client, and being color-blind—that is, thinking that treating everyone as the same assures fair and equitable treatment—are examples of covert, or unintentional, bias.

In our experience as counselor educators, we have found that the unintentional forms of racism, sexism, and homophobia are far more salient than intentional bias and discrimination. Students and supervisees wish to see themselves as caring and accepting people. Their discovery of racist or sexist attitudes and beliefs within themselves often comes as an unexpected and unwelcome surprise to them. It is difficult for many people to reconcile their personal prejudices with their self-images as decent and moral human beings. This cognitive dissonance is what makes unintentional prejudice difficult to address, that is, the mistaken belief that finding prejudice in one-self somehow makes one a "bad" person. Counselor educators must give students "permission" to uncover and examine their biases, create a safe environment for doing so, and recognize the potential impact of those biases on the therapy process. Exercises 8.1 and 8.2 are designed as icebreakers for discussions of race in the counselor education classroom.

Racial identity development models (Hardiman, 2001; Helms & Cook, 1999; Jackson, 2001; Parham, 1989) provide a useful framework for beginning the process of self-examination for unintentional bias. These models propose "stages" of consciousness about the manner in which race has been constructed in the United States and its psychological impact. The identity development models make the assumption that everyone, regardless of race, is affected by systems of racial stratification that have been in place in our society for generations. That everyone has been affected by race is not to say that everyone is aware of its impact. Indeed, models for people of color and Whites typically begin with a stage of naïveté, that is, lack of awareness of the salience and consequences of racial dynamics. As individuals become aware of racial differences, often at an early age, the potential for racial understanding and connection grows. Unfortunately, so, too, does the potential for intolerance.

We suggest that students acquaint themselves with the various models of racial identity development. Helms and Cook (1999) is a good resource for models pertaining to Whites and people of color. Wijeyesinghe and Jackson (2001) is an excellent resource as well, with the advantage that it

---

Exercise 8.1   Starting the Conversation About Race

Part I

Pose the following question to participants: What makes it hard for you to talk about race?

Ask participants to take a few moments to think about the question silently before sharing their responses. Assure them that there are no "right" or "wrong" responses. Encourage them to be as honest with themselves and the class as they can.

Ask participants to share their responses as you write them on the board. Discuss the responses. Are there any apparent patterns?

Discuss their internal reactions to the question itself. Did you feel uncomfortable with the question? Challenged by it? Confused?

Part II

Pose the question: What do you need to feel safe when talking about race?

(Follow the same steps as above.)

Exercise 8.2   How Have I Been Affected By Race?

Consider the following questions:

1. What has been my experience(s) talking about racial issues with people of the same race? Of another race?
2. How have these experiences affected my willingness to continue to talk about race with other people?

Share your responses with others in the group. Afterward, engage in the following small group discussion:

1. Tell your group about your multicultural experiences.
2. What impact have your experiences had on your feelings about other racial groups?
3. With which racial groups do you feel *least* familiar? *Most* familiar?
4. How well do you think your experiences have prepared you for multicultural work with individuals and families?

Table 8.1   Resources on White Racial Identity Development

Fine, M., Weis, L., Powell, L. C., & Wong, L. M. (Eds.). (1997). *Off-White: Readings on race, power, and society.* New York: Routledge.

Frankenberg, R. (1993). *White women, race matters: The social construction of whiteness.* Minneapolis: University of Minnesota Press.

Helms, J. E. (Ed.). (1990). *Black and White racial identity: Theory, research, and practice.* New York: Greenwood.

Johnson, A. G. (2001). *Privilege, power, and difference.* New York: McGraw-Hill.

Katz, J. H. (1978). *White awareness: Handbook for anti-racism training.* Norman: University of Oklahoma Press.

Kiselica, M. S. (Ed.). (1999). *Confronting prejudice and racism during multicultural training.* Alexandria, VA: American Counseling Association.

Kivel, P. (1996). *Uprooting racism: How White people can work for racial justice.* Gabriola Island, British Columbia, Canada: New Society.

Ponterotto, J. G. (1988). Racial consciousness development among White counselor education trainees: A stage model. *Journal of Multicultural Counseling and Development, 16,* 146-156.

Reynolds, T. L., & Ginter, E. J. (Eds.). (1999). *Racism: Healing its effects* [Special Issue]. *Journal of Counseling and Development, 77*(1).

Ridley, C. R. (1995). *Overcoming unintentional racism in counseling and therapy: A practitioner's guide to intentional intervention.* Thousand Oaks, CA: Sage.

Rowe, W., Bennett, S. K., & Atkinson, D. R. (1994). White racial identity models: A critique and alternative proposal. *The Counseling Psychologist, 23,* 364-367.

Schneider, B. (Ed.). (1998, Spring). *Whiteness: What is it?* [Special Issue]. *Hungry Mind Review.* St. Paul, MN: R. David Unowski.

Terry, R. W. (1970). *For Whites only.* Grand Rapids, MI: Eerdmans.

also covers models of identity development for multiracial individuals. Other resources are cited in Table 8.1.

Familiarity with the models can assist students in identifying phases in their own journeys and current status with regard to racial consciousness. These identity models normalize the notion that each of us carries prejudices of which we may be unaware. Recognition of this can help to increase students' comfort in uncovering and sharing their unintentional biases. Tables 8.2, 8.3, and 8.4 present summarized versions of three models of racial identity development.

Exploration and discussion of students' journeys toward increased racial understanding is an important step toward reducing unintentional bias. Exercise 8.3 is designed to facilitate such exploration and discussion. I (CBW) usually prepare students for this exercise by providing many examples of progressive, regressive, and parallel (Helms & Cook, 1999)

Table 8.2 Racial Identity Development Model for People of Color

Naive

- Little or no conscious social awareness of race or racism
- Vulnerability to worldviews of influential others, such as parents
- Curiosity about obvious racial differences without hostility or fear

Preencounter/Conformity/Acceptance

- Internalized racism; feelings of inferiority, inadequacy, shame
- Preoccupation with overcoming stigma of race and seeking White approval
- Eurocentric cultural perspective (i.e., identification with Western values)
- Dualistic thinking (White is good; non-White is bad)
- Social goal: assimilation-integration with Whites
- Anti-Black sentiment (extreme stance)

Encounter/Dissonance/Resistance

- Active questioning about one's personal racial identity
- Triggers may include events, workshops, personal encounters, or being the target of racism
- Self-examination of internalized racism
- Person begins to reinterpret his or her world and validate his or her new perceptions
- Period of conflict, confusion, cognitive dissonance
- Person decides to start the journey toward a new racial identity

Immersion/Redefinition

- A stage of psychological metamorphosis
- Rejection of "old self" in which racism was internalized
- Thirst for learning about one's racial group
- Intensive period of self-discovery
- Period of unlearning internalized racism (confronting the racial anti-self)
- For some, rejection of White people and values
- Formation of new referent group reflecting one's own race
- Dualistic thinking (non-White is good; White is bad)
- Social withdrawal from Whites sometimes necessary
- Demonstrative displays of racial identity (i.e., "proving" oneself to others)
- Anger, guilt, insecurity in new identity

Internalization/Introspection

- Affective and cognitive openness (rather than either/or thinking)
- Ideological flexibility; pluralistic and nonracist perspective

(Continued)

Table 8.2 (Continued)

- Integration and synthesis of new worldview into all areas of one's life
- Reduction of psychological stress related to racial identity
- Self-confidence
- Concern with ethnocentric basis of judging others
- Critical, complex thinking about self and others
- Resolution of conflicts between old and new identities

Commitment/Integrative Awareness

- Action toward social change

SOURCE: Synthesis of Cross, Parham, and Helms (1991); Helms and Cook (1999); Jackson (2001); Parham (1989).

therapist-client interactions based on racial identity stages. *Progressive therapeutic interactions* are those in which the therapist's response reflects a more advanced stage of racial identity development than the client's; *regressive interactions* reflect therapist responses at a less developed stage than client's; and *parallel interactions* are those in which therapist and client interactions are at similar stages of racial consciousness. Helms and Cook (1999) provide useful examples of therapist-client interactions at the various levels and suggests that all three levels may be evidenced in a single therapeutic session.

Codes of ethics for the three mental health professions are clear in their admonitions against the imposition of therapists' cultural biases on clients. These codes do not limit their statements to race and ethnicity but also include gender, age, language, sexual orientation, and other potential areas of cultural bias. Exercises and discussions similar to those suggested throughout this chapter can be applied to these areas. Furthermore, models of gender consciousness development (Downing & Roush, 1985) and lesbian/gay identity development (Cass, 1990) can be helpful resources for practitioners interested in uncovering unconscious biases toward women and sexual minorities. An activity designed to begin exploration of students' language, age, gender, religious, and other biases is presented in Exercise 8.4.

A final point about unintentional bias we wish to make before turning to the ethical incidents is the importance of understanding that racial oppression occurs on at least four levels: individual, interpersonal, institutional, and cultural (Ponterotto & Pedersen, 1993). *Individual oppression,* or prejudice, refers to people's attitudes about others, which may or may not be overtly expressed. *Interpersonal prejudice* is present when people base their overt interactions with others on personal attributes about which they harbor negative thoughts and feelings. *Institutional oppression* is

Table 8.3 White Racial Identity Development Model

Naive

- Chronologically, up to 5 years old
- Innocent curiosity about racial differences
- Seeing racial difference without negative evaluation

Acceptance/Contact

- Learning cultural evaluations about racial difference (begins around age 3)
- Accepting "Whiteness" as normative: "Others" (i.e., people of color) have differences; "we" (i.e., Whites) don't
- Absorbing the cultural myths about race (e.g., who is beautiful, dangerous, smart, or lazy)
- In its active form: expressing racial hatred, belonging to hate group, engaging in hate crimes, etc. (small percentage of population)
- In its passive form: not confronting racism
- Denial of racism, defensiveness ("I'm not racist")

Resistance/Disintegration

- Triggered via personal encounter, confusing moral dilemmas regarding racial disparities, enlightenment through education, etc.
- Questioning and challenging racism
- Uncertainty about how to relate to people of color (e.g., overly friendly, color-blind, color-conscious)
- Examination of White privilege and own participation in racism
- Examination of unconscious internalization of White norms (e.g., paternalism, "Let me help you")
- Isolation from other Whites (sometimes due to not fitting in anymore, being ostracized, feeling more enlightened than other Whites)
- "Change-back" pressure from other Whites (difficulty maintaining new awareness; need contact with and support from other like-minded Whites)
- Easy to revert back to acceptance (Both Hardiman and Helms contend that most Whites cannot tolerate sense of estrangement from other Whites associated with this stage)
- Anger, self blame, guilt (you "see and know too much")

Reintegration (Helms & Cook)

- Process of mitigating the anxiety of the disintegration stage
- Reduction of cognitive dissonance by conforming to surrounding social standards with regard to race
- Selective perception and distortion of information

(Continued)

Table 8.3   (Continued)

Pseudo-Independence (Helms & Cook)

- Identification with nonracist Whites
- Being racist seen as being a "bad" person
- Belief that people of color who conform to White standards are better, more competent, or less threatening

Redefinition/Immersion

- Learning about one's White ethnic background
- Redefining one's relationship with other Whites and with people of color
- Reading autobiographies of others who have made the same journey
- Involvement in antiracism training
- Connecting with other Whites on same journey
- Separating being White from being racist (establishing a nonracist White identity)
- New worldview becomes part of one's every role
- Mission no longer is to "save" people of color, but to understand "Whites" (i.e., redirection of energy toward self rather than helping others)
- Sorting out issues around being in a socially constructed "superior" group
- Empathy rather than defensiveness regarding the anger felt by many people of color toward Whites
- Proactive stance against racism, yet picking your battles
- Understanding that White norms are but one set among many

Internalization/Autonomy

- Clear self-interest in challenging racism and White privilege
- Understanding connections among "isms"
- Cultural and racial identity continue to be explored and understood
- Development of multicultural interpersonal connections
- Cognitive flexibility in viewing oneself and others with regard to racism

SOURCE: Synthesis of Hardiman (2001) and Helms and Cook (1999).

visibly reflected in the dominance of White people in positions of leadership and power in the United States and less visibly in the cultural norms and values that underlie institutional practices. *Cultural oppression* is the hardest to articulate because it permeates almost every aspect of the social climate in which we live. It is evidenced, for example, in the preponderance of negative and stereotypical media portrayals of racial minorities, women, and sexual minorities. It is also embedded in our language. The terms

---

Table 8.4   Types of White Racial Consciousness

Avoidant

Dismisses racial issues as irrelevant. Issues concerning people of color are not viewed as affecting one's day-to-day life. Little to no consciousness about how race shapes one's life experience as a White person.

Dependent

Adopts the thinking of influential others. Beliefs about people of color are absorbed from one's social context. Little independent thinking operates at this stage.

Dissonant

Is confused and ambivalent about minority issues. Politically correct statements may be made without much conviction. Attempts are made to find answers to troubling questions about racial disparities.

Dominative

Feels a sense of entitlement and racial privilege. Negative evaluation and/or overt belittling of the cultures and customs of people of color. Belief in the superiority of white values.

Conflictive

Supports equality. Belief in equal opportunity as long as minorities are not too demanding. Sees affirmative action as creating unfair advantages for people of color.

Integrative

Values cultural pluralism. Believes in racial and cultural integration. Race and culture do not negatively affect one's choice of colleagues, friends, and other acquaintances.

Reactive

Exhibits consciousness about racism at all levels: personal, interpersonal, institutional, and cultural. Believes in processes and procedures that ensure equal access for persons of color in social, political, and economic arenas. May be unconsciously paternalistic toward people of color.

SOURCE: Adapted from Rowe, Bennett, and Atkinson (1994).

Exercise 8.3   My Racial Identity Development

Discuss the following issues:

1. Where would you place yourself now and at earlier points in your life?

2. What you would have to "give up" to move to the next status?

3. Potential counseling process and content issues for clients at various statuses.

4. What counseling might be like with clients at various stages given your present stage.

5. Which client stage do you feel you could counsel most effectively?

6. Which client stage do you feel you would work with least effectively?

---

minorities, culturally different, Hispanic, and *homosexual* are examples of language determined and defined by those in power but not always embraced by the targeted groups.

Questions for Reflection and Discussion

1. In what ways do service delivery systems unintentionally reflect a White, male, heterosexual, middle-class bias?

2. What is the responsibility of mental health centers to have services available to non-English speakers? What is their responsibility if practitioners speaking the client's language are not available?

3. Why is treating every client the same not the same thing as treating every client equitably? In what ways might mental health services have to be adjusted to respond to a culturally diverse clientele?

4. What is the responsibility of individual practitioners to ensure they are practicing in a nonbiased manner?

5. At what point(s) on the developmental models of racial identity development would you place yourself? What are the implications, both positive and negative, of your level of awareness for your work as a practitioner?

6. What stages of racial identity development for counselor and client are most likely to foster parallel therapeutic interactions? Regressive? Progressive?

Exercise 8.4   Circle of Sharing

Step 1

Divide the group into two equally sized subgroups. Ask one group to form a circle in the middle of the room, then turn around and face outward. The second group forms an outer circle around them. Each person should be facing another.

Step 2

Explain to the group that you will pose a series of questions. Starting with the first question, participants will share their responses with their partners. Allow 2 to 3 minutes per dyad per question.

Step 3

With each subsequent question, participants in the outer circle move counterclockwise to the next person to their right.

Circle of Sharing Questions:

1. Share a time in your life when you felt different from others around you. What was it like for you?
2. Share your first memory of racism. What was the impact on you and others?
3. Share a recent incident of homophobia you witnessed. What was your reaction, and how do you feel about it now?
4. What biases about gender are you aware you hold?
5. Share the messages you learned as a child about your own and other people's religious beliefs.
6. Talk about your first encounter with someone with a disability.
7. Tell your partner about a recent incident when you interacted with someone who had difficulty speaking English. How did you feel? How do you usually feel?
8. What racial or other targeted group are you most fearful about counseling?

The following critical ethical incident is the first in which an expert's response appears. Refer to Table 7.1 in the previous chapter for a review of the questions to which the expert responded. We asked experts to give readers a glimpse into their thinking; that is, to reveal in their written responses the thoughts that came to mind as they approached the case. We thought it would be helpful, especially for practitioners-in-training, to be privy to what experts ponder when they consider the interface between ethical and cultural issues. Thus, you will note examples of this "thinking out loud" manner in each of the experts' responses. Our aim is to demystify the ethical decision-making process by making it a very human endeavor that is not always strictly linear. We hope that this unfiltered manner of presentation will help students and practitioners to free themselves to think creatively when exploring alternative solutions to ethical dilemmas related to cultural concerns.

Ethical Dilemma 1

Mickey is a 16-year-old Latina, the firstborn of three girls in a tight-knit Puerto Rican family. Mickey is very popular in her large urban high school in the East. She is a bright, engaging young woman who is active in school clubs and community service. Her goal is to get into a good college to study architecture because she is "fascinated by old buildings and the relationship between urban buildings and lifestyles." Mickey's close friends are a multiracial group of young women and men who recently went on a summer trip together to Europe as a "last fling" before their senior year.

During the trip, Mickey was surprised to find herself developing a crush on Molly, one of her longtime friends. Her feelings persisted after they returned and began their senior year. Mickey finds herself thinking about Molly "all the time" and fantasizing being physically intimate with her. She and Molly continue to spend a lot of time together. She has not expressed these feelings to Molly, scared that Molly will be "freaked out" if she knew what Mickey was feeling. Nor is Mickey herself certain what to make of her feelings, since she has always had boyfriends. In fact, she is currently dating a young man, a senior in her school, whom she would never wish to hurt.

Mickey is scared that she might be a lesbian and can't imagine how she would handle it. She is pretty certain her parents would be devastated. Her friends are actually fairly accepting of gays and lesbians; at least, that's what they say. She decides to make an appointment with Ms. Erin Brady, the school counselor, to talk about the emotional turmoil she has felt since the trip to Europe. Mickey likes and trusts Erin and has often confided in her. She wants Erin to tell her that everything's okay and that she's not a "freak." Erin is a White heterosexual woman in her late 20s, well liked by students at the school and new to her career as a school counselor. Erin has no idea of what might be going on with Mickey but responds to Mickey's almost palpable anxiety by assuring her that she probably is not a lesbian. Erin tells Mickey that what she is going through is a normal stage of late adolescence and will likely pass soon. Mickey is visibly relieved.

Questions for Classroom Discussion

1. What "unintentional cultural bias" is evident in this incident?

2. What would have been a more ethically sound direction for Erin to take in her session with Mickey?

3. How might culture, both the client's and counselor's, play a role in this case?

Expert's Discussion

Colleen Logan, Ph.D., LPC
Assistant Professor, University of Houston-Victoria
Private Practice, Houston

The purpose of this discussion is to explore how mental health practitioners can unknowingly and perhaps even unintentionally discriminate against clients who are different from them. Counselors are particularly susceptible to the negative influence of stereotypes and misinformation when working with clients who are exploring their sexual identities. Like all of us, mental health practitioners are raised and educated in a society that teaches us that homosexuality is immoral and inferior to heterosexuality. Without adequate training, counselors often find themselves stymied when working with sexual minorities, forced to try to fit clients into inappropriate and largely ineffective heterosexual paradigms, and potentially causing great harm to the client. Dismissing, discounting, or even worse, trying to "repair" or change a homosexual client are all symptoms of an uninformed and unethical practitioner. Therefore, it is the ethical responsibility of mental health practitioners to educate themselves regarding the myriad issues facing sexual minorities.

The Client's Story

As with all counseling relationships, the initial task involves listening carefully and empathically in order to gain understanding of the client's world. With clients who are different from us, arguably all clients, special attention to the details and nuances of their stories is mandatory. It is critically important that mental health practitioners listen without prejudice, suspending biases and stereotypical judgments in order to be fully present and available to help their clients.

Critical factors of Mickey's case that must be carefully attended to include the fact that she is Puerto Rican, the eldest of three girls in a "tight-knit" family, and greatly confused by a recent "crush" she has on her longtime female friend, Molly. These feelings are scary and overwhelming to Mickey because prior to the emergence of these feelings, she has always had boyfriends, and in fact she is currently dating a young man. Because of these foreign "same-sex" feelings, Mickey is afraid she is a lesbian. She is mortally afraid to tell her parents because they would be "devastated." She is afraid to tell Molly in case she would "freak out." Her circle of friends appear to be accepting of gay people, but she isn't quite so sure that they would be accepting of her if she were to share her feelings of attraction for Molly. Mickey's internal strife is exacerbated by the fact that not only is lesbianism considered taboo in the dominant White culture, but in the Hispanic minority community it is also strictly forbidden. Mickey is so absolutely frightened by the mere possibility of being a lesbian that she probably hasn't even considered that her feelings are normal and may not necessarily mean that she can no longer consider herself heterosexual. The bottom line is that being a lesbian is not acceptable and her "tight-knit" family and friends are likely to react negatively or, even worse, disown or reject her.

Mental health professionals from the dominant White culture may miss the real significance of Mickey's fears regarding her family and friends. Discussing her same-sex feelings with family and friends could mean rejection and ostracism from the very unit from which she gains her strength and self-identity. To work effectively with Mickey, it is important to understand how the Puerto Rican community views homosexuality. This is important regardless of whether Mickey is indeed a lesbian, because her deep-rooted fear of rejection and ostracism may prohibit her from fully exploring her feelings, thereby delaying or even prohibiting her ability to accept her sexual orientation, be it homosexual, bisexual, or, indeed, heterosexual. As a White counselor, Erin may or may not be familiar with the Puerto Rican culture. She may not understand or recognize the importance of family and friends, as well as the culturally ingrained heterosexual assumptions, and therefore might completely miss the enormity of Mickey's dilemma, missing the anger, pain, and frustration Mickey must feel as she grapples with the possibility of being Latina and lesbian.

Unintentional bias may also be introduced simply by way of the counselor's own sexual orientation. For example, heterosexual counselors may fail to explore and challenge their own internalized homoprejudice (Logan, 1996) and end up dismissing and discounting their clients' sexual identity explorations by attempting to convince clients that they really are heterosexual. On the other hand, gay and lesbian therapists may err on the opposite side, assuming that anyone who questions his or her sexual identity is gay or lesbian, denying the client the opportunity to explore his or her feelings in a safe and affirming atmosphere. In Erin's case, because she is heterosexual, it is likely that she has not taken the time to explore her own internalized homoprejudice, and thus she is operating from the faulty assumption that everyone is heterosexual and therefore Mickey's feelings and struggles are easily discounted and dismissed. Moreover, Erin may feel justified in dismissing Mickey's feelings as a "phase" because blinded by the cloak of heterosexual bias, she fails to realize that some youth have begun to crystallize their awareness of same-sex attraction during puberty. In fact, according to McClintock and Herdt (1996), same-sex attraction begins about age 10, the same age when heterosexual youth begin to feel sexual attractions, while the age of self-labeling of same-sex orientation varies between ages 13 and 16 (D'Augelli & Hershberger, 1993; Hershberger & D'Augelli, 2000). It is possible, therefore, that Mickey is in the initial stages of the coming-out process, and Erin's assurances that she is heterosexual would then be clearly misguided and unethical.

When listening to a client's story with a finely tuned "cultural ear," the following issues stand out as critical milestones that are paramount to Erin's ability to work effectively with Mickey:

1. It is important to recognize and understand Mickey's cultural background, that is, what it means to Mickey to be Puerto Rican. Erin must ascertain Mickey's sense of ethnic identity as well as the degree to which she and her family are acculturated to United States society. Moreover, it is essential to understand how strongly her family influences Mickey, including extended family members as well as the powerful cultural influences of sex role socialization and religion (Lee, 1997).

2. In addition, it is important to explore Mickey's beliefs, myths, and stereotypes regarding homosexuality. Accurate and unbiased information regarding what being lesbian means and doesn't mean is critically important to Mickey's ability to understand and appreciate her sexual identity. Messages decrying homosexuality bombard Mickey from all sides, from within both the minority culture and the dominant culture. The powerful and detrimental impact of these negative messages must be attended to and understood.

3. As with any cross-cultural counseling experience, counselors must explore their own beliefs, biases, and values about the minority culture. In working with Mickey, it is also critically important that Erin explore the myths and stereotypes that she has internalized regarding sexual minorities. We are all raised in a homoprejudiced society that teaches us that homosexuality is immoral and inferior to heterosexuality. Left unchecked, counselors can find themselves acting unethically and unprofessionally, as the projection of these internal biases can have an extremely detrimental impact on the health and growth of the client.

Cultural Considerations

First and foremost, it is important to understand the enormity of Mickey's feelings and the courage it took for her to share her dilemma with Erin. One cannot underestimate the power of the cultural context that serves as a backdrop for Mickey's struggle. If Mickey is, indeed, in the process of coming out or accepting her lesbian identity or even if she is merely exploring her feelings, the following issues must be considered.

First, it is important to recognize the historical prejudice both the minority and majority cultures have held toward homosexuality. Mickey is likely to have learned negative stereotypes about homosexuality long before she considered whether she might be lesbian or not. In fact, like all of us, she has literally been bombarded by negative messages about homosexuality since she was a child, and it's no wonder she is scared and confused about her feelings. Trusted family members, who otherwise challenge the White dominant culture's stereotypes and misinformation about their own ethnic group, often propagate and confirm stereotypes and biases about sexual minorities. This apparent incongruency is often confusing, making the coming-out process that much more difficult and more complex for dual minority clients (Greene, 1997).

Espin (1987) stresses the challenges of exploring one's sexual identity as an ethnic minority by stating, "Coming out to self and others in the context of a sexist and heterosexist American society is compounded by the coming out in the context of a heterosexist and sexist Latin culture in a racist society (p. 35)." There is great pressure to remain closeted in minority communities, because coming out is literally viewed as an act of treason against culture and family (Greene, 1994). Coming out as a lesbian could mean losing a primary source of support and identity, as ethnic minority families traditionally provide an oasis of affirmation and understanding in a world ruled by the dominant White culture.

Mickey's dilemma is exacerbated by her status as a Puerto Rican female. Latina women are expected to be passive, nurturing, submissive, respectful of elders, and deferent to men. Emotional and physical closeness with females, or *amigas intimas,* is expected, yet lesbianism is strongly rejected (Espin, 1987). In fact, physical and emotional closeness with women is culturally designed to diminish contact with males, as Latina women are expected to remain chaste until marriage. In a culture that denies the sexuality of women, lesbianism is seen as blatant and conscious participation in sex—not out of duty to a man or husband, but out of wanton desire. Lesbians are considered to be man-haters, a blight against the natural order of things, and worse yet, active participants in a sordid attempt to overthrow the authority of men (Green, 1994).

Moreover, Mickey is taking enormous risks by verbalizing her feelings. Public disclosure of homosexuality shames the family, not just the immediate biological family but also the distant kinfolk (Espin, 1987). Coming out to others affects many generations and carries an enormously heavy cultural burden. If indeed Mickey is a lesbian and begins to consider coming out to her friends and family, care must be taken to ensure Mickey's safety and well-being. Again, ethnic minority families are usually places of support and safety; however, coming out as a lesbian could have major repercussions, placing Mickey in jeopardy or even physical peril (Barret & Logan, 2002). This is why it's so important for Erin to know the local gay and lesbian resources and organizations, where Mickey could find support and affirmation as she navigates the coming-out process.

Given these cultural dynamics, it is easy to understand why Mickey's anxiety was "almost palpable." The idea that she might discover that she is a lesbian, something so taboo and anathema to her cultural identity, must be absolutely terrifying. It's no wonder she is visibly relieved when Erin dismisses her struggle as an adolescent phase, assuring her that she is probably not lesbian. This swift dismissal of Mickey's feelings is clearly an indication of Erin's internalized homoprejudice and her obvious lack of training in this area. As a heterosexual woman, Erin errs greatly by assuming heterosexuality and thereby prohibiting Mickey from exploring her feelings in a safe and nonjudgmental atmosphere. It is essential to remember that adolescence is a time of exploration. Mickey should be afforded the opportunity to explore her same-sex feelings. To ignore her struggle with sexuality is to dismiss a very important part of her adolescent development and is likely to bring with it enormous conflict and inner turmoil for Mickey.

In a homprejudiced society, it is not uncommon for sexual minority youth to delay crystallizing their sexual orientation until late adolescence. This is particularly true for adolescent girls because of societal sanctioning of close female friendships, intensified in Mickey's case by cultural mandates of physical and emotional intimacy with girls. On the other hand, it is important to be aware that same-sex feelings and behaviors don't automatically imply homosexuality either. For example, boys may engage in group masturbation, competing to see who can have an orgasm first, and girls can be very affectionate with each other, holding hands, walking with their arms around each other, and even kissing. This does not necessarily mean they are gay or lesbian; it does mean, however, that youth must be afforded the time and space necessary to explore their feelings.

Ethical Concerns and Questions

It is clear that Erin violated ACA ethics code, Section A.2.a, "Counselors do not condone or engage in discrimination based on age, color, culture, disability, ethnic group, gender, race, religion, sexual orientation, marital status, or socioeconomic status."

According to Hershberger and D'Augelli (2000), counselors are engaging in unethical practice when they interfere with youth development because they hold uninformed and biased views about same-sex sexual orientation and do not allow youth the opportunity to discuss their concerns without fear of judgment or rejection.

Erin acted unethically when she automatically assumed that Mickey is heterosexual. It is inappropriate and unethical to prematurely label and categorize questioning youth. Rather, questioning youth should be afforded opportunities to explore, meet, and interact with other questioning youth in safe and affirming environments.

Erin also violated ACA ethics code Section A.2.b,

> Counselors will actively attempt to understand the diverse cultural backgrounds of the clients with whom they work. This includes but is not limited to, learning how the counselor's own cultural/ethnic/racial identity impacts her/his values and beliefs about the counseling process.

Erin's blatant and rapid dismissal of Mickey's concerns is a clear reflection of her lack of understanding and appreciation for Mickey's dilemma. Assuring her of heterosexuality does not take into account her fears and concerns about being a lesbian, nor does it take into account the cultural context. Erin's response to Mickey clearly reflects her own values and beliefs as a White heterosexual woman. Erin has not taken the time to explore her own internalized homoprejudice and how it may affect her ability to be empathic and understanding of Mickey's concerns. Erin needs to take time to explore her own feelings about sexuality, sexual identity, and behavior as well as assess her comfort level with her own sexuality and sexual identity.

In addition, Erin violated ACA ethical code, Section C.2.a,

> Counselors practice only within the boundaries of their competence, based on their education, training, supervised experience, state and national professional credentials and appropriate and professional experience. Counselors will demonstrate a commitment to gain knowledge, personal awareness, sensitivity and skills pertinent to working with a diverse client population.

It has been clearly documented that counselors receive little, if any, training in their graduate programs (Buhrke, 1989; Buhrke & Douce, 1991). It is Erin's responsibility to educate herself about the concerns of youth who are struggling with sexual identity and orientation issues. She could do so by reading literature and books or by attending workshops and other types of continuing education programs. In recent years, there have been a number of programs at both the local and national level related to the issues facing gay, lesbian, bisexual, or questioning youth.

Monocultural and Multicultural Perspectives

As noted earlier, it is likely that Erin received little, if any, training regarding the myriad issues facing sexual minorities in her graduate program. Only in recent years has more attention been given to these issues, although, still today, these issues are often relegated to a small subsection of a multicultural class. Because sexual orientation cuts across gender, race, ethnic background, and socioeconomic status, it is essential that counselor educators infuse discussion of sexual identity and orientation into all courses, including multicultural courses. Culturally responsive courses must include a discussion of sexual orientation in every dialogue about every ethnic and cultural group. In this way, students could begin to understand the issues associated with dual and triple minority status and learn to respond appropriately and sensitively to these clients.

Options for Appropriate Action

To respond appropriately to Mickey, Erin must first conduct a thorough self-examination. Doing so will help her discover how she has internalized societal homoprejudice and incorporated the associated myths and biases into her thoughts and feelings toward gay, lesbian, and questioning youth. Erin must also explore her values, thoughts, and feelings about different ethnic groups, in particular the Puerto Rican community. Failing to do so puts her in jeopardy of responding unethically and insensitively to Mickey and any other future clients who might struggle with these same issues.

Erin needs to educate herself regarding the myriad issues facing gay, lesbian, and questioning youth. Options for education include consultation with educated peers or a supervisor or attending workshops or presentations on sexual minority youth. Doing so will help her to objectively facilitate the process of clients who are questioning their sexual identities, rather than assuming heterosexuality and squelching the growth process.

In conclusion, it is clear that Erin acted unethically by dismissing Mickey's struggle with her same-sex feelings. By doing so, she denied Mickey the opportunity to explore her feelings in a safe and affirming environment, and she blatantly ignored the cultural context and its impact on Mickey's dilemma. Albeit her response may, indeed, have been "unintentional," this seems like a lame excuse in this day and age, as claiming "I didn't know" can no longer be tolerated when working with our sexual minority and questioning youth.

Ethical Dilemma 2

Sandy Lawson is a White, master's level clinician who practices in a mental health center located in a racially and ethnically diverse city in the Midwest. The clinicians at the mental health center are predominantly White individuals at the master's and doctoral levels. After a few months in this position, Sandy begins to notice that the population seeking services at the clinic is primarily White middle class. Lower socioeconomic status (SES) Whites and people of other racial backgrounds are few and far between among the clinic's clientele. Ms. Lawson wonders whether the clinic is inadvertently engaging in discriminatory practices.

Questions for Classroom Discussion

1. What "standard" practices of community mental health centers are you aware of that might contribute to poor people and people of color not seeking services?

2. Let us assume that the clinic staff at the mental health center is willing to examine whether they are engaging in unintentional cultural bias. What steps might they take to facilitate their self-examination?

3. What strategies could make the center's mental health services more equitable to their community?

Ethical Dilemma 3

Maya, a 15-year-old recent refugee from Bosnia, is living temporarily with a White family, the Mastersons, whose church sponsored her relocation to the United States. Maya's English skills are limited, although she is able to understand more than she can speak. Mr. and Mrs. Masterson have assisted Maya in seeking mental health assistance because she is having difficulty sleeping, is constantly on edge, cries frequently, and often has flashbacks to scenes of torture she witnessed in Bosnia before her passage to this country. Maya is concerned about becoming a burden to her host family, who has so graciously opened their home to her.

The Mastersons accompany Maya to a community mental health center, where they are told that no one on the staff speaks Slavic. Maya and her American family are distressed that no one at the clinic is prepared to work with her. They leave the clinic wondering what steps to take to get Maya the help she needs. The next day, the clinic director follows up with a phone call offering to find an interpreter. Although the Northeast town they live in is not large, the clinic director explains that the local high school has a small population of Slavic students, many of whom are refugees like Maya. Perhaps one of these students could serve as an interpreter so that Maya can receive treatment. Maya feels very uncomfortable with this arrangement, embarrassed to talk about her problems in front of someone her age and from her country whom she fears will judge her as weak. Maya does not share her concerns with her family, feeling she has already caused enough problems.

Questions for Classroom Discussion

1. Maya faces a conflict in that she wishes to please her host family yet feels uncomfortable with the solution offered by the mental health center. Are there more viable solutions to this dilemma?

2. In your view, what responsibility does the mental health center have to provide or locate appropriate services for clients like Maya?

Classroom Exercises

1. Ask students to identify common institutional practices in the mental health field that reflect a Western cultural bias.

2. Set up a series of role plays in which students in the therapist role have an opportunity to practice working with a challenging client of another culture.

3. Ask students to role-play their responses to question 5 under "Questions for Reflection and Discussion" (identify and discuss the implications of your stage of racial identity development for unintentional or indirect expressions of cultural bias in the therapy setting). Specifically, create "therapist" and "client" role plays that demonstrate parallel, regressive, and progressive therapy interactions.

Summary and Key Points

Ethical mental health practice demands that practitioners refrain from discriminating against clients based on race, gender, sexual orientation, and other diverse characteristics. In our experience, it is the rare practitioner who engages in overt racial and other forms of discrimination. It is more likely that practitioners think and/or behave in a biased manner unintentionally rather than intentionally. These covert forms of discrimination are the most difficult to identify yet are probably more prevalent. Racial identity development models can be useful tools for examining the indirect manner in which racism and other "isms" manifest in clinical practice and everyday experience.

Key processes for practitioners to engage in include the following:

- Identification of what they need to feel safe when revealing their prejudices and cultural biases in training and supervision

- Thoughtful reflection on how they have personally participated in individual, interpersonal, institutional, and cultural oppression of various target groups
- Reflection on the extent to which they make room in their world for "differences" with regard to ethnicity, race, and sexual orientation
- Self-exploration of how willing they are to examine the potentially deleterious effects of not recognizing their own privilege—be it racial, gender, or sexual orientation—on their work with clients who do not share the same cultural privilege.

9

Client Welfare

ACA Code

Section A.1.b of the American Counseling Association code (ACA, 1995) states, "Counselors encourage client growth and development in ways that foster the client's interest and welfare; counselors avoid fostering dependent counseling relationships."

APA Code

Principle E of the American Psychological Association ethics code (APA, 2002) includes the statement, "Psychologists respect the dignity and worth of all people, and the rights of individuals to privacy, confidentiality, and self-determination."

NASW Code

The National Association of Social Workers code (NASW, 1996) contains an ethical principle valuing the "inherent dignity and worth of the person." Consistent with this value, social workers are required to "treat each person in a caring and respectful fashion, [being] mindful of individual differences and cultural and ethnic diversity."

* * *

Certainly, the overarching principle contained in these sections of the mental health codes of ethics is protection of the welfare, or best interest, of the client. This, however, is a broad statement that leaves much room for interpretation—and misinterpretation. For example, reports abound of therapists engaging in sexual relationships with clients under the guise of serving the best interest of the client. Indeed, a frequent defense by unethical practitioners is that such relationships were in the service of the client's growth and recovery. Who determines what is in the client's best interest? Is it unethical, for example, for a happily married couple to have been formerly in a client-therapist relationship?

In the case of race, gender, ethnicity, and sexual orientation, the issues can be even less clear. The mental health ethics codes, because they are based on principles of self-determination, individualism, and clear relational boundaries, advocate a professional stance that may be at odds with the more interdependent, self-in-relation patterns of some ethnic and women-centered cultures' ways of being. These contradictions may cast practitioners in a double bind; that is, doing what is in the best interest of the client may conflict with various ethical codes. For example, clients from collectivist cultures for whom self-identity is inseparable from kinship systems may bring family members with them to group therapy sessions. This may pose a dilemma for the therapist cognizant of the importance of maintaining the confidentiality of group members but wishing to be culturally sensitive at the same time.

Pedersen (1995) raised another potential source of conflict between ethical codes and culture in his discussion of the concept of dependency. For many cultures, dependency on others is a way of life. Strong networks of interdependence have been critical to the economic and psychological survival of many immigrants as well as people of color whose history in the United States goes back many generations. The ethics codes, however, advise against therapeutic relationships in which clients feel dependent on the counselor. But is it not possible that such relationships might be in the client's best interest at least temporarily? Is it not possible that a strong, even dependent, relationship with a counselor could serve as a bridge toward greater self-efficacy for a client who feels little personal power? And if these possibilities seem viable, then where does one draw the line between what is in the client's best interest and critical to his or her healing and that which ultimately is psychologically damaging to the client? We pose these questions in an effort to examine the parameters placed around the therapist-client relationship.

Another important issue to consider with regard to client welfare is that of social activism on the part of practitioners. The counseling and psychology professions have historically been narrowly focused on the individual client, apart from family, social group, and cultural context. Even group and family work often are limited to intragroup and intrafamilial dynamics without deliberate analyses of social, political, and economic systems and their impact on clients. Many multicultural experts have advocated for therapist involvement in social activist endeavors, particularly those that challenge institutional oppression (Arredondo et al., 1996; Sue, 1995; Sue & Sue, 1999). These experts have pointed to inherent inequalities in the distribution of power in our society and its impact on the psychological, not to mention economic and political, well-being of many historically stigmatized populations. They argue for increased activism by mental health practitioners against institutional and cultural barriers to power sharing across racial, class, and gender lines.

Sue (1995) advanced a strong argument for expanding the counseling role to one that embraces social and political change efforts. He stated, "The counseling profession must realize that although individual change and development are important goals, true lasting change can occur in our society only if our organizations also change and develop" (p. 490). Sue advocated that counselors become involved in efforts to attack biases, prejudices, and stereotypes inherent in institutional practices. He suggested several possibilities, including the roles of advocate, consultant, and change-agent. The ACA has endorsed this notion with the establishment in 2000 of the division of Counselors for Social Justice. How comfortable are you with the idea of extending the traditional therapist roles to include system change efforts? Exercise 9.1 is designed to explore your comfort level. The critical ethical incidents below address this and other questions regarding client welfare.

Questions for Reflection and Discussion

1. Are there groups of people whom I have difficulty according dignity and respect? Is my attitude based on my religious beliefs, cultural socialization, personal experiences, or other factors? How do I reconcile conflicts between my beliefs and the expectations of my profession?

2. How would I work with a client who does not adhere to the importance of self-determination? For example, how would I work with clients whom I believe are negatively affected by their conformity to religious tenets and expectations?

3. How familiar am I with different cultural definitions of mental health? How adaptable is my therapeutic orientation to non-Western cultural norms and patterns related to help-seeking behavior?

4. How do I determine the difference between client behavior that is culturally appropriate and behavior that is problematic? For example, when does the "healthy cultural paranoia" exhibited by some African Americans among Whites become problematic for them? How do I make that determination from a culturally sensitive stance?

Exercise 9.1   Counselor Advocacy

Identify the activities you (a) have engaged in and/or (b) would feel comfortable engaging in as part of your role as a therapist:

Activity:	Done	Would Do
1. Educated clients about oppression.		
2. Recommended antiracism readings to clients.		
3. Displayed antiracism materials in your office.		
4. Recommended political involvement to clients.		
5. Displayed antisexist materials.		
6. Shared anti-oppression views with clients.		
7. Worn a gay affirmative button in session.		
8. Participated in anti-oppression activities.		
9. Advocated for client rights.		
10. Participated in social justice causes.		
11. Worked with clients on their racism, sexism, or homophobia.		
12. Worked actively on your own racism, sexism, or homophobia.		
13. Assisted clients in dealing with institutional barriers.		
14. Worked with institutions to make them less exclusionary.		
15. Challenged your own agency or school on diversity issues.		

5. How do I balance my professional obligation to support client autonomy with respect for clients whose cultures accord therapists a great deal of power and authority?

Ethical Dilemma 1

Marc, a 27-year-old Navajo man, is in his second year in family medicine at a prestigious medical school in the Northwest. From shortly after starting medical school, Marc has questioned whether this is the career that will ultimately be most fulfilling for him. He wants to give something back to his Indian community and had planned to use his degree to help make a difference in stemming the acute medical problems his community faces. However, the more he remains in medical school, the more Marc feels his spirit is being boxed in and eventually will die altogether or be replaced with a set of values he presently rejects. He wonders who he is and whether he will be of any help to his people feeling as psychically wounded as he does. He decides that medical school is not for him and speaks to one of his professors about his decision to drop out of his program.

Marc's professor, a White man who was instrumental in recruiting Marc into medical school, suggests that Marc put his decision on hold until he speaks to a counselor. His professor refers him to Dr. Mandalay, an American Indian counselor, also Navajo, hoping she will talk Marc into finishing his residency. Dr. Mandalay believes that greater numbers of professionally trained American Indians are needed on reservations and hopes Marc will change his mind. She admires his commitment to his people as well as his resistance to what they both label as "Western values." She wants to honor Marc's decision, even if it is to terminate his medical training, but also is looking at the bigger picture of the plight of American Indians. Dr. Mandalay knows that Marc's medical skills are sorely needed. Dr. Mandalay does not want her biases to affect her treatment with Marc, but she also knows from experience that a person can go through a Western training program and still retain his or her ethnic values. She would like to help Marc see that this is possible for him.

Questions for Classroom Discussion

1. How can Dr. Mandalay proceed in an ethical manner given her biases?

2. What are the cultural and ethical conflicts in this case?

Ethical Dilemma 2

Danni is a 15-year-old White girl who has been referred to the school counselor, Ms. Baines. Danni had always been a rather shy and reserved student and had always felt "different" from other kids. But teachers begin to notice a change during Danni's senior year. Throughout her senior year, Danni has been wearing a lot of black clothing, wearing very white face makeup, and writing essays about macabre thoughts and feelings. Her grades have begun to drop from A's to B's. She is socializing during breaks with a group of students whom many school officials have been worried about because of their "bizarre" appearance. When she visits Ms. Baines, Danni explains that this group has been very accepting of her, while others have not. She says she feels comfortable socially for the first time in her life and has a better handle on what's really important in life. Ms. Baines is sure that this group, because it appears to her to be at the fringes of normalcy, is not the best place for Danni to explore herself and make sense of her life. She wants to find a way to help Danni disengage from her new friends and find more acceptable ways of developing a sense of self and belonging.

Questions for Classroom Discussion

1. What are your thoughts about Danni's capability of making her own decisions about what is best for her?

2. What are the cultural issues in this incident?

3. Applying the multicultural ethical decision-making steps, what would be your first clue about a potential ethical dilemma if you were seeing Danni? Which ethical principles apply in this case? How would you balance sensitivity to Danni's decision with your concern about her welfare?

Ethical Dilemma 3

Tommy is a 12-year-old African American boy brought by his father for treatment with Ms. Mary Collins, an African American psychology intern. Tommy's mother passed away when he was 8 years old. Since then his father, Lawrence, who has not remarried and seldom dates, has raised Tommy with occasional assistance from members of the extended family. Lawrence is concerned about Tommy's lack of energy and interest in most things. Tommy has no close friends, and except for going to school and sports events with his father, he remains fairly isolated. He is quiet and shy and appears to Lawrence to be "lost and afraid." Lawrence says that Tommy's withdrawal seems to worsen every year around the anniversary of his mother's death. Lawrence tries to do special father-son things with Tommy at these times but admits he still has difficulty himself with his wife's unexpected death and sometimes has to force himself to "be there" for his son. This year, Tommy appears more depressed than usual.

Mary begins a course of psychotherapy with Tommy and is immediately successful in building an alliance with him. Mary is a single woman in her early 30s who enjoys children and finds Tommy very engaging. She is surprised at how verbal he is given his father's initial description. After only a few sessions, Tommy's affect is remarkably improved; he is cheerful, energetic, and very invested in his therapy. His relationship with his father, which had always been respectful, gradually becomes closer. Mary helps Lawrence find ways to talk openly about the death of Tommy's mother. Mary is aware of Tommy's attachment to her and shares with Lawrence her interpretation that Tommy has a positive mother transference toward her. Mary believes Tommy's transference to be therapeutic at this point in his treatment and encourages Tommy's openness and vulnerability with her. Her goal is to help Tommy begin to replace his dependency on her with a deeper emotional connection with his father, extended family members, and eventually friends.

One afternoon at the end of Tommy's session, Tommy tells Mary his father will be unable to pick him up and that he must take the bus home. He forgot his bus money and asks Mary if he can borrow 50¢. Mary does not hesitate to lend Tommy the money, making sure he knows where to wait for the bus before sending him off. Later in supervision, Mary's supervisor Dr. Faith Manning, a White, psychoanalytically oriented psychologist, expresses concern about Mary's gesture. Faith believes that Mary is stepping into a mothering role that will be emotionally harmful to Tommy when it is time to terminate therapy.

Dr. Manning suggests that she and Mary devote the next several sessions in supervision to Mary's countertransference issues as a single woman wanting a family of her own. Mary is not opposed to this, but firmly believes she is acting in Tommy's best interest and not from her personal needs. In Mary's experience, mothers in Black families are at the hub of the emotional and spiritual well-being of the kinship network. Mary believes that Tommy's close relationship with her has enabled him to more fully grieve his mother's death and find renewed faith in himself and his ability to connect with others. She would like to discuss with Faith how cultural dynamics enter into her approach to treatment. However, she and Faith have never broached the issue of race or culture, and Mary is not certain that Faith would understand or accept her perspective.

Questions for Classroom Discussion

1. What are the potential risks in Tommy's dependency on Mary? What are the potential benefits?

2. As indicated in the scenario, Mary and Faith have never discussed race, ethnicity, or culture in supervision, yet these factors appear to be significant. Is this an ethical concern? Whose responsibility is it to raise these issues?

3. Applying the multicultural decision-making steps to this case, (a) how significant is cultural knowledge and sensitivity in Tommy's treatment? (b) what signs are there of possible ethical conflicts? and (c) which ethics codes are relevant to this case?

4. Would a White female therapist with little multicultural training have been as successful as Mary in working with Tommy?

5. How would you advise Faith to balance culture and ethics in her supervision of Mary? How would you advise Mary to do the same in her work with Tommy?

Classroom Exercises

1. Ask students to share experiences they have had with human rights or other types of advocacy. What was the impact of their actions? What connection do they draw between human rights advocacy and working with clients from targeted groups?

2. Role-play a client-therapist scenario in which the client challenges the therapist about his or her stance and actions with regard to women's rights. How would you respond? How do you feel about the client's inquiry?

3. In small-group discussions, ask students to generate a list of topics related to diversity they have discussed in the context of clinical supervision. Indicate whether the topic was initiated by them or their supervisors and whether their race or the race of the supervisor or client was a factor in raising the topic.

Summary and Key Points

Fostering the dignity and welfare of clients is an enterprise fraught with cultural nuances. That is, dependency, self-determination, and privacy—posited in ethics codes as cornerstones of client welfare—have different definitions from different cultural perspectives. Is what is important to a Vietnamese refugee's welfare the same as what is important to the welfare of a seventh-generation African American professional woman? Or to a 14-year-old White lesbian adolescent whose parents are threatening to "disown" her because of her sexual orientation? Where do practitioners place themselves vis-à-vis their clients and cultural systems that impede their empowerment?

The following are key points for practitioners to consider:

- How willing they are to engage in social/political advocacy to promote the welfare of clients in target groups.
- How diligent they are about attending to the inherent power differences between them and the clients who seek their assistance.
- How they would distinguish between a strong therapeutic alliance and client dependency and from what cultural lens this distinction is being drawn.
- How they would determine the "best interest of the client" and how they would handle clients' disagreements with them about what is in their best interests.
- How they would relate to the notion that client welfare may be culturally determined.

10

Bartering for Services

ACA Code

Section A.10.c of the American Counseling Association code (ACA, 1995) addresses the issue of bartering:

> Counselors ordinarily refrain from accepting goods or services from clients in return for counseling services because such arrangements create inherent potential for conflicts, exploitation, and distortion of the professional relationship. Counselors may participate in bartering only if the relationship is not exploitative, if the client requests it, if a clear written contract is established, and if such arrangements are an accepted practice among professionals in the community.

APA Code

Standard 6.05 of the American Psychological Association code (APA, 2002) states, "Psychologists may barter only if (1) it is not clinically contraindicated, and (2) the resulting arrangement is not exploitative."

NASW Code

Section 1.13.b of the National Association of Social Workers code (NASW, 1996) states,

> Social workers should avoid accepting goods or services from clients as payment for professional services. Bartering arrangements, particularly involving services, create the potential for conflicts of interest, exploitation,

and inappropriate boundaries in social workers' relationships with clients. Social workers should explore and may participate in bartering only in very limited circumstances where it can be demonstrated that such arrangements are an accepted practice among professionals in the local community, considered to be essential for the provision of service, negotiated without coercion and entered into at the client's initiative and with the client's informed consent. Social workers who accept goods or services from clients as payment for professional services assume the full burden of demonstrating that this arrangement will not be detrimental to the client or the professional relationship.

* * *

In each of the ethics codes, bartering in exchange for therapy is not prohibited altogether, but is permitted within specified circumstances and conditions. According to Welfel (1998), bartering for services is problematic because it inherently creates dual relationships; that is, an employer-employee arrangement exists alongside the therapeutic relationship. Conflicted feelings on the part of either party about the worth of the services provided vis-à-vis the value of therapy complicate such arrangements. The ACA code (1995) states that bartering is acceptable "if such arrangements are an accepted practice among professionals in the community" (Section A.10.c). NASW code contains a similar statement. Professionals working in communities in which bartering is practiced are urged to consult with experienced colleagues for guidance about how best to handle these agreements. Bartering goods rather than services for therapy can be less problematic, although assessing the value of goods in relation to specific numbers of therapy sessions in a way that both counselor and client deem to be fair may not be a simple process (Welfel, 1998). Even if this is satisfactorily negotiated, similar concerns may arise as when services are bartered, that is, concerns about the value of goods in relation to the value of therapy.

The ethics codes' stance on bartering contains implicit assumptions. First, there is the assumption that the therapist's economic level affords him or her the option of receiving goods or services rather than monetary payment from the client. Although this undoubtedly is true for many, it certainly is not the case for all therapists, limiting the pool of therapists available to clients for whom bartering is the only viable option. Although this issue does not speak directly to the manner in which bartering is handled, it has relevant sociocultural—particularly socioeconomic class—implications. It raises the question of who is in a position to accept clients on a non–fee-paying basis. This raises concerns about class differences and how they might affect the therapist-client relationship.

The influence of class and therapist-client class differences in the treatment arena is rarely discussed in the general mental health literature and often not examined in depth in the multicultural therapy literature. Yet classism—along with racism, sexism, and homophobia—are worth exploring, especially in a class-stratified society like the United States. Helms and Cook (1999) are among the few scholars (see Sue & Sue, 1999) who explore the impact of socioeconomic class in treatment. Their discussion of "affluent guilt" on the part of therapists suggests one way that this dynamic may play out in terms of countertransference. This can be especially problematic for financially successful therapists who are members of targeted groups with histories of economic hardship. They may feel particularly pressed to assist their clients economically without fully examining the implications of their decisions for both their clients and themselves.

Another assumption is that therapists and clients have equal access to resources to redress problems that may arise from bartering arrangements. In the standard fee-paying arrangement, if clients are dissatisfied with therapy, they have the option of not returning. They also have the option of filing grievances against therapists with a number of different bodies: state licensing and grievance boards and state and national professional associations. Although clients who use bartering as a method of payment have the same options, their economic circumstances may limit their mobility and access to these resources to redress grievances. The therapist's options for formal action may, too, be limited due in part to confidentiality constraints.

A final point we wish to raise is one we would place under the category of "food for thought." Throughout this book, we have encouraged those engaged in mental health practice and supervision to actively question dominant mental health paradigms reflected in the codes of ethics. In this spirit, we raise the following questions: How would it look if North American professional mental health practice grew out of indigenous cultural patterns of sharing and trading goods; if services were provided, where and when needed, with no expectation of monetary remuneration; or if mental health practice were conducted in such a way that pro bono services were not merely a portion of one's work, but the bulk of one's caseload? Of course, you might understandably wonder how one would earn enough to make a living in this imaginary scenario. We ask you to think about possible responses from a multicultural perspective.

Questions for Reflection and Discussion

1. On what bases would I determine (for myself, not in terms of what the codes state) that bartering for services is appropriate?

2. How could I ensure that the bartering agreement does not compromise the therapy relationship?

3. What if I am dissatisfied with the service the client has provided in exchange for therapy? Do I raise this with the client in therapy, outside of therapy, or at all?

4. How do I make sure that my own need for quality goods or services does not compromise the therapy?

5. How do I monitor possible power imbalances between the client and me in (a) the therapy relationship, (b) the service agreement, and (c) the relationship between them?

Ethical Dilemma 1

Dr. Sam Martson, an American Indian psychologist, is the only therapist in a rural community in the West. He frequently has bartered goods and services with his low-income clients in exchange for payment, supplementing his income through other professional ventures such as teaching and consulting. These arrangements have always worked out to everyone's satisfaction. However, lately Sam's businesses have taken a downward turn financially. Sam is not particularly concerned about this at first. He grew up in a poor family and learned very early in life how to survive tough financial times. Besides, Sam's lifestyle is fairly simple; most of his basic living needs are met through the income generated by his consulting and teaching.

Rick Daniels, a fairly successful White contractor and one of Sam's favorite clients, has been in therapy with Sam for 4 months to deal with an expensive divorce that caused a temporary financial setback for Rick. Rick does repairs on Sam's ranch in exchange for therapy sessions to deal with his depression about his divorce. Rick grew up in the 1960s, when kids in his hometown played "cowboys and Indians." Rick has always been fascinated with American Indian cultures, and Sam is the first "real" American Indian Rick has ever known.

Rick's depression about his divorce is lifting, and Sam decides to bring up termination. Rick responds by telling Sam that he is definitely benefiting from his therapy sessions and says that even the repair work he is doing for Sam is therapeutic. Rick jokes that their arrangement benefits both of them and that he would like to continue his therapy.

Questions for Classroom Discussion

1. What are the ethical and cultural issues in this incident?

2. What transference and countertransference issues affect ethical decision making in this case?

Expert's Discussion

Michael Tlanusta Garrett, Ph.D.
Associate Professor of Counseling
Department of Human Services
Western Carolina University

The Client's Story

Listening to the client's story with a "cultural ear," it is important to consider both the client's story and the relationship between the client and therapist. What do we know about them? First of all, it is helpful to consider the client's worldview. We know that the client is a White middle-aged man and therefore possesses certain societal privileges that go along with being a member of the majority. We know that the client has been financially "successful" to this point and may or may not be accustomed to a lifestyle associated with higher socioeconomic status (SES) as well as the privileges that go along with that status. We also know that Rick was married, is now divorced, and has probably gone through many difficult changes associated with divorce and the loss he may have experienced as a result. Some of these, according to the case description, include depression and financial strain. The mental and emotional stress of Rick's divorce may have created questions for him about relationships in general and his identity at this point.

We also know that Rick most likely grew up with stereotypical views of "Indians" perpetuated through the media of the time ("cowboys and Indians") and that these stereotypes (be they good or bad) may not have ever been challenged, considering that his interaction with Sam is his first with a Native American person. Rick's fascination with Native cultures and possible intrigue with his therapist as a member of one of those cultures might say something about the internal process of searching that Rick's circumstances have offered to him as an opportunity to learn more about himself, about others, and about life. However, given the current client/therapist relationship, it may also be creating a dependency that could impede therapeutic progress.

It might be helpful to consider the therapist's worldview in order to better understand the dynamics of the relationship as well. What do we know about the therapist? Sam is a Native American man who grew up in a lower-SES family but who has obviously achieved a great deal in terms of educational and financial "success."

However, it also seems as if Sam may have grown up with some very traditional Native values such as kindness, generosity, attention to harmony in relationships, and offering help to others in need, as demonstrated by his "frequent bartering of goods and services with his low-income clients." Sam knows firsthand what it is like to be a person in need, given his background, and it is probably an important part of his cultural identity to be there for others in whatever way he can while also trying to balance his own survival needs, sometimes even making sacrifices of the latter for the former. However, the fact that Rick is one of Sam's favorite clients also seems significant. There may be dynamics on both the part of the client and therapist that need to be explored. Listening to the situation from my own cultural background as a Native doctoral-level counselor and counselor educator, I am struck by what seems like a familiar dynamic in the relationship between a White client and a Native therapist. With no disrespect toward the client, I am reminded of comedians Williams and Ree, who describe a tribe known as the Wishiwas (i.e., "I wish I was"). The client's intent in the therapeutic relationship seems suspect through transference at a time when he is probably vulnerable and looking for some way to reconcile his own identity. Probably in his own naïveté and depending on his own stage of cultural identity development at this point, Sam may or may not be aware of this dynamic of the relationship being played out and indeed may have set himself up for this merely by being a "good Indian" and trying to be helpful.

Cultural Considerations

What are the questions therapists need to be asking about the cultural issues suggested in the incident? What might therapists want to explore about their own and/or the client's cultural backgrounds that would affect their handling of this incident? Are the cultural backgrounds of other people involved in the incident relevant? There are a number of questions therapists might want to ask themselves about the cultural issues suggested in the incident:

1. What are some of Rick's most deeply held values and beliefs as a person? What are some of Sam's most deeply held values and beliefs as a person and as a professional?

2. What are some of the privileges that Rick and Sam have or do not have as a result of their cultural characteristics (e.g., race, ethnicity, gender, sexual orientation, age, class, religion/spirituality, exceptionalities, attractiveness, language, nationality, geographic origin)?

3. How do similarities or differences in privilege affect both the content and process that occur in therapy between Rick and Sam?

4. How has oppression affected the lives of both Rick and Sam, and how does this affect the therapeutic relationship?

5. Given his cultural worldview, how does Rick view his therapist? Given his cultural worldview, how does Sam view his client?

6. From a cultural perspective, how does Rick define healing? From a cultural perspective, how does Sam define healing?

7. How are the respective communication styles of Rick and Sam similar or different?

8. In what stage of racial identity development is Rick? In what stage of racial identity development is Sam?

9. What are the implications for counseling based on Rick's and Sam's respective stages of racial/cultural identity development?

10. Based on Rick's cultural identity, what is it that he wants from therapy in general and from the therapist specifically? Based on Sam's cultural identity, what is it that he expects from therapy in general and from his client specifically?

These are a number of questions that therapists might want to ask themselves to better understand some of the cultural issues pertinent to the incident. In addition, therapists might want to ask themselves some of these same questions to further explore their own cultural backgrounds and how this would affect their handling of this or any similar incident.

Ethical Concerns and Questions

What are the important ethical issues to consider in the incident? Which ethics codes might have been violated? Do cultural elements affect how ethics codes might apply in this incident? Are the ethical questions or issues different when culture fails to be considered?

There are a number of important ethical issues to consider in this incident. Based on the ACA (1995) code of ethics, the following standards seem to apply for consideration.

A.1.b. Positive Growth and Development. This standard states in part that, "Counselors avoid fostering dependent counseling relationships." By allowing and even encouraging Rick to exchange his services as a contractor for therapy, Sam has not only put himself in a financial bind in which he might be tempted to create dependency in order to stay afloat financially but he has also potentially allowed Rick to become emotionally dependent on the therapeutic relationship in a way that may or may not benefit Rick. (Also note A.6.a, "Dual Relationships.")

A.1.c. Counseling Plans. This standard states that, "Counselors and their clients work jointly in devising integrated, individual counseling plans." Given the current state of affairs between Rick and Sam, both client and therapist seem to be at a point where they view the counseling plan very differently, and that needs to be addressed.

A.5. Personal Needs and Values. This standard states in part that, "Counselors . . . avoid actions that seek to meet their personal needs at the expense of the client." Although in the incident, both parties seem to be benefiting from the current arrangement, clearly, Sam has created a situation in which he is meeting his own personal needs for repairs on his ranch. (Again, also note A.6.a, "Dual Relationships.")

A.10.b and A.10.b. Fees and Bartering. This standard indicates that counselors should attempt to provide comparable services of acceptable cost when a fee structure is inappropriate for clients and that, "Counselors may participate in bartering only if the relationship is not exploitive, if the client requests it, if a clear written contract is established, and if such arrangements are accepted practice among professionals in the community." Clearly, both Rick and Sam agreed to the current arrangement, which is still desirable on the client's part. The only part we do not know is whether a clear written contract was established concerning the arrangement to exchange repair services for therapy sessions.

Also, it is important to consider that Sam is the only therapist in this rural community, where exchange of goods or services for therapy might not only be commonplace but also may be a necessity given the SES of clientele. So, bartering for goods and services might not only be a natural approach given Sam's cultural background and identity but may also be necessitated by the context. In this manner, cultural elements are an important consideration in whether the arrangement between Rick and Sam is appropriate.

It is important to note, in addition, that this standard also says, "Counselors ordinarily refrain from accepting goods or services from clients [due to the] inherent potential for conflicts, exploitation, and distortion of the professional relationship" (A.10.c). Part of the underlying issue here is not whether bartering for goods and services is appropriate, but more important, what effect it has on the therapeutic relationship.

A.11.c. Appropriate Termination. This standard states that, "Counselors terminate a counseling relationship, securing client agreement when possible, when it is reasonably clear that the client is no longer benefiting, when services are no longer required." Although in this case, the client indicates that he is still benefiting from therapy and from the current arrangement to exchange services, it is the therapist's prerogative whether he believes that therapy is still of benefit or necessary for the client based on therapeutic goals established with the client. We do not know in the current incident what specific therapeutic goals were established from the beginning between client and therapist. Nonetheless, it is still the therapist's prerogative to terminate at this point.

Monocultural and Multicultural Perspectives

How are Western/monocultural and multicultural perspectives similar and different when applied to this incident? How do Western mental health education, training, and practice aid and/or hinder in examining the incident from a multicultural perspective?

A Western monocultural approach based on mainstream American values and beliefs emphasizes the importance of objectivity in professional relationships and the payment of fees for goods or services. This is based on an underlying value placed on capitalism, competition, individualism, and the acquisition of wealth and status as being evidence of a "successful" member of society. From a multicultural approach, taking into consideration Native traditions from which Sam may be coming, there is more emphasis on the importance of subjective relationships that focus more on people than on progress; more emphasis on sharing and cooperation for the good of all those involved; and more emphasis on community needs over individual needs, all of which contribute to the underlying social and spiritual importance of harmony and balance.

Western mental health education, training, and practice tend to assume a culture-based norm with the therapeutic process concerning dimensions such as monetary payment for therapeutic services, with a specific system of equivalence to maintain fairness for the exchange; the structured approach to time; and the focus on talking through one-way self-disclosure from client to counselor in an objective relationship that is intended to produce insight for the client and create better health and more effective functioning indicated in part by more independence. From a Native traditional perspective, seeking healing from a Medicine person involves approaching that person with a great deal of respect and humility; having a comfortable, familiar relationship with that person either directly or through a close family member, friend, or respected elder; giving gifts to that person of a number of goods that are considered appropriate, such as tobacco, blankets, ceremonial items, crafts, food, and so on (typically not money per se; however, money may be part of an offering that is made without any discussion of such and without any expectation of equivalence); involvement of family members and/or community as a part of the healing process; the sharing of a meal; and the implementation of ceremony to restore or maintain harmony and balance in personal, family, and community relationships, as well as environmental and spiritual relations. Of course, this is a generalization for both cultural contexts that can vary depending on specific people and circumstances involved; however, it tends to be true from a larger perspective.

One thing is certainly true: One must clearly define healing from a cultural perspective and examine to what extent client and therapist definitions match. Without looking at the helping process as a culture-based process, it is easy to overlook the relative nature of both content and process as well as the very framework within which therapeutic change is expected to occur. Ethical questions or issues may be very different when culture is considered for any given instance. What is ethical or appropriate or even desirable in one cultural context may not be in another. Often, the challenge may lie in creating a balance between the needs presented by varying cultural contexts and worldviews. This seems to be the case with the incident presented here.

Options for Appropriate Action

What are some options for ethical thinking and behavior in this incident? What does it look like when culture and ethics are brought into balance? What does it look like when they're not?

Both Rick and Sam have reached a very difficult place in the therapeutic process: One wants to continue with the therapeutic relationship, whereas the other does not feel that it is needed any longer. Looking at it from the client's point of view, why leave something that has been working well for you and that feels comfortable as a way to deal with life's most difficult challenges? Looking at it from the therapist's point of view, why continue therapy unnecessarily when the client seems to have made the desired progress?

From both an ethical and therapeutic standpoint, it seems important to validate the client for the progress he has made to this point, to review what progress has been made, and to relate that back to original therapeutic goals. Also, it would seem to be important to address any anxiety that the client has about leaving the comfort of the therapeutic relationship and facing life on his own. It might be helpful to explore ways that the client can get his needs met "out there in life" without having to rely on therapy, since therapy cannot continue forever. It might also be helpful to explore the dynamics of the relationship between client and counselor at this point to address and resolve any transference/countertransference issues that exist in creating a dependency on the part of client or therapist.

Regardless of what action is taken at this point, first and foremost, it needs to be taken keeping the client's best interest in mind. Part of the purpose of the therapeutic process is to help clients deal not only with the current issue or difficulty but also deal better with themselves, others, and life, as well as any similar issues or difficulties that may arise in the future. Ironically, we create a temporary dependency to create a more long-lasting independence for the client. That is a cultural value in and of itself. However, as one Native put it, "Knowledge is like the wind, once obtaining it, you can go anywhere" (Yellow Horse, as cited in Padilla, 1994, p. 12). That truth seems to apply to both client and therapist, but the challenge seems to be how to do it together until the time arrives when it is important to do it apart.

Ethical Dilemma 2

Mrs. Barbara Wilson, an African American woman in her 40s, is referred by her pastor for therapy to Mr. Steven Adelmann, a 27-year-old Jewish social worker. Steven has chosen to practice in an economically depressed African American community in the South in an effort to follow a family history of involvement in civil rights and service to the poor.

Steven's family instilled in him a strong sense of social justice and the importance of helping those less fortunate than oneself. He has reached out to elders and other leaders in the community and has gained their trust. Pastor Jones refers many members of his Southern Baptist congregation to Steven for family problems. Barbara has been seeking counsel from Pastor Jones since the death of her son a year ago in a car accident in which she was driving. Barbara has begun to feel despondent again and recently has had suicidal thoughts. Pastor Jones sends Barbara to Steven for more intensive mental health treatment.

Barbara agrees to meet with Steven on Pastor Jones's urging but is very concerned with how she will pay for his services. Barbara cleans houses for a living and has limited financial resources. Steven suggests a reduced fee, but Barbara is unable to pay even a small amount at this point. Barbara is not comfortable with Steven's suggestion of dropping the fee and offers gardening services in exchange for 12 therapy sessions. Steven has no problem with this arrangement; he is very comfortable financially and, moreover, believes that gardening may be therapeutic for Barbara. After six sessions, Steven realizes that due to Barbara's depression, she is unable to handle any kind of work. He is not concerned that Barbara has not begun gardening for him. What concerns him is whether Barbara's not following through is an indication not only of her depression but also of how she feels about her therapy.

Steven decides to bring the matter up with Barbara, asking her directly whether she is benefiting from therapy. Barbara initially felt very guarded and remains somewhat uncomfortable self-disclosing to this young White man, whom she isn't sure could ever understand the pain and sorrow she has felt for so many years as a poor, unmarried Black woman. However, she concurs with her pastor's view of Steven as an earnest and honest young man who genuinely wishes to help. Barbara confesses her early reservations and her present commitment to her treatment. Six additional sessions transpire, bringing treatment to its agreed-upon termination point. Steven raises this issue with Barbara, concerned that she still appears fairly depressed. Barbara tells him she does not wish to terminate until she feels more emotionally stable and self-confident. Barbara still has not begun gardening for Steven.

Questions for Classroom Discussion

1. What are the cultural factors Steven brings to his work with Barbara? In what ways might family messages positively affect Steven's approach? In what ways might they be of concern? If you were supervising Steven, how would you broach these issues?

2. How do Barbara's race, socioeconomic status, and spirituality potentially affect the course of treatment? What "red flags" are evident in this scenario?

3. If you were treating Barbara, would you handle anything differently? How would you address her guardedness?

4. What ethical concerns are reflected in Barbara's and Steven's bartering arrangement? How would you handle "payment" as her therapist?

5. Given the steady source of referrals from Pastor Jones, what are the areas of cultural awareness, sensitivity, and knowledge that Steven needs to be aware of to competently and ethically treat his clients?

Classroom Exercises

1. Have students share with the class their thoughts and comfort level with regard to bartering. Set up several role plays in which they have an opportunity to practice explaining their "policies" to clients.

2. In small groups, have students draft statements about fees and bartering that might appear on a disclosure form.

Summary and Key Points

Although the APA, ACA, and NASW ethics codes do not prohibit bartering for mental health services, several caveats are identified that might make practitioners think twice before commencing with such arrangements. We suggest that the caveats themselves, while certainly reasonable, stem from a particular cultural, specifically SES, standpoint. We encourage practitioners to be mindful of the socioeconomic class implications of fee agreements they make with clients.

Practitioners are urged to act as follows:

- Explore their own attitudes about money and finances: How was money handled in their families? What feelings about money were modeled by family members: guilt, entitlement, or anxiety? How might these early messages play out in their arrangements with clients?
- Discuss with other practitioners and supervisors their thoughts about bartering, the conditions under which it might make sense, and how to prepare for the possibility of missed "payments."
- Consider the point at which they might make the decision to terminate a client for failure to pay for services, either monetarily or via bartering.

11

Fostering Dependency

ACA Code

Section A.1.b of the American Counseling Association code of ethics (ACA, 1995) states that, "Counselors avoid fostering dependent counseling relationships." Also, much like other mental health codes, references in the ACA code to avoiding client dependency are incorporated in other sections as well. For example, the section of the code (Section A.6.a) cited in an earlier chapter on dual relationships advises counselors not to exploit clients' dependency. Also, in Section A.5.a, counselors are advised to, "Avoid actions that seek to meet their personal needs at the expense of clients."

APA Code

Similarly, the American Psychological Association code (APA, 2002) contains sections cautioning psychologists against exploiting clients' trust by offering or continuing treatment when personal problems on the part of the psychologist might interfere with treatment (Standard 2.06). This includes circumstances in which psychologists may develop inappropriate feelings, interest, or dependency on clients.

NASW Code

The National Association of Social Workers code of ethics (NASW, 1996) addresses the importance of collectivism when it states,

> Social workers understand that relationships between and among people are an important vehicle for change. Social workers engage people

as partners in the helping process. Social workers seek to strengthen relationships among people in a purposeful effort to promote, restore, maintain, and enhance the well-being of individuals, families, social groups, organizations, and communities.

*   *   *

Successful counseling and therapy practice inherently has the potential for fostering dependency at least temporarily as the client comes to rely on the therapist for assistance and guidance. This natural dependency on—or trust in—the therapist is counter to Western proscriptions against being "needy" in relation to other people. We receive many messages about the virtues of standing on your own two feet, keeping a stiff upper lip, not depending on anyone but yourself, and doing the job yourself if you want to get it done right. The ethical principles underlying much of mental health practice reflect the values of autonomy and independence. In mainstream culture as in much of psychotherapy, the self is at the core of human "be-ing," at the center of our experience. Even in group and family practice, although interpersonal dynamics are typically explored, goals of personal development of group and family members and assisting the "identified patient" reflect an emphasis on individualism.

In an earlier, related chapter (Chapter 9) on client welfare, we discussed dependency, or interdependence, as a core component of collectivist cultures. In many ethnic cultures, the individual self is viewed as secondary to the importance of the family, the community, and one's race (Helms & Cook, 1999; Sue & Sue, 1999). Interdependence rather than independence is the norm in these cultures. Thus, it behooves counselors working with clients whose cultures value collectivism to assess their approaches, perhaps by placing themselves on a continuum between individualism and collectivism. Counselors also may benefit from exploring their personal experiences with and feelings about autonomy and dependency. Exercise 11.1 is a self-assessment tool for examining these values. The purpose of the exercise is not to argue that either interdependence or independence is a better way of being than the other. In fact, most of us operate from both modalities at different times, in different circumstances, with different people, and sometimes with the same people in different instances. The purpose of the exercise is to derive a clearer sense of how you experience your independence and your interdependence. The more aware you are of your biases, the less likely they will negatively affect your work with others operating from different perspectives.

It is also important for counselors to explore the way they feel about others' dependency on them. Like it or not, therapists hold a position of power in the eyes of many clients by virtue of their education, training, and perceived wisdom. Clients may become dependent on therapists for advice, believing that the therapist knows what is best for them. Therapists who feel

---

Exercise 11.1   Assessing the Value of Interdependence and Independence

---

Part 1: Experiences

Divide a sheet of paper in half lengthwise, making two columns. In the left column, identify as many examples as you can of your personal experience with independent action and decision making. Possibilities might include the following:

- A project you worked on independently
- Being evaluated by another for independent work
- A challenge you confronted alone
- A major decision you made without outside input
- Something you accomplished that made you feel proud
- An athletic achievement

In the right column, list your experiences with team or group work. These might include:

- Collaborative work with other professionals
- Team sports
- A decision for which you elicited significant input from others
- Family or group therapy
- A grassroots organizing effort
- Community service
- Committee participation

List as many activities or events in each column as possible.

Part 2: Feelings

Look over each of your lists. Identify and make note of feelings associated with the items you listed. Were there feelings of accomplishment, connection to others, pride, resentment, shame, anxiety, comfort, or anger? After identifying your feelings, review your lists and note any patterns. For example, do you tend to enjoy group work more than independent effort, or vice versa; only under certain circumstances, or in certain settings? Which activities tend to give you greater satisfaction?

Part 3: Values

Now identify values that stem from the activities and feelings associated with them. Explore the following questions:

(Continued)

Exercise 11.1   (Continued)

- Who or what influenced my values?
- Am I comfortable with my values; that is, if confronted on them, would I affirm my beliefs?
- How do my beliefs regarding independence and interdependence affect my view of people with different orientations?
- How do my values affect my approach as a therapist?

---

insecure or unsupported in their personal lives may begin to enjoy a sense of power from clients' deference to them. This may be particularly problematic when working with clients whose cultural values reflect high esteem for elders, educated people, and those in positions of authority. Balancing cultural sensitivity with ethical treatment can be very challenging.

It is critical that trainees be given the opportunity to think through these dilemmas before they arise in the treatment setting. Exercise 11.2 is designed to encourage students to think about the impact of cultural norms concerning dependence and independence on their lives and work.

Analyzing cultural norms such as dependence and independence and their impact on our beliefs and experiences certainly is a useful activity. However, engaging in self-examination can remain merely an intellectual process without really changing our views of ourselves or others. Actual contact with cultures different from our own can move us beyond intellectualizing, force us to reevaluate our beliefs, and possibly change our beliefs about and behavior toward others (Bohan, 1996; Diaz-Lazaro & Cohen, 2001). Diaz-Lazaro and Cohen (2001) described an immersion activity in which students in their multicultural counseling course (a) attended cultural events in which they were a minority in a culturally different group, (b) became exposed to organizations and community settings populated by the group, and (c) had meaningful interactions with members of the culturally different group. Data generated by this study suggested that cross-cultural contact is important in developing multicultural competency.

In the context of our discussion of ethical approaches to the issue of client dependency, it may be useful for practitioners to make a point of spending time in cultural settings—this could include religious or spiritual settings, neighborhood celebrations, or community events—in which collectivism is actively practiced and engages people in discussion about their experiences. It can be helpful to identify a person (e.g., a colleague) to serve as a liaison in order to reduce the possibility that the practitioner's interest will be seen by members of the group as voyeuristic or exploitative.

Exercise 11.2   Early Messages About Dependence and Independence

---

I. In small groups, identify as many cultural messages, sayings, and proverbs as you can about the value of independence:

1.

2.

3.

4.

5.

Identify as many cultural expressions as you can about the value of dependence:

1.

2.

3.

4.

5.

II. Place an asterisk next to the messages that are reflected in your relations with others.

III. Discuss the potential impact of what you have learned about dependence and independence on your work with (a) clients with similar views and (b) clients with different views.

The question we would ask practitioners to consider while engaging in these activities is whether alternatives to Western practices of independence, separation, and autonomy can be more emotionally healthy for some of the people with whom they work.

Questions for Reflection and Discussion

1. How do I define dependency? By what criteria do I determine that a client is too dependent? How do I distinguish between appropriate trust in the therapeutic relationship and dependency?

2. What is my feeling about cultures in which the distinction between self and other is less emphasized than in Western cultural practices? How do I view those who rely on the views of others when making difficult life decisions? How do I view those whose decisions are based on their families' perspectives and not their own?

3. What is my attitude about adults living with their parents? Do I view them as being unable to "make it on their own"? Is making it on one's own always preferable? Do I have a bias in favor of individuals who make their own way in life? Do I view myself as having made it on my own?

4. How have I handled situations in which I've been granted some measure of power? What did I like and dislike about those experiences? How might my experience with and feelings about power affect how I work with clients?

5. What warning signs might come up to alert me to the possibility that I am using a client to meet my own emotional or dependency needs?

6. How have I handled periods in my own life when I have felt emotionally alone? Do I tend to reach out to others, withdraw farther, experience myself as "needy," or get involved in activities that distract me? How might my behavior be played out with clients?

Ethical Dilemma 1

Ms. Chau Thuong is a Vietnamese American social worker in a community mental health clinic serving a predominantly Asian and Asian American clientele. Chau sees most her of clients in the community setting because of their discomfort with the idea of visiting her in a mental health clinic, despite the large numbers of Asian American staff. Chau's clients range in age from young children to the elderly, many of whom have experienced severe psychological trauma and economic hardship related to their relocation from their home countries to the United States. Chau works closely with various community resources, such as churches, schools, and other institutions, in an effort to coordinate support services for her clients. Chau has made herself very available to her clients over the years she has worked at the mental health center, and her clients have developed a great deal of trust in her.

One of Chau's clients, Li-Song, a woman in her mid-50s, is having a particularly difficult time. Her husband died recently after a long illness. Li-Song was her husband's primary caretaker after his discharge from the hospital. She wishes she could have done more to help her husband. Shortly after her husband's death, Li-Song's flashbacks to her last several months in Vietnam began again—her experience at two relocation camps and the brutal death of a family member she witnessed, all years ago—and she consequently feels increasingly suicidal. Chau suggested temporary hospitalization and medication, both of which Li-Song is suspicious of and refuses to do. Li-Song likewise rejected Chau's suggestion that she move in with one of her children. Li-Song does not wish to be a burden to her children, who are adults with their own families and lives.

Consequently, Chau spent most of the night at Li-Song's house caring for her and making sure she was safe. Chau hospitalized Li-Song involuntarily the following day because she was still suicidal. Dr. Dugan, the admitting psychiatrist, a White man in his 30s, was alarmed that Chau had spent the night with the patient rather than admitting her sooner. He has decided to file a grievance against Chau for inappropriate boundaries and fostering dependency in her patient.

Questions for Classroom Discussion

1. How do ethnicity and culture affect Chau's actions with regard to her client, Li-Song?

2. How do ethnicity and culture affect Dr. Dugan's decision to file a grievance?

3. What additional information would you seek about this case if you had the responsibility of making a decision about whether an ethical violation had occurred?

Ethical Dilemma 2

Margot is a 30-year-old White attorney who has entered therapy with Dr. Mike Barton, a 40-year-old African American psychologist, for treatment of anorexia. Mike's approach to working with eating disorders is to isolate clients for a period of time from their social milieus, believing their daily environments to be the main source of reinforcement for their unhealthy eating behavior. Mike's method of social isolation is to place clients for several weeks in a retreat center he established, staffed with mental health workers, medical personnel, and nutritionists. Mike gradually reintroduces clients to their social settings while helping them to disengage from what he refers to as "toxic" people in their lives. While clients are isolated at the retreat center, Mike and other staff members meet with them daily to work therapeutically with them. Mike's approach has been successful with a great number of clients, earning him a solid professional reputation in his field.

While treating Margot, Mike begins to get reports from other staff members that Margot refuses to work with anyone but him, feeling that he is the only one who really understands her problem. Staff members also report to Mike that they suspect Margot has erotic feelings for him. They tell him they have no concrete evidence for their suspicions, simply their clinical hunches based on innuendo from Margot. This is not the first time Mike has had to deal with clients wanting to work with him alone, and he has always managed to discourage it. However, Margot is not responding to his insistence that she work with others at the retreat. Today in their session, Margot threatens to stop eating altogether unless Mike complies with her request. Mike does not want to jeopardize the trust he has established with Margot yet is concerned that she may be becoming too dependent on him. He is considering terminating their individual sessions, concerned not only about Margot's dependence but also about the possibility of staff misconstruing his actions with Margot.

Questions for Classroom Discussion

1. What are the relevant ethical codes in this scenario?

2. What are the racial and cultural issues? Specifically, how might stereotypes about Black males be a variable in the dynamics among Mike, his staff, and his patients?

3. How might Mike have better prepared himself for the dilemma he faces with Margot? That is, were there any warning signs suggested by the scenario, and if so, how could he have handled them?

4. How should Mike address Margot's reported erotic transference?

Ethical Dilemma 3

Cynthia Mendoza is a single, Chicana family social worker in her 30s whose main professional interest is in working with Mexican American families in a working-class, rural community in the Southwest. She lives in the same community as most of her clients and, when she is not treating families, is actively involved in local politics. Cynthia is especially concerned about what she perceives to be racist practices in the predominantly White school where Latino children are often placed in lower academic tracks. She sees herself as an advocate for her people, a bridge between them and the local school board. Mexican American citizens in the community have come to see Cynthia as a powerful ally and depend on her to speak on their behalf. Cynthia feels honored by the trust her families have placed in her. She is a strong, intelligent woman who feels passionate about empowering her people.

Questions for Classroom Discussion

1. What are the cultural issues in this scenario?

2. Are there any ethical "red flags"? For example, is her community's dependence on her advocacy for children an ethical problem?

3. How can Cynthia guard against potential ethical violations while advocating for the rights of the Mexican American families?

Classroom Exercises

1. Divide students into small groups. Ask each group to propose a scenario in which (a) client dependency makes good clinical sense, (b) therapist detachment works against client welfare, and (c) therapist detachment is clinically indicated. Have students discuss their scenarios with the entire class. Role-play one of the scenarios generated by the students.

2. In small groups, ask students to create a vision of what therapy might look like if based on collectivist norms and practices.

Summary and Key Points

Codes of ethics admonish therapists against fostering dependency in their therapeutic relationships with clients—both their own dependency on clients as well as client dependency on therapists. Yet at the same time, therapists are encouraged to view therapy as a partnership that promotes clients' well-being.

The following are key points for practitioners to consider:

- Healthy ways to take care of their own needs so that their therapeutic relationships with clients remain focused on clients' needs
- Ways in which interdependence can operate effectively in the therapy setting.

12

Boundaries of Competence

ACA Code

Section A.2.b of the American Counseling Association (ACA, 1995) states, "Counselors will actively attempt to understand the diverse cultural backgrounds of the clients with whom they work. This includes, but is not limited to, learning how the counselor's own cultural/ethnic/racial identity impacts her/his values and beliefs about the counseling process."

APA Code

Standard 2.01(b) of the American Psychological Association code (APA, 2002) states,

> Where scientific or professional knowledge in the discipline of psychology establishes that an understanding of factors associated with age, gender, gender identity, race, ethnicity, culture, national origin, religion, sexual orientation, disability, language, or socioeconomic status is essential for effective implementation of their services or research, psychologists have or obtain the training, experience, consultation, or supervision necessary to ensure the competence of their services, or they make appropriate referrals.

NASW Code

Standard 1.05 of the National Association of Social Workers code (NASW, 1996) states,

> Social workers should understand culture and its function in human behavior and society, recognizing the strengths that exist in all cultures.

Social workers should have a knowledge base of their clients' cultures and be able to demonstrate competence in the provision of services that are sensitive to client's cultures and to differences among people and cultural groups. Social workers should obtain education about and seek to understand the nature of social diversity and oppression with respect to race, ethnicity, national origin, color, sex, sexual orientation, age, marital status, political belief, religion and mental or physical disability.

* * *

Multicultural counseling knowledge and skill are viewed as vital for competent practice in our culturally diverse society. Each of the mental health codes clearly standardizes the expectation for focused education and training with regard to cultural diversity. Failure to acquire appropriate training increases the risk of being sanctioned for unethical practice. Both the ACA and APA have published documents identifying explicit guidelines for competent multicultural practice (APA, 1993; Arredondo et al., 1996). The guidelines identify dimensions of culturally competent counseling (i.e., awareness of one's own biases, knowledge of diverse cultures, and skill in the application of culturally responsive counseling techniques and approaches) and delineate key skills associated with each of the dimensions. (Refer to Chapter 4 for a discussion of the guidelines.) The ACA and APA guidelines are useful resources for training students to meet the challenges they will face in multicultural settings. Emphasis on multicultural competency is not limited to standards set by professional mental health organizations. Many state licensing entities list coursework in sociocultural foundations as a prerequisite for obtaining a mental health practice license. Oral licensing examinations may include areas of inquiry that tap practitioners' cultural competency. Also, accreditation entities for counseling, psychology, and social work programs dictate inclusion of multicultural content in curricula. Thus, the mental health professions and related regulatory agencies have taken decisive steps toward ensuring multicultural competency among practitioners.

Despite broad-based consensus about the importance of multicultural competency, such consensus is lacking with regard to a clearly defined course of training. Consequently, there is no standardized curriculum for multicultural competency and no clear research findings supporting a particular approach or sequence of training experiences resulting in cultural competency. Empirical evidence also is lacking that connects cultural competencies as defined by published guidelines to treatment efficacy and outcome. These realities make the task of determining when practitioners are practicing competently and when they are not challenging at the very least. This is complicated by discrepancies among individual practitioners' personal assessments of their competence. Some professionals may feel that a generalist counseling education and training background is sufficient for working effectively with a range of cultural groups. Others may work actively to bolster their levels of cultural competence even after years of experience with diverse clients. The question of whether specific training in cultural competencies is necessary and how much is enough continues to be debated among mental health educators.

Welfel (1998) identified three components of professional competency in mental health practice: education, formal training, and supervised experience. These components are clearly reflected in each of the ethics codes' sections that appear at the beginning of this chapter. What remains to be defined is how much of each component is enough for competent multicultural practice. Should one course in multicultural counseling serve as a minimum requirement for competency? Should training programs be required to demonstrate diversity among their faculty? Should trainees be required to complete practica and internships in culturally diverse settings? Should training programs be expected to develop partnerships with practitioners in local agencies serving diverse clients? Do these elements lead to cultural competency? Further research addressing these questions, we hope, will lead to greater clarity and consistency in multicultural training and reinforce ethical multicultural practice.

We advocate the need for minimum standards for multicultural training along with clear expectations for additional ongoing supervision and training. Currently, counseling and psychology accreditation requirements in this area are fairly general. They include an expectation for curricula that address multicultural issues and practicum experiences with diverse client populations. The extent, focus, and depth of these experiences are not specified. Thus, training programs range in quality from meeting the minimum accreditation requirements to making multicultural training an integral part of the curricular and supervision experience of students. Training programs also vary widely in terms of the diversity of faculty. Our hypothesis is that those with the greatest cultural diversity, particularly racial diversity, among faculty are likely to be the most diverse in terms of student population and most focused with regard to cultural content in the curriculum. We hypothesize further that practitioners whose graduate training included more than one multicultural therapy course taught by a diverse faculty and who avail themselves of continuing education in multicultural issues are more likely to practice ethically and competently. See Exercise 12.1 for a checklist of training experiences.

Questions for Reflection and Discussion

1. Am I familiar with the multicultural counseling competencies? If not, why not? How prepared am I to work with clients who are culturally different from me? What has been my education and training, and do I seek out opportunities for continuing education in this area?

2. Am I familiar with the controversies and debates in multicultural counseling theory? For example, do I understand the difference between

---

Exercise 12.1   Checklist of Multicultural Training Experiences

---

Mark each item in the following list according to whether you participated one time only or on an ongoing basis. Each item refers specifically to the area of multicultural counseling and therapy:

	One Time	Ongoing
1. Reading	——	——
2. Workshops, seminars, or in-service training	——	——
3. Continuing education workshops	——	——
4. Graduate courses	——	——
5. Personal experiences with cultural differences	——	——
6. Professional experience	——	——
7. Supervision	——	——
8. Focused training or postdoctoral work	——	——
9. Peer discussion	——	——
10. Consultation	——	——
11. Conference sessions	——	——
12. Advanced training institute	——	——

---

multicultural and diversity counseling? Am I familiar with arguments for and against cultural relativism?

3. Do I favor etic or emic approaches to the issue of culture? What is my stance on "color-blind" approaches to counseling?

4. What are the resources in my area for consultation and supervision on cultural issues in treatment? Do I know whom to contact if I were to encounter an unfamiliar or difficult multicultural case involving ethnic, sexual orientation, gender, or disability issues?

5. Will I need to have some measure of fluency in another language to be effective with certain client populations? Am I aware of the availability of trained bilingual translators in the area in which I wish to practice?

6. If a grievance were filed against me for not practicing in a culturally competent manner, what educational, training, supervision, and continuing education experiences could I cite?

Ethical Dilemma 1

Ms. Delia Rodriguez, a former client of Dr. Henry Alcott, is very unhappy with the treatment she received while in therapy with Dr. Alcott.

Delia is considering reporting Dr. Alcott to the ACA for breaching Section A.2.b of the code of ethics. Delia was in treatment with Dr. Alcott for 8 months for chronic generalized anxiety. Just prior to entering therapy with Dr. Alcott, Delia had graduated from a major university with a degree in journalism. Delia had relocated from the East Coast to a predominantly White community in the West to pursue her career as a television news reporter.

Delia, a third-generation Mexican American, grew up in a poor family in Southern California. Delia's family recognized her intellect and talents from the time she was a child. They saved what money they could to put toward her college education. Delia's family is very proud of their daughter's success. She is the only member of a large extended family to have graduated from college. Delia is very close to her family and grateful for the sacrifices her family has made for her. She becomes angry when she thinks about the ethnic discrimination her parents had to endure as they struggled to create a decent life for their children. Delia is determined to confront racism whenever she encounters it, rather than suffer the indignities her parents did.

Delia's therapy with Dr. Alcott was prompted by the high stress she experienced in the first few months of her new job. On one hand, Delia felt confident of her ability to be successful; on the other hand, at times she felt lost and anxious in the competitive world she had entered as a journalist. During her treatment with Dr. Alcott, Delia recounted subtle incidences of exclusion from colleagues despite her efforts to be a team player. Delia also found it difficult to make new friends and felt very lonely. Her family was far away, and the demands of her new job precluded family visits. Dr. Alcott, a behaviorist, focused Delia's therapy on strategies she could use to connect more with others at her work and in social settings. Delia's therapy with Dr. Alcott ended 6 months ago at Dr. Alcott's suggestion that they terminate so that she could try out some of the new behaviors on her own.

Delia is now seeing a new therapist, Dr. Felicia Sanchez, also a Latina—a Cuban American—with whom she is actively exploring her racial and cultural identity. It has been through her work with Dr. Sanchez that Delia has come to realize that Dr. Alcott never explored the possibility that racial, gender, and cultural issues might be at the core of the conflicts she experiences in her work and social settings. In the grievance she is considering against Dr. Alcott, she identifies Dr. Alcott's failure to raise issues of race, gender, and culture. Delia believes Dr. Alcott to be incompetent to treat clients of color. Dr. Sanchez has encouraged Delia to explore these feelings before making a decision about which direction to take with regard to the grievance.

Questions for Classroom Discussion

1. Was Dr. Alcott practicing outside the limits of his competence when he treated Delia? What experiences would he have to document to support a claim of cultural competence?

2. In what ways might ethnic and racial identity be at the core of Delia's conflicts? How could Dr. Alcott have addressed these issues?

3. Assume that Dr. Alcott is able to document education and training in multi-cultural counseling. What then might explain his failure to explore ethnic issues with Delia?

4. If Dr. Alcott were to claim that behavioral therapy does not focus on socio-cultural issues, but directly on changing behavior, would he still be guilty of incompetent practice?

5. Let's assume that you, too, are a behaviorist and have only six sessions to treat Delia. How would you address ethnic and racial issues?

6. What is Dr. Sanchez's ethical responsibility given Delia's report about her previous therapy?

7. Do you agree with Delia's assertion that Dr. Alcott is not qualified to treat clients of color?

Expert's Discussion

Sandra I. Lopez-Baez, Ph.D., NCC, CCMHC, LPCC
Charlottesville, Virginia

I am a mental health counselor functioning in multiple roles as counselor educator, practicing clinician, consultant, and public speaker. Upon reading Incident 1, my first impression was that Dr. Alcott's practice of "behaviorism" reflects a theory-bound approach that disregards the client's reality and cultural context. Such an approach focuses on expressed symptomatology to the exclusion of contextual variables. The client's cultural context is of importance in this case because it provides information as to whether the symptom, in this case anxiety, is occurring without an accompanying process. Were Dr. Alcott to have included Ms. Rodriguez's cultural background and current life situation among his considerations for a prescribed treatment, then this client's anxiety could be considered a by-product of acculturative stress, which is adaptive, rather than "chronic generalized anxiety," which is maladaptive. Here is the question: Is behaviorism a relevant and appropriate treatment modality for acculturative stress, and is it relevant to this case?

Dr. Alcott's approach fails to consider Ms. Rodriguez's knowledge and understanding regarding mental health systems and therapeutic services. This lack of "psychological mindedness" (Garcia & Zea, 1997) creates a barrier to treatment. The client's knowledge and expectations of the therapeutic relationship and process do not match the therapist's. What the therapist perceives as his or her role may not be part of the client's role expectation for a therapist. An example would be that if Ms. Rodriguez expected "advice" from Dr. Alcott as a "role-appropriate" behavior, she may have misconstrued his treatment methods as advice rather than an approach to alleviate symptoms. Sue and Sue (1999) address this issue in their statement, "A therapist's credibility is dependent upon the psychological set or frame of reference of the minority client." Thus, understanding the client's context is vital to delivering therapeutic services to minority clients. Dr. Alcott's choice of treatment is important because it illustrates a failure to fully understand Ms. Rodriguez's situation as a culturally relevant one, in which anxiety is a normal by-product, rather than a pathological entity.

The Client's Story

When using a "cultural ear" to listen to Ms. Rodriguez's story, the "etic/emic" model seems appropriate. This model provides a framework to examine and observe cultural norms of different groups. The emic approach observes behavior of only one culture from within that culture and takes into account only what the group members assign importance to. Conversely, the etic approach studies a culture from the outside of that particular group or system so that only universal aspects of behavior are considered. This model supports the notion that the context upon which the client's symptoms are manifested is as important as what the symptoms themselves tell the therapist.

As a Puerto Rican woman who is a practicing mental health counselor, I am part of the Latina/Hispanic group to which Ms. Rodriguez belongs as a Mexican American. My ethno/racial identification is integrated into who I am and what I do as a person and professional. As a therapist, I explore the various pertinent aspects of my clients' lives. This process includes assessment of their ethno/racial identity, acculturation, and adaptation to the dominant culture. These variables affect clients' support systems (family, friends, church) and may be a contributing factor to their symptomatologies.

When focusing on culture, the client's story takes on a new meaning. Stories will contain explanations of how the client has coped with oppression, discrimination, managed to straddle two cultures, and modified his or her systems of belief to better adjust to new environments. The client's adaptation to a new culture is a transition that requires a skill base many clients lack and therapists frequently ignore. Transitioning from one culture to another taxes the individual's coping skills. This process requires gaining insight into the unspoken rules of the new environment while at the same time functioning at work and home. To a "naive" observer, this process may seem to be of clinical significance rather than an adjustment required by the dominant cultural group that can be distressing to minorities.

Cultural Considerations

Dr. Alcott's failure to ask Ms. Rodriguez what she expected to resolve in therapy, her goals for her visits, and information of how they would relate is significant. Such information gives the therapist insight into the client's role expectation. Questions about past experiences in therapy, family background, ethnic, and racial or cultural identity are essential in understanding the client's worldview. Worldview permeates the individual's values, beliefs, feelings, and behaviors, constructs that the therapeutic relationship aims to modify. Furthermore, the therapist also brings a set of assumptions determined by his or her worldview. Differences and commonalities in client-therapist worldview orientation provide the necessary depth to set up a treatment plan consonant with a minority client's experience.

Ms. Rodriguez's case illustrates how failure to address worldview variables may contribute to lack of progress in the therapeutic relationship. Behaviorism, in its simplest form, presupposes that all behavior is learned through conditioned responses and can be unlearned through rehearsal of new behaviors. There is an element of assumed control (by the therapist) on the part of the client that ignores the sociopolitical reality of oppression in today's world. Ms. Rodriguez's accounts of exclusion, lack of support from coworkers and the work environment, and inability to receive support from her extended family constitute a set of problems brought on by her move and new environment. This "lack of balance" in her life prompted stress and anxiety brought on by the process of acculturation, which results in new equilibrium or balance. As Ms. Rodriguez finds adequate support systems that encourage and help her acculturate, her symptoms signal this process in action.

The new therapist, Dr. Sanchez, recognizes the acculturative process with its concomitant symptoms. By actively exploring the issues producing the symptoms, a higher level of adjustment is attained. Thus, the symptoms subside or disappear altogether. It is this writer's belief that a therapist need not be "ethnic" to understand this process, but rather aware of ethnocultural variables, age, gender, and differences that exist between clients and their therapists. This information is available and can be acquired through training and appropriate supervision.

Ethical Concerns

The use of behavioral theory and interventions by Dr. Alcott fails to take into account individual differences among clients, specifically their cultural backgrounds and identities. This is in conflict with the principle of beneficence endorsed by all codes of ethics, This principle is reflected in the ACA code of ethics (1995) by the statement, "The primary responsibility of counselors is to respect the dignity and promote the welfare of clients" (Section A.1.a). The use of behavioral interventions fails to address the client's cultural background and her background story of exclusion. Furthermore, Section A.2.b, "Respecting Differences," recommends that counselors "understand the diverse cultural background of the clients with whom they work." Dr. Alcott's choice of behaviorism as his theory does not excuse him from acknowledging cultural differences and incorporating such knowledge into his treatment plans.

According to Baruth and Manning (1999), people of all cultures adapt to their environments by either changing themselves (autoplastic approach), by changing the environment (alloplastic approach), or by combining both. These approaches then raise the question concerning the extent to which multicultural psychotherapy or counseling leans toward changing the client, as opposed to helping the client change the environment. Is it healthy to help a client adapt to an oppressive environment? Is it in their best interests?

Ms. Rodriguez's "rights as a client" are addressed by Section A.3.a of the ACA (1995) code of ethics in their "Disclosure to Clients" section. This section of the ACA code specifies that counselors inform clients of the purposes, goals, techniques, procedures, and limitations of counseling services. This requirement facilitates clients' understanding of the counseling process in order to provide "informed consent" for treatment. It is vital that Ms. Rodriguez understand the process, techniques used, and in particular whether Dr. Alcott had knowledge and understanding of her cultural background. Otherwise, her consent was based on faulty knowledge of the process.

Section E.5.b of the ACA (1995) code of ethics addresses counselors' cultural sensitivity. It specifies that, "Counselors recognize that culture affects the manner in which clients' problems are defined." This includes clients' socioeconomic and cultural experiences as important variables that will affect the diagnosis and treatment recommended for a client's problem.

Monocultural and Multicultural Perspectives

Mental health practitioners must become aware of the sociopolitical dynamics that form not only the worldviews of their clients, but their own as well. This is vital to recognizing that in a pluralistic society, multiple worldviews coexist. The risk of therapists who espouse a monocultural worldview is that they may become "culturally encapsulated" and "theory bound." Encapsulation denotes a denial of a pluralistic reality in which individuals must navigate various sets of values and perspectives. From a "theory-bound" perspective, only one theory and set of techniques are applied to all clients, regardless of individual differences. This no-choice option is applied to all clients, regardless of their distinctiveness or variations.

Racial and cultural dynamics enter the helping process and, when ignored, may result in misdiagnosis, confusion, and additional pain for clients, along with reinforcement of biases. For minority clients to survive oppression, they must learn how to discern gross and subtle prejudicial racial attitudes of others in order to minimize their vulnerability. Such behavior, when poorly understood by a therapist, can be mistakenly labeled as hypervigilance, defensiveness, or even paranoia. Lack of training in working with diverse clients reinforces the notion of monoculturalism and the assumption of universality of the values reinforced by the dominant cultures.

Ethnocentric monoculturalism is dysfunctional in a pluralistic society (Sue & Sue, 1999). Mental health professionals must deconstruct the values, biases, and assumptions that reside in the beliefs that one group is superior to all others, the dominant group is empowered to impose its standards on everyone, and under the notion of universality, condoning institutionalized oppression is a "nonissue."

The counseling profession holds us accountable for possessing the knowledge and understanding required to render services in a diverse society. Becoming a multiculturally aware counselor requires personal growth and a form of "stretching" of the self to make room for understanding the various worldviews that exist. A linear, dichotomous, hierarchical worldview is only one of the multiple possibilities that is available; it is up to us as professionals to rise to this challenge.

Options for Appropriate Action

Dr. Alcott needs training and supervision in working with minority clients. His therapeutic approach, though effective for certain problems, is not universally applicable to all concerns that clients bring. Furthermore, an understanding of how culture and race affect the process of diagnosis and treatment planning is vital to an effective therapeutic process. The universal principles guiding ACA's code of ethics include autonomy, beneficence, nonmaleficence, justice, and fidelity. These principles hold counselors accountable for providing the highest standards of care to their clients. To accomplish this, counselors must be knowledgeable about the current social situation and the impact it has on clients.

As American society becomes more pluralistic, counselors will be rendering services to a growing diverse client population. Thus, counselors must seek the necessary knowledge and information to offer effective therapeutic services. Asa Hilliard (1984) best summarized it in this statement: "Cultural sensitivity is a prerequisite to professional competence. This is not merely a fairness issue" (p. 20). Understanding and sensitivity to cultural issues in clients is directly related to the provision of ethical services.

Ethical Dilemma 2

Dr. Marybeth Donnolan is a White feminist psychologist specializing in relationship issues with couples. Her approach to working with couples is based on the principle that egalitarian roles in which each partner's feelings and wishes are taken into account and communicated are at the heart of successful relationships. Dr. Donnolan is aware that not all cultures share her philosophy. She has made it a practice to refer couples from cultures in which there is a hierarchical relationship between partners.

Over the last few years, Dr. Donnolan's practice has begun to be negatively affected by general changes in mental health practice, including the increasing presence of managed care. Also, the community in which her practice is located has recently had a large influx of Eastern European and Asian immigrants. Dr. Donnolan decides to expand her practice into the area of multicultural counseling. She has neither the time nor the inclination to take more courses or seek supervision in multicultural counseling. She feels her graduate training, which consisted of a course in multicultural counseling, has prepared her well to work with a range of client populations. Furthermore, she knows of no training opportunities or supervisors in her area with expertise in the ethnic populations residing in her community. Dr. Donnolan is aware that many practitioners in her area regularly see clients of different cultures without special supervision or training. Dr. Donnolan decides to read books and journal articles about the norms and patterns of different cultural groups to prepare for her new clients. She assumes that her years of expertise in couples work will serve as a strong foundation for working with ethnic clients.

Questions for Classroom Discussion

1. What sort of training and education is required for practitioners to work with diverse ethnic and racial populations? Does Dr. Donnolan's training meet the requirements?

2. One measure of competent practice is consistency with community standards. Does the fact that other practitioners in the area treat ethnically diverse clients without special training support her claim that the training she has is sufficient?

3. Let's assume Dr. Donnolan decides to call her profession's ethics committee to double-check her decision about not seeking additional training or supervision. If you were sitting on the committee, how would you advise her?

Ethical Dilemma 3

Mr. Barry Sanderson is a Black clinical social worker whose expertise is anxiety management with adolescents. Scott, a 16-year-old high school student, has come to Barry for help in dealing with feelings of overwhelming anxiety about his sexual orientation. Scott, who has never been interested in girls, recently met another boy his age, Tom, to whom he feels very attracted. He would like to approach Tom but is anxious because he has never tried to "pick up another guy." Scott doesn't know if Tom is gay, and if he is gay, whether Tom would be interested in going out with him. Another concern Scott has is whether Tom, who is White, is open to an interracial relationship with Scott, who is Black. Scott's anxiety has been so great for the past several weeks that he is having trouble concentrating, to the point that his schoolwork is beginning to suffer. He is also losing weight and sleeping poorly. Scott has not told his parents about his attraction to other boys because he is very fearful of their reactions. In fact, Scott has told no one about his feelings.

Scott meets with Barry and is relieved to finally have an opportunity to talk to someone. Barry listens to Scott's story, and as Scott shares his homosexual feelings, Barry becomes concerned about his ability to work with him. Barry has never worked with gays before and is uncomfortable with homosexuality. He is aware that his profession's ethics do not condone discrimination on the basis of sexual orientation, so he wonders whether referring Scott because he is gay would be an ethical violation. Barry is confident he could help Scott manage his anxiety but is afraid his own homophobia would be problematic for both of them. Scott tells Barry that one of the main reasons he chose Barry is because Barry is the only Black therapist available. Since racial issues are among Scott's concerns, he thought Barry would be the perfect person to help him sort through these issues.

Questions for Classroom Discussion

1. What are Barry's options in terms of treating Scott ethically?

2. How would you respond to a client's discomfort with you on the basis of race alone? How would you handle the client's request for a racially similar therapist when you have the expertise to treat him or her?

3. What is a therapist's ethical obligation to clients about whom the therapist has deep-seated prejudices?

Classroom Exercises

1. Role-play a scenario in which the "client" requests a therapist of a different racial group, gender, or sexual orientation from yours. Assume that such a therapist is not available and that you are willing to treat the client.

2. In small groups, outline the steps you would take if you had the opportunity to treat someone who presented a problem area in which you have little expertise, but a great desire to gain experience. Share with your group an example of such an area of practice and its appeal to you. How would you justify to an ethics board your decision to treat such a client? Share your small-group discussion with the class.

3. Interview local multicultural experts about their preparation and training. Ask them what they consider to be the most helpful aspects of their training.

Summary and Key Points

The need for practitioners to exhibit multicultural counseling competence is underscored in all the mental health codes of ethics. However, there are considerable differences across training programs about what constitutes multicultural competence and, therefore, what characterizes ethical multicultural practice. Despite the appearance of guidelines and definitions of cultural competencies and state licensing requirements concerning knowledge about sociocultural phenomena, levels of cultural competency in practitioners vary widely due to inconsistencies in training. The risk of practicing unethically is notable in a professional climate marked by a lack of standardization in multicultural training.

Thus, key points for practitioners to address are as follows:

- Their commitment to increasing their professional competence with a range of culturally different clients
- Identifying strategies for furthering their cultural competence
- Whether their education and training provide a sufficient foundation for ethical multicultural practice
- Being thoughtful about how they will know whether their education, training, and worldviews about cultural differences provide them with the competence to treat a client from a dissimilar culture or whether their ethical obligation is to refer

References

American Counseling Association. (1995). *Code of ethics and standards of practice.* Alexandria, VA: Author.

American Psychological Association. (1992). *Ethical principles of psychologists and code of conduct.* Washington, DC: Author.

American Psychological Association. (1993). Guidelines for providers of psychological services to ethnic, linguistic, and culturally diverse populations. *American Psychologist, 48*(1), 45–48.

American Psychological Association. (2002). Ethical principles of psychologists and code of conduct. Washington, DC: Author. Available on the World Wide Web at: www.apa.org.ethics.

Arredondo, P. A., & Arciniega, G. M. (2001). Strategies and techniques for counselor training based on the multicultural counseling competencies. *Journal of Multicultural Counseling and Development, 29*(4), 263–273.

Arredondo, P., Toporek, R., Brown, S., Jones, J., Locke, D. C., Sanchez, J., & Stadler, H. (1996). *Operationalization of the multicultural counseling competencies.* Alexandria, VA: American Counseling Association.

Barret, B., & Logan, C. (2002). *Counseling gay men and lesbians: A practice primer.* Pacific Grove, CA: Brooks/Cole.

Baruth, L. G., & Manning, M. L. (1999). *Multicultural counseling and psychotherapy: A lifestyle.* Upper Saddle River, NJ: Merrill.

Basic Behavioral Science Task Force of the National Advisory Mental Health Council. (1996). Basic behavior science research for mental health: Sociocultural and environmental processes. *American Psychologist, 51,* 722–731.

Bernal, M. E., & Castro, F. G. (1994). Are clinical psychologists prepared for service and research with ethnic minorities? *American Psychologist, 37,* 780–787.

Bernard, J. M., & Goodyear, R. K. (1998). *Fundamentals of clinical supervision* (2nd ed.). Boston, MA: Allyn & Bacon.

Bohan, J. (1996). *Psychology and sexual orientation: Coming to terms.* New York: Routledge.

Brown, L. S., & Root, M. P. P. (Eds.). (1990). *Diversity and complexity in feminist therapy.* New York: Harrington Park.

Brown, S. P., Parham, T. A., & Yonker, R. (1996). Influence of a cross-cultural training course on racial identity attitudes of White females and males: A preliminary perspective. *Journal of Counseling and Development, 74*(5), 510–516.

Buhrke, R. A. (1989). Incorporation of lesbian and gay issues into counseling training: A resource guide. *Journal of Counseling and Development, 68,* 77–80.

Buhrke, R. A., & Douce, L. (1991). Training issues for counseling psychologists in working with lesbian women and gay men. *The Counseling Psychologist, 19,* 216–234.

Casas, J. M. (1984). Policy, training, and research in counseling psychology. The racial/ ethnic minority perspective. In S. D. Brown & R. W. Lent (Eds.), *Handbook of counseling psychology* (pp. 785–831). New York: John Wiley.

Cass, V. C. (1990). The implications of homosexual identity formation for the Kinsey model and scale of sexual preference. In D. P. McWirther, S. A. Sanders, & J. M. Reinisch (Eds.), *Homosexuality/heterosexuality: The Kinsey scale and current research* (pp. 239–266). New York: Oxford University Press.

Collins, P. H. (1990). *Black feminist thought: Knowledge, consciousness, and the politics of empowerment.* New York: Routledge.

Comas-Diaz, L., & Greene, B. (Eds.). (1994). *Women of color: Integrating ethnic and gender identities in psychotherapy.* New York: Guilford.

Corey, G., Corey, M., & Callanan, P. (1993). *Issues and ethics in the helping profession* (4th ed.). Pacific Grove, CA: Brooks/Cole.

Coser, L. (1956). *The functions of social conflict.* New York: Free Press.

Cross, T. L. (1988, Summer). Services to minority populations: What does it mean to be a culturally competent professional? *Focal Point.* Portland, OR: Portland State University, Research and Training Center.

Cross, W. E. (1991). *Shades of black.* Philadelphia: Temple University Press.

Cross, W. E., Parham, T. A., & Helms, J. E. (1991). In R. L. Jones (Ed.), *Black Psychology* (pp. 319–338). Berkeley, CA: Cobb & Henry.

D'Andrea, M., Daniels, J., & Heck, R. (1991). Evaluating the impact of multicultural counseling training. *Journal of Counseling and Development, 70,* 143–150.

D'Augelli, A. R., & Hershberger, S. L. (1993). Lesbian, gay and bisexual youth in community settings: Personal challenges and mental health problems. *American Journal of Community Psychology, 21,* 1–28.

Diaz-Lazaro, C. M., & Cohen, B. B. (2001). Cross-cultural contact in counselor training. *Journal of Multicultural Counseling and Development, 29*(1), 41–56.

Downing, N. E., & Roush, K. L. (1985). Passive acceptance to active commitment: A model of feminist identity development for women. *Counseling Psychologist, 13,* 695–709.

Espin, O. M. (1987). Issues of identity in the psychology of Latina lesbians. In the Boston Lesbian Psychologies Collective (Eds.), *Lesbian psychologies: Explorations and challenges* (pp. 35–56). Chicago: University of Illinois Press.

Estrada, D., Frame, M. W., & Williams, C. B. (2002). *Journal of Multicultural Counseling and Development.* Submitted for publication.

Garcia, J. G., & Zea, M. C. (Eds.). (1997). *Psychological interventions and research with Latino populations.* Boston: Allyn & Bacon.

Goodyear, R. K., & Guzardo, C. R. (2000). Psychotherapy supervision and training. In S. D. Brown & R. W. Lent (Eds.), *Handbook of counseling psychology* (3rd. ed., pp. 83–108). New York: John Wiley.

Greene, B. (1994). Lesbian women of color: Triple jeopardy. In L. Comas-Diaz & B. Greene (Eds.), *Women of color: Integrating ethnic and gender identities in psychotherapy.* New York: Guilford.

Greene, B. (1997). Ethnic minority lesbians and gay men: Mental health and treatment issues. In B. Greene (Ed.), *Ethnic and cultural diversity among lesbians and gay men.* New York: Guilford.

Hardiman, R. (2001). Reflections on White identity development theory. In C. L. Wijeyesinghe & B. W. Jackson III (Eds.), *New perspectives on racial identity development: A theoretical and practical anthology* (pp. 108–128). New York: New York University Press.

Helms, J.E. (Ed.). (1990). *Black and white racial identity: Theory, research, and practice.* Westport, CT: Greenwood Press.

Helms, J. E., & Cook, D. A. (1999). *Using race and culture in counseling and psychotherapy: Theory and process.* Needham Heights, MA: Allyn & Bacon.

Herlihy, B., & Corey, G. (1996). *ACA ethical standards casebook.* Alexandria, VA: American Counseling Association.

Hershberger, S. L., & D'Augelli, A. R. (2000). Issues in counseling lesbian, gay, and bisexual adolescents. In R. N. Perez, K. A. Debord, & K. J. Bieschke (Eds.), *Handbook of counseling and psychotherapy with lesbian, gay, and bisexual clients.* Washington, DC: American Psychological Association.

Hilliard, Asa. (1985). Multicultural dimensions of counseling and human development in an age of technology. *Journal of Non-White Concerns in Personnel and Guidance, 13,* 17–27.

Ibrahim, F. A., & Arredondo, P. M. (1986). Ethical standards for cross-cultural counseling: Counselor preparation, practice, assessment, and research. *Journal of Counseling and Development, 64,* 349–352.

Ibrahim, F. A., & Kahn. H. (1987). Assessment of worldviews. *Psychological Reports, 60,* 163–176.

Ivey, A. E. (1987). Reaction: Cultural intentionality: The core of effective helping. *Counselor Education and Supervision, 26,* 168–172.

Ivey, A. E., Ivey, M. B., & Simek-Morgan, L. (1997). *Counseling and psychotherapy: A multicultural perspective.* Needham Heights, MA: Allyn & Bacon.

Ivey, A. E., Pedersen, P. B., & Ivey, M. B. (2001). *Intentional group counseling: A microskills approach.* Belmont, CA: Wadsworth.

Jackson, B. W., III. (2001). Black identity development: Further analysis and elaboration. In C. L. Wijeyesinghe & B. W. Jackson III (Eds.), *New perspectives on racial identity development: A theoretical and practical anthology* (pp. 8–31). New York: New York University Press.

Jordan, A. E., & Meara, N. M. (1990). Ethics and the professional practice of psychologists: The role of virtues and principles. *Professional Psychology: Research and Practice, 21*(2), 107–114.

Kitchner, K. S. (1984). Intuition, critical evaluation and ethical principles: The foundation for ethical decisions in counseling psychology. *The Counseling Psychologist, 12,* 43–55.

Kluckhohn, F., & Strodbeck, F. (1961). *Variation in value orientation.* Evanston, IL: Row Pedersen.

LaFromboise, T. D., Foster, S., & James, A. (1995). Ethics in multicultural counseling. In P. B. Pedersen, J. G. Draguns, W. J. Lonner, & J. E. Trimble (Eds.), *Counseling across cultures* (4th ed., pp. 47–72). Thousand Oaks, CA: Sage.

Landrine, H. (Ed.). (1995). *Bringing cultural diversity to feminist psychology: Theory, research, and practice.* Washington, DC: American Psychological Association.

Lappin, J., & Hardy, K. V. (1997). Keeping context in view: The heart of supervision. In T. C. Todd & C. L. Storm (Eds.), *The complete systemic supervisor: Context, philosophy, and pragmatics* (pp. 41–58). Boston: Allyn & Bacon.

Lee, C. C. (1997). The promise and pitfalls of multicultural counseling. In C. C. Lee (Ed.), *Multicultural issues in counseling: New approaches to diversity.* Alexandria, VA: American Counseling Association.

Leventhal, G. S. (1979.) Effects of external conflict on resource allocation and fairness within groups and organizations. In W. G. Austen & S. Worchel (Eds.), *The social psychology of intergroup relations.* Monterey, CA: Brooks/Cole.

Lloyd, A. (1987). Stimulus paper: Multicultural counseling: Does it belong in a counselor education program? *Counselor Education and Supervision, 26,* 164–167.

Logan, C. R. (1996). Homophobia? No, homoprejudice. *The Journal of Homosexuality, 31*(3), 31–53.

MacDonald, C. (2001, November). *A guide to moral decision making.* Retrieved December 13, 2001, from the World Wide Web at: http://www.ethics.ubc.ca/chrismac/publications/guide.html.

McClintock, M. K., & Herdt, G. (1996). Rethinking puberty: The development of sexual attraction. *Current Directions in Psychological Science, 5,* 178–183.

Merta, R. J., Stringham, E. M., & Ponterotto, J. G. (1988). Simulating culture shock in counseling trainees: An experiential exercise for cross-cultural training. *Journal of Counseling and Development, 66,* 242–245.

Mio, J. S. (1989). Experiential involvement as an adjunct to teaching cultural sensitivity. *Journal of Multicultural Counseling and Development, 17,* 38–46.

Mio, J. S., & Iwamasa, G. (1993). To do, or not to do: That is the question for White cross-cultural researchers. *The Counseling Psychologist, 21,* 197–212.

Mio, J. S., & Morris, D. R. (1990). Cross-cultural issues in psychology training programs: An invitation for discussion. *Professional Psychology: Research and Practice, 21,* 234–241.

National Association of Social Workers. (1996). *Code of ethics.* Washington, DC: Author.

O'Byrne, K., & Rosenberg, J. I. (1998). The practice of supervision: A sociocultural perspective. *Counselor Education and Supervision, 38,* 34–42.

Opotow, S. (1990). Moral exclusion and injustice. An introduction. *Journal of Social Issues, 46,* 1–20.

Pack-Brown, S. P. (1999). Racism and White counselor training. Influence of White racial identity theory and research. *Journal of Counseling and Development, 77*(1), 87–92.

Pack-Brown, S. P., Whittington-Clark, L. E., & Parker, W. M. (1998). *Images of me: A guide to group work with African-American women.* Boston, MA: Allyn & Bacon.

Pack-Brown, S. P., Whittington-Clark, L. E., & Parker, W. M. (2002). *Images of me: A guide to group work with African-American women.* Framingham: Microtraining Associates.

Pack-Brown, S. P., & Williams, C. B. (2000). To discriminate or not to discriminate: Culture and ethics. *Counseling Today.* Alexandria, VA: American Counseling Association.

Padilla, S. (1994). *A natural education: Native American ideas and thoughts.* Summertown, TN: Book.

Parham, T. A. (1989). Cycles of psychological Nigrescence. *The Counseling Psychologist, 17,* 187–226.

Parham, T. A. (1993). Reaction: White researchers conducting multi-cultural counseling research: Can their efforts be "Mo Betta"? *The Counseling Psychologist, 21,* 250–256.

Parker, W. M. (1987). Reaction: Flexibility: A primer for multicultural counseling. *Counselor Education and Supervision, 26,* 176–180.

Pedersen, P. (1987). Ten frequent assumptions of cultural bias in counseling. *Journal of Multicultural Counseling and Development,* 16–24.

Pedersen, P. (1988). *A handbook for developing multicultural awareness.* Alexandria, VA: AACD.

Pedersen, P. (1995). *A handbook for developing multicultural awareness.* Alexandria, VA: American Counseling Association.

Pedersen, P. B. (1997a). The cultural context of the American Counseling Association Code of Ethics. *Journal of Counseling & Development, 76,* 23–28.

Pedersen, P. B. (1997b, July). The positive consequences of a culture-centered perspective. *Counseling Today, 40*(1), 20.

Pedersen, P. B. (1998). *Multiculturalism as a fourth force.* Philadelphia: Brunner/Mazel.

Pedersen, P. B. (2000). *A handbook for developing multicultural awareness* (3rd ed.). Alexandria, VA: American Counseling Association.

Pedersen, P. B., & Hernandez, D. (1997). *Decisional dialogues in a cultural context.* Thousand Oaks, CA: Sage.

Ponterotto, J. G., & Pedersen, P. B. (1993). *Preventing prejudice: A guide for counselors and educators.* Newbury Park, CA: Sage.

Remley, T. P., & Herlihy, B. (2001). *Ethical, legal, and professional issues in counseling.* Upper Saddle River, NJ: Merrill/Prentice Hall.

Ridley, C. R. (1995). *Overcoming unintentional racism in counseling and therapy: A practitioner's guide to intentional intervention.* Thousand Oaks, CA: Sage.

Robinson, T. L., & Howard-Hamilton, M. R. (2000). *The convergence of race, ethnicity, and gender. Multiple identities in counseling.* Upper Saddle River, NJ: Prentice Hall.

Rowe, W., Bennett, S. K., & Atkinson, D. R. (1994). White racial identity models: A critique and alternative proposal. *The Counseling Psychologist, 23,* 364–367.

Staub, E. (1987). *Moral exclusion and extreme destructiveness: Personal goal theory, differential evaluation, moral equilibrium and steps along the continuum of destruction.* Paper presented at American Psychological Association meeting, New York.

Steinman, B. O., Richardson, N. F., & McEnroe, T. (1998). *The ethical decision-making manual for helping professionals.* Pacific Grove, CA: Brooks/Cole.

Sue, D. W. (1995). Multicultural organizational development: Implications for the counseling profession. In J. G. Ponterotto, J. M. Casas, L. A. Suzuki, & C. M Alexander (Eds.), *Handbook of multicultural counseling* (pp. 474–492). Thousand Oaks, CA: Sage.

Sue, D. W., Arredondo, P., & McDavis, R. J. (1992). Multicultural counseling competencies and standards: A call to the profession. *Journal of Counseling and Development, 70,* 477–486.

Sue, D. W., & Sue, D. (1999). *Counseling the culturally different: Theory and practice* (3rd ed.). New York: John Wiley.

Sue, S. (1991). Ethnicity and culture in psychological research and practice. In J. D. Goodchilds (Ed.), *Psychological perspectives on human diversity in America* (pp. 51–85). Washington, DC: American Psychological Association.

Sue, S. (1999). Science, ethnicity and bias: Where have we gone wrong? *American Psychologist, 54*(2), 1070–1077.

Sue, S., & Zane, N. (1987). The role of culture and cultural techniques in psychotherapy. A critique and reformulation. *American Psychologist, 42,* 37–45.

Thompson, A. (1990). *Guide to ethical practice in psychotherapy.* New York: Wiley Interscience.

Welfel, E. R. (1998). *Ethics in counseling and psychotherapy: Standards, research, and emerging issues.* Pacific Grove, CA: Brooks/Cole.

Wijeyesinghe, C. L. (2001). In C. L. Wijeyesinghe & B. W. Jackson III (Eds.), *New perspectives on racial identity development: A theoretical and practical anthology* (pp. 129–152). New York: New York University Press.

Wijeyesinghe, C. L., & Jackson, B. III (Eds.). (2001). *New perspectives on racial identity development: A theoretical and practical anthology* (pp. 108–128). New York: New York University Press.

Williams, C. B. (1999). Claiming a biracial identity: Resisting social constructions of race and culture. *Journal of Counseling and Development, 77,* 32–35.

Williams, C. B. (2001). Ethics complaints: Procedures for filing and responding. In E. R. Welfel & R. E. Ingersoll (Eds.), *The mental health desk reference* (pp. 441–447). New York: John Wiley.

Glossary of Terms

Afrocentric worldview A set of presuppositions and assumptions grounded within a cultural context that provides guidelines for how a person views (a) the world, (b) "self" in relation to the world, and (c) the world's relationship to "self." Common values include a holistic approach to life, emotional vitality, interdependence, collective survival, and oral tradition in history. The concept of "self" is couched within the context of being a member of the community. Self-esteem and empowerment are promoted via the reality of "self in relation."

Assume To take for granted, suppose to be a *fact* (e.g., assume the sun will shine tomorrow).

Assumption A taking for granted; supposition.

Culture An accumulation of values and moral standards of a society. Includes patterns of learned thinking and behavior communicated across generations through media such as traditions, language, and artifacts.

Cultural values The totality of beliefs and behaviors that are common to a group of people and held in high esteem. Examples include language, customs, and traditions.

Difference State or quality of being dissimilar, and distinct from.

Discrimination The display of partiality or prejudice based on factors other than merit. This partiality influences how an individual treats another individual or collective group.

Diversity Individual differences (e.g., gender, socioeconomic status, sexual orientation) that may be drawn on and developed to promote the goals of an organization or community.

Ethics   The discipline dealing with what is "good" and "bad," moral duty, and obligation. A set of moral principles or values. A theory or system of moral values. The principles of conduct governing an individual or a group.

Ethnicity   A dimension of human identity that includes one's social, cultural, and national heritage (e.g., language, religion, geography, morals, race), passed from generation to generation.

Ethnocentrism   The prioritizing of the attitudes, beliefs, and customs of one's own group, nation, or people, which serves as a basis for judging all other groups.

Eurocentric worldview   A set of presuppositions and assumptions grounded within a cultural context that provide guidelines for how a person views (a) the world, (b) "self" in relation to the world, and (c) the world's relationship to "self." Common values include an individualistic approach to life, control of emotions, independence, individualism, and written history. The concept of "self" is couched within the individual perspective and view of the world. Self-esteem and empowerment are promoted via the reality of "self" as an individual.

Gender   A dimension of human identity in which traits of masculinity and femininity are assigned to individuals on the basis of their biological sex.

Goal   A point toward which effort or movement is directed.

Homophobia   Fear of same-sex relationships or of gays and lesbians.

Homoprejudice   Negative judgment and/or stereotypes about gays and lesbians; preferred by some over the term *homophobia*.

Moral   Of or relating to principles of right and wrong in behavior. Sanctioned by or operative of one's conscience or ethical judgment.

Morality   A moral discourse, statement, or lesson. Conformity to ideals of right human conduct.

Multicultural   A reference to the five major ethnocultural groups in the United States and its territories: African/Black, Asian and Pacific Islander, European/White, Hispanic/Latino, and Native American. All individuals are believed to be ethnic, racial, and cultural beings.

Multicultural counseling   The preparation and practices that integrate multicultural and culture-specific awareness, knowledge, and skills into counseling interactions.

Oppress   To crush, trample, or overpower via abuse of power or authority over another person or group of people.

Oppression   Unjust or cruel exercise of authority or power over another person or group of people. A sense of heaviness or obstruction in one's body, mind, or spirit due to unjust or cruel exercise of power of one person(s) over another person(s).

Personal culture   The organized totality of an individual's identity. This identity comprises historical, political, and economic dimensions, including religion, work experience, parental status, sexual orientation, gender, and so forth. The interaction of these dimensions makes for a dynamic rather than a static personal culture.

Presume To take for granted or assume to be true until disproved (e.g., I presume you are right).

Presumption The act of forming a *judgment on probable grounds, awaiting further evidence;* also, the judgment so formed, or a ground or reason for it. That which may be logically or legally assumed to be true until disproved (e.g., the presumption of guilt).

Principle A general truth or law. Inherent/determining essential character. Moral standard.

Race Refers to the social construction of a dimension of human difference that creates distinctions between people on the basis of genetic physical characteristics such as skin pigmentation, facial features, and hair texture. There is no scientific validity for the classification of races, and many in the field question its validity in multicultural counseling.

Racism The doctrine that race is the basic determinant of human abilities and that racial groups are organized along a hierarchy in which one group is deemed superior to others. A critical point is that there is no scientific validity to the classification of races.

Social construction Refers to socially sanctioned agreements about the meaning and significance of various human traits, notably race, gender, and sexual orientation.

Spirituality An emphasis on the spirit as the essence of humanity.

Supposition A hypothetical proposition offered to explain a particular fact, relating facts, or deducting consequences. A hypothesis.

Worldview Comprises presuppositions and assumptions held by an individual specific to the makeup of her or his world. It exemplifies how a person perceives his or her relationship to the world (nature, institutions, other people, things, etc.) as well as how the world perceives its relationship to the person. Worldview is culturally based and learned.

Index

About the Authors

The accomplishments of **Sherlon P. Pack-Brown,** Ph.D., (L)PCC, include 14 publications; coauthorship of a book titled *Images of Me: Group Work With African-American Females;* and more than 36 presentations at the international, national, and state levels in the area of multicultural and diversity counseling and competence. Prior to her academic appointment at Bowling Green State University, in Ohio, she was a counselor for 5 years with the University of Toledo Counseling Center, in Ohio. She has had a part-time private practice for 15 years specializing in diversity competent group counseling, specifically with African American females. Dr. Pack-Brown served as cochair of the American Counseling Association Ethics Committee and past president of the Association for Multicultural Counseling and Development (a division of the American Counseling Association), and was the recipient of the Sam Johnson Award. She is associate professor in counselor education at Bowling Green State University. Her primary area of research, teaching, supervision, and consultation is multicultural and diversity competent counseling.

Carmen Braun Williams, Ph.D., is associate professor in counseling psychology and counselor education at the University of Colorado at Denver. She received her doctorate in clinical psychology from Pennsylvania State University in 1980 and has been licensed as a psychologist in Colorado since 1983. Prior to her academic appointment at CU-Denver, Dr. Williams had a psychotherapy practice for 15 years specializing in adult women's issues and racial/cultural issues with adolescents and adults. Her primary area of research, teaching, supervision, and consultation is multicultural therapy. Her accomplishments include more than 20 publications and 100 presentations at international, national, and state conferences. Dr. Williams's professional appointments include Board Member for the Colorado Psychological Association (2001–2002), Chair of the Colorado Board of Psychologist Examiners (1989–1991), Chair of the American Counseling Association Ethics Committee (1998–2001), and Chair of the International Association of Marriage and Family Counselors Professional Training and Development Task Force (1998–2000). She has received several professional awards in teaching, writing, and service at both state and national levels.